AROUND THE
WORLD IN
80 TRADES

AROUND THE WORLD IN 80 TRADES

CONOR WOODMAN

MACMILLAN

First published 2009 by Macmillan
an imprint of Pan Macmillan Ltd
Pan Macmillan, 20 New Wharf Road, London NI 9RR
Basingstoke and Oxford
Associated companies throughout the world
www.panmacmillan.com

ISBN 978-0330-46787-2 (HB)
ISBN 978-0330-46956-2 (TPB)

1 3 5 7 9 8 6 4 2

A CIP catalogue record for this book is available
from the British Library.

Printed and bound in Great Britain by
CPI Mackays, Chatham ME5 8TD

Map Artwork by Hemesh Alles

AN IMG ENTERTAINMENT COMPANY

Visit **www.panmacmillan.com** to read more about all our books
and to buy them. You will also find features, author interviews and
news of any author events, and you can sign up for e-newsletters
so that you're always first to hear about our new releases.

CONTENTS

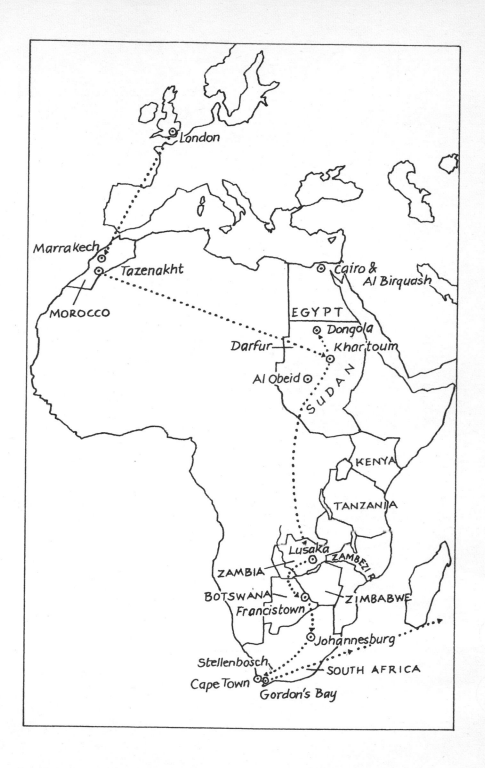

London

Marrakech
Tazenakht
MOROCCO

Cairo &
Al Birquash

EGYPT

Dongola
Darfur
Khartoum

Al Obeid

S U D A N

KENYA

TANZANIA

Lusaka
ZAMBIA
ZAMBEZI

BOTSWANA
Francistown
ZIMBABWE

Johannesburg

Stellenbosch
SOUTH AFRICA

Cape Town
Gordon's Bay

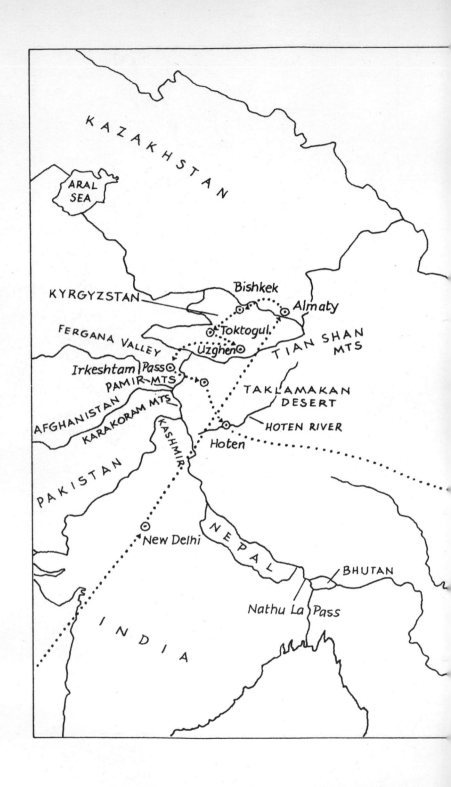

CHINA

JAPAN

Tokyo
& Tsukiji

Fukuoka
& Kamasaki

Suzhou   Shanghai

YANGTZE RIVER   Yongkang

Taipei
TAIWAN

Lishan

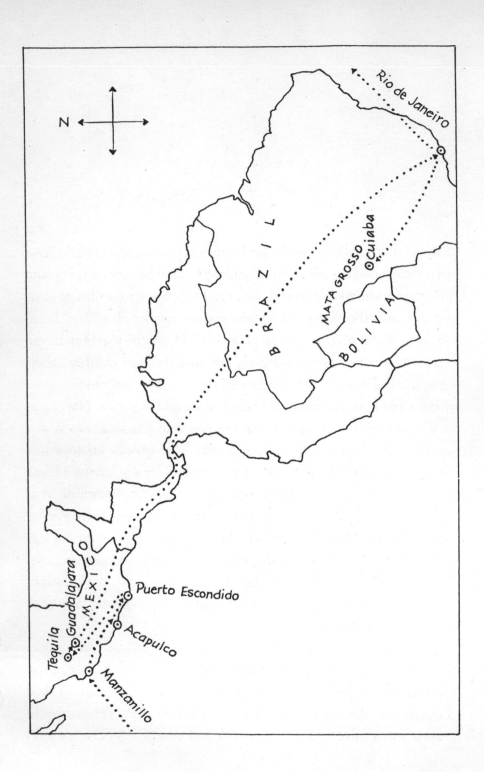

PROLOGUE

If the Gatlang valley were in the English countryside, it would have been designated an 'area of outstanding natural beauty', a successful Victorian industrialist would have erected a stone monument at its summit and thousands of holidaymakers would marvel at it on family walking holidays every year. As a foothill in the Himalayan region of northern Nepal it merely falls into the 'just another valley' category and is seemingly populated by no one. Save, that is, for a wrinkly old man I'd almost literally just stumbled across. Naygar, as he introduced himself to me, was employed by the local monk as a caretaker for the monastery, outside which we quietly sat together. Naygar's onerous duties seemed to involve drying lumps of yak meat he'd found, snorting a type of herbal amphetamine that he'd made from the local vegetation, and keeping a close eye on neighbouring Tibet. I passed on the raw meat, but I was curious about the herbal snuff and so just to be sociable I'd taken a nose-full. I found myself feeling slightly heady, listening to the sound of cowbells and watching a caravan of traders leading their yaks over the hills in the distance.

'Where are the yaks headed?' I asked my translator and guide, Ram. After a discussion with Naygar that lasted the best part of five minutes he turned to me and simply answered, 'Tibet'. I had thought that the border with Tibet was firmly shut. Permission to cross it was a minefield of paperwork and counter-paperwork with no guarantee that in the end anyone would actually let you through. When I raised this with Ram another lengthy discussion ensued. 'They do not know there is a border there,' Ram explained, this time at more length. 'They have been trading over this pass for centuries.'

I was immediately intrigued. These ancient traders used yaks to transport carpets, furs and spices over the pass and traded with Tibetans who brought precious salt from the north. Once a deal had been struck, they returned to sell their stock at the market back on the Nepalese side of the border for a profit. How did they price their goods? Did they negotiate or were prices set? What were the risks and profit margins that made this market work? These are the questions an economist asks himself when he encounters human behaviour with which he is not familiar. And the best way of finding the answers to these questions is to see for yourself.

*

'I'm sorry to tell you all that with immediate effect you are to be made redundant. You will be entitled to £200 for each year of service with the company as a statutory entitlement, although this will be capped at a maximum of £800. You are also entitled to apply for Jobseeker's Allowance and unemployment benefit with immediate effect.' I looked up from my notes at twenty confused, angry, defeated faces in the room, staring back in disbelief. But as the words dropped out of my mouth I knew that I was only doing what had to be done. The company to which most of the assembled craftsmen had given the best part of their working lives was no longer profitable, and it was simply my job to sell it for as much as I could.

It was the summer of 2004. I was thirty, single and living in a swanky pad in central London with a job in the City that paid me the kind of salary most young men dream of, although I was working so many hours a week that, some months, finding time to spend any of it was a real problem. I was a corporate finance analyst in a large American firm, working on a deal to restructure a glass manufacturing company in the north of England. The company had defaulted on its recent loan payments. I'd done the sums in the office and the harsh economic reality was that the company had no real future. My boss had decided that I needed some 'field experience' and so I'd been dispatched with a small team to make 400 people redundant; a necessary step towards realizing the company's full potential.

The harsh economic reality wasn't in dispute, that these people were only entitled to £800 compensation for a lifetime of loyalty wasn't up for negotiation, but what suddenly hit me was the certainty that I was in the wrong place. I was not the person who was supposed to deliver news like this. This was not why I studied economics. I had to get out of this job and I had to do it today, but today wouldn't be finished until another 380 people had been given the bad news.

*

That chance moment when I was trying to escape from it all in Nepal saw me become hooked on the idea that trying to understand ancient markets was the answer to my crisis back home. How do people operate in an ancient commodity market compared with the harsh world of corporate finance? Would it be just as ruthless? What have we forgotten – or never learned? And, daringly, could I use the knowledge that I had developed as an economist and analyst to compete and make a profit myself, or would I simply be too white, too green – or too yellow, even?

Economics teaches us about relationships and interactions. Trade has always provided us with the motivation to interact with people from other cultures. Three thousand years ago, early traders were inspired to travel in order to find new markets for their goods, and in doing so they exposed themselves to new and exciting cultures. It has often been said that the pursuit of money is the root of all evil. Well, I couldn't disagree more, because without that profit motive there would be no trade. Without trade we would know nothing of the world beyond our own front door.

I couldn't think of a better way to really understand both business and people than to put myself in the place of those traders crossing the border over the hills in the distance, to become like them, see for myself how they interacted, and form relationships of my own.

On returning home I began to research the idea further and I realized there were countless markets all over the world that I could get involved in. I wanted to see if I could travel the whole globe, starting with a handful of cash, trade with some of the world's wiliest traders and come back with a tidy profit. Little did I know what I'd be letting myself in for.

At that stage, all I wanted was to test the theory – about understanding people better through trading with them and what an economist's eye can tell you about the way the world works. So, I set myself a little challenge.

One

EVERY CARPET
TELLS A STORY

The souks of Marrakech are home to one of the oldest and most cut-throat markets in the world. If I was going to pass muster circumnavigating the globe through trading, I decided I'd have to pass muster here first.

I landed in Marrakech and wasted no time in doing a recce of the markets to work out how the hell I was going to make some money. I'd decided to bet that the future of my project lay on the success of this challenge: to hold my own in an ancient market. If I could make it work on a small scale here in Morocco then I would think about how to increase the stakes and take it further afield. The trouble was, I had set myself a limit of only £500 to invest, and just three days to turn a profit.

I met Adnan, my translator and guide, at the airport. He was a dead ringer for Tom Selleck in his Magnum PI guise, right down to his Wayfarer Ray-Bans. Morocco has developed a thriving film industry over the last ten years as a desert location for blockbuster franchises such as *Star Wars* and *The Mummy*, and Adnan listed the various film projects that he'd worked on in the past. The fallout for guys like him has been great; he takes home more in a week than most Moroccans earn in a year. I immediately liked him: he knew English, French and Arabic, and a fair bit about carpets, too . . .

Carpets are to Morocco what coal used to be to Newcastle: a life-blood. Everyone in Morocco knows about carpets; their brother, uncle, father and neighbour are all experts and everyone seems to belong to a family with a carpet business where they sell the very best. You needn't look any further, they'll find you the carpet you want and then you can all sit down over a mint tea while they wrap it, pack it and post it back home for you (duty-free, of course). The reason for all this is simple: tourists. And Marrakech has developed a neat trick. Just as every tourist going to Rome wants to see the Colosseum, every tourist going to Marrakech wants to see the souk and have a haggle to get a bargain. The carpet sellers here have actually made buying something from them a 'must-do' for every tourist who wants to cross Marrakech off their list.

You might think that with so many buyers the job of buying and selling a carpet in Marrakech would be a simple one. I was at least sensible enough not to be under any such illusion. After explaining to Adnan what it was that I intended to do, we agreed that the best starting point was a look around the market itself. I wanted to see as many different outlets as possible and speak to the traders to understand how the supply chain worked and where the profits were.

Marrakech is a citadel town. The layout follows a unique and economically ordered structure. The town is built around its mosque, which sits at the centre, and everything radiates outwards from there. First there is a ring of stalls selling religious paraphernalia – incense and religious texts – then come the tailors, then the carpet sellers, and so on until you reach the city walls. Outside, there are still more traders, selling things that travellers to the town would have historically wanted, such as animal feed. Although Marrakech is now a modern city, the structure of its souks is still based on its economic history. Thus finding the souk selling carpets involves battling through the crowds right to the centre. I was glad to have Adnan to guide me once we hit the dark inner alleys; without him I'd have needed a trail of breadcrumbs to find my way out again.

All the carpet sellers sit together. After a brief introduction from Adnan, one trader, Faraz, a short, fat, hairy man, was happy to explain to me how their market works. The carpets for sale in Marrakech fall into two categories. First, there are the factory-produced carpets made in the north of the country, predominantly styled with gaudy colours and geometric patterns. These are popular with Moroccans and hardly ever sell to tourists. Second, there are carpets handmade by the indigenous Berber women of the Atlas mountains, woven from wool coloured with local organic dyes and designed in such a way as to tell the story of the woman who made it. It is these that tourists want to buy, and which the traders charge a premium for. The next important idiosyncrasy of this market is the notion of price. Nobody in the souk puts a price tag on anything. You ask, 'How much?' They tell you a price that represents about ten times what they paid for it, so you have to take time to argue them down. That is how it's done round here, and it's the power of his argument that makes one trader better than the next. I already knew that if I was going to get into this market I needed the right product and the right sales technique.

I sat in the souk with Adnan, chatting to Faraz, for about an hour. During that time a few tourists walked past but no one was seriously looking to buy anything from Faraz or any of the other fifty or so adjacent carpet sellers. I was worried. I asked Faraz how many carpets he usually expected to sell in a day. He explained that some days he didn't sell any, some days he sold three. As the profit he made on each carpet depended on the moving target of price, he was always unsure about how much money he'd make in any given week. This was fine if you had a month to wait, but I only had three days.

As we left the souk and headed back out of the medina towards our van, I noticed that there were a number of coaches parked near us. Adnan explained that many of the hotels and travel agencies in Marrakech organized shopping trips, the coaches taking groups of up to fifty tourists at a time from shop to shop. The vendors gave the tourists the shopping experience they'd heard about, and if anyone actually bought anything the tour guide would get a kickback. A few enterprising businesses had grown up outside the medina and were offering a very different experience to the souk. I was keen to take a look.

Bouchaib is the Harrods of Marrakech: instantly impressive, a slick and manicured five-star shopping experience. The usual, rather ugly sight of commission being given openly to tour guides who bring tourists to a shop or stall had been replaced here by a classier, more subtle system whereby women with walkie-talkies relayed the details of every arrival to an office upstairs. The tourists need never know that their guides were earning commissions on top of what they were already being paid. As I waited to meet the boss, Samir, a busload of around thirty tourists was shepherded in and shown to a ring of seats where, in keeping with warm Moroccan hospitality, they were instantly offered a cup of mint tea to soften them up before the main event. I discovered that in a quiet, dark room next door a team of salesmen waited to see who was 'up'. Between them they can speak every language, from Japanese to Swedish, and their remarkable skills are well rewarded. Carpet selling at Bouchaib is regarded as one of the best jobs in Marrakech.

Bouchaib represents Morocco's adaptation to global market and trading trends better than anywhere else. The sellers in the souk have traditionally made more profit by never revealing the asking price for their carpets. Some days they will have a good day and sell a carpet for way more than they paid for it, but this comes at a cost. Many tourists are suspicious. While some tourists buy from the souk for the very challenge of paying a fair price, Bouchaib has recognized another type of tourist. Here, the carpets have prices attached to them. Samir has calculated that most serious buyers of his carpets don't want to haggle; they regard it as stressful and will actually pay a premium to *not* haggle. He has found a niche in his own market by copying exactly what we do in the West.

But I observed that the process hasn't become fully westernized. The tourists are still treated to a performance from one of the shop's multilingual maestros. On this occasion, Rashid, a keen young man sporting a crisply ironed shirt, was the chosen seller and he launched straight into his patter. One after another, carpets were presented at the feet of the audience as Rashid explained first the region of origin, then the age and then the story behind each one. The first was made by a woman with a fence around her field, he said, which was depicted by the border in the pattern; the next was made by a pregnant woman who already had three children, depicted by the three stars in the weave. And so it went, on and on. Rashid knew how to tell the individual story of each and every one of the fifty or so carpets he presented. The tourists were not simply being asked to buy a carpet, they were being asked to buy a story.

I was curious as to how Rashid, Samir, or indeed anyone, could be so sure that the stories they were telling were true. But as I cross-examined Samir, I was careful not to cause offence, as I knew I would also need to ask him for a favour. However, he just laughed at the idea that I thought all the stories were true; of course they weren't, and they certainly didn't expect the tourists to believe each individual story. The idea was to explain the patterns, and these historically represented what was going on in a woman's life, but now as carpet manufacture had become big business there could no longer be any guarantee that a carpet with a border *actually* was made by a woman with a fence around her field.

9

But I had seen an opportunity, a way to make some money in this market. I would need to be able to use his shop for an afternoon. I explained to Samir that I intended to go to the Atlas mountains and return with one carpet to sell. If I could use his premises to sell it within a few hours I would give him 20 per cent of the profit. No need, he said, there was no way I would succeed. Instead, he proposed a wager. Yes, I could use his shop. If I sold the carpet in the time I had left, then all the profit was mine. But if I failed to sell it then the carpet was his.

The gauntlet had been dropped at my feet. It was time to go and find a carpet.

My favourite carpets in Rashid's demonstration had all originated from the Tazenakht region of southern Morocco, in the High Atlas mountains, home of the Berber people. This is where I was going shopping. Adnan arranged a driver who could speak Berber and we set off at dawn the next day. It took a full day's drive through the desert to get there, and we only arrived in the mountains after dark.

After a hot, sweaty night in a poorly ventilated hotel room, I awoke to find myself in a dusty old town high up in the dry, arid landscape of the Atlas mountains. In this part of the world all the buildings are made from the local sandstone, so villages and towns have an eerie sense of having grown out of the ground. All houses are walled and family life traditionally happens exclusively and privately within the home. Berber women only leave the home twice in their lives: first, on their wedding day, when they leave their father's house for their husband's house; second, when they leave their husband's house for their grave. They don't even go to the market for foodstuffs – the men do all that. What I really wanted was to meet one of these women, buy a carpet directly from her, and hear her real story in the process.

Our driver, Barak, asked around in the town about where we might be able to buy a locally produced carpet and we were helpfully directed towards a village a few miles down the road. But after what seemed like an encouraging start I found that the village was already one step ahead of me. A sophisticated co-operative had been established where each woman in the village had strengthened her bargaining position by joining together as a group and using a local middleman to represent them. There was a 'showroom' in the centre where buyers are invited to view the carpets, and the profits are shared out between the woman who made the carpet and the other women, to ensure that no one ever goes hungry. This was great for the village but it didn't give me any room to negotiate a good price, nor did it give me the very thing I'd come to find: a no-bullshit story. I needed Adnan and Barak to gain access to a real Berber family home.

How do you get into a Berber home? A simple question with a simple answer: knock on the door. From Jehovah's Witnesses to electricity companies, we're used to telling people to go away here in the UK. The Berbers, however, are not used to strangers knocking and asking if they have any carpets that they'd like to sell, so were a little on the back foot when I started to do exactly that. Despite Barak's assertions that this approach would never work, it didn't take more than a few tries before we were granted access to the home of an admittedly slightly suspicious Berber man. I'm never surprised at how adaptable people are when there's money to be made, and this man was no different. He was actually prepared to sell one of the carpets from his own house and, incredibly, he was also agreeable to us coming inside. I was delighted, Barak absolutely stunned. So far, so good.

After the usual offering of mint tea in the courtyard and an explanation of what I was doing conducted in a mixture of English, Berber and Arabic, the man instructed his two sons to go into the house and come out with every floor covering they possessed. It was as if they were preparing to do a really good spring clean. In no time at all, we were looking at ten or so carpets neatly arranged in the courtyard outside. Every one of these carpets had been made on the loom in the house by the women of the family, but they had several different styles. I was relying on my own Western taste to inform me of what would sell back in Marrakech. After that, I was relying on Adnan to recognize good craftsmanship. The last carpet out of the house was laid in the middle of the courtyard, a beautifully understated black and white geometric rug with a subtle border in saffron that I would happily throw on the floor of my own flat in north London. If there's a good story attached to this one then we may have a deal, I thought.

The Berber people start negotiating the second they're born. I can imagine them as infants delaying the inevitable weaning programme by offering to be quiet for their mothers. So I knew I was the underdog in a scrap the second I declared interest in the carpet and asked for a price. You don't start to haggle with a Berber unless you're committed to seeing it through to the bitter end. Now, Samir had told me not to pay more than €300 for a 6 foot by 4 foot carpet (they speak French up here, which means they also deal in Euros). The opening price I'm given is €600. It's the last carpet that his mother ever made, the only thing he has to remember her by, some of her finest ever work . . . My God, I thought, when will this ever end? Enough! He was playing hard ball. But I guessed that all this was meant to soften me up and stop me asking for a lower price. In the Western world we're either too polite or too scared to ever ask for money off anything. Since we've lost the art of negotiation, tourists come to places like Morocco and pay way over the odds for everything they buy. Moroccans laugh at us all the way to the bank. But I couldn't afford to be polite.

There's a classic three-step negotiation technique that is often quoted in business literature. Many theorists and lecturers re-brand it with a catchy name and pass it off as their own unique insight, but it basically always boils down to the same thing. First, before you go into any negotiation tell yourself what your bottom line is – you must never settle for less than this. If the negotiation looks like it falls short of this, then walk away! Second, have in your mind what you think is the likely outcome of the negotiation. This will be a benchmark for you to judge how well the negotiation went. Lastly, consider your 'best case scenario'. This should include price but might also include extra elements of the deal such as free delivery or fancy packaging, and these should be reflected in your opening position. You shouldn't be afraid to ask for them right from the outset.

I decided that €400 was my walk-out point. I simply couldn't make a decent profit back in Marrakech if I paid more than that. I thought it more likely that I'd pay €300–350 and my best case scenario was nearer to €200. So I would start at €200, but not until I'd brought him down a bit first. There's great mileage in giving someone the silent treatment in a negotiation. As soon as he threw out the price of €600, I knew that it would be too difficult to get him down to where I thought the negotiation should end up, so instead I said nothing. I simply asked him to give me a better price. This is not the Berber way and he was unsettled. He had expected me to make a counter-offer but instead I had refused to play his game. Yet our game had undoubtedly begun – there was no going back.

Mr Berber, Adnan and Barak continued to discuss my position in a mixture of Arabic and Berber. Time and time again, Adnan asked me what my price was but I stayed firm: I'd give my price once I received a fair opening price. Eventually he cracked: €450 – a 25 per cent reduction without me giving anything away. Now I was ready to counter. I offered €200 in line with my best case estimate. This prompted another round of Arabic, Berber and English negotiations, prices went up and down and eventually I resorted to telling him to talk to his wife.

This was, I later discovered, a potentially insulting gambit as a

Berber man never consults his wife over business. However, this one did exactly that. I have no idea what she said to him but he came back with his final price: €350. I was now near to my anticipated likely outcome, and he was adamant that there was no more room to manoeuvre on price. So I needed to be inventive to get more value from the deal.

One thing that had fascinated me while the family had been showing me the carpet was the story of how their grandmother had used the wool from her own sheep. This was the kind of detail I'd need to sell the carpet myself. So as a final gambit I asked for a bag of wool, and for us to have a picture taken together. Done. We shook hands and I had a carpet, a bag of wool and proof of the authenticity of my transaction for the princely sum of €350. Now all I had to do was sell it.

Back at Bouchaib, I sat waiting for Samir. The first test of how I'd fared in the village was going to be Samir's critique of not just the rug's quality, but also the price I'd paid. He was as close to an expert opinion as I was ever going to get, so his approval was very important to me. He greeted me with his usual warm, charming smile. It was easy to see how this man had made his money as a salesman; he was instantly likeable and sharp as a tack. He wasted no time in getting me to show him the goods.

I watched for his reaction as I unfurled the carpet. He seemed impressed; the carpet was a 'good one'. But the crucial detail was: how much did I pay for it? I hesitated. I didn't want to tell him, I wanted to know what he would have paid. '€300–500.' Bingo, I hadn't been ripped off. In fact, Samir himself would have been happy to have negotiated the carpet for €350. The first half of the job had been completed well enough that I could now ask for €600, a 40 per cent mark-up, and the sort of profit Samir would have made.

Given the choice between being a buyer and a seller, I'd be a buyer every time. Buying something is the easier end of the process to control; you're in the driving seat because you have options. You can always walk away and look elsewhere. Of course it's important to get a good deal and that can require careful negotiation, but it's small beer compared to the pressure you feel when it comes time to sell. The tables are turned, and you must do everything you can to appear in control. The seller is a bit like the map reader: he has to convince the driver to trust him and then lead him where he thinks he wants to go. Having a good product helps because it gives you what you need most: confidence. I was confident that my carpet was of good quality and reasonably priced. I knew that because Samir had told me. But I now had to convince a complete stranger of it.

My first attempts at showing French tourists my wool and the pictures of the Berber family from whom I'd bought the carpets went badly. Faced with people not engaging with the story, doubts were beginning to creep into my mind. I wasn't getting anywhere and I knew it was because I wasn't getting my passion for the carpet and its story across to my customers. The guides were bringing in busloads of tourists but my carpet and I were being ignored time and time again. It sunk in: I might know a fair bit about economics and trading, but if I didn't learn the ease of a natural salesman fast, I'd be stuck with a carpet – or rather, a nice present for Samir – and a nasty taste of failure.

The only way was to approach it as an act. I'd done a fair bit of amateur theatrics in my day so I drew a deep breath and put on a face, like Samir. At first, I continued to struggle. It wasn't easy to engage with the serious buyers, and groups of tourists were starting to die off as it was getting late in the day. I felt a sense of dread, because trying again tomorrow just wasn't an option. The whole point of this test was to show that it was possible for a person from somewhere like London to trade in a traditional and demanding foreign market, and then move on. After all, if I seriously expected to do this all over the world then I had to be able to buy, transport and sell for a profit all in a few days, whether it was carpets or camels. The pressure was on and I was feeling it, but no one wants to buy from a nervous salesman.

Suddenly, I spotted a couple who looked like serious buyers on the other side of the shop. They'd already put a couple of carpets to one side and were looking at more. I could hear from their conversation that they were Italian so I grabbed one of the salesmen in the shop who could speak English and Italian and strode over with my carpet under my arm. It was time for a full-on charm offensive, and I realized quickly how a smile and a confident demeanour will turn someone on to you. I now had the approach to go with the goods and the story. In a flash, I got them intrigued by the pictures of the family: a real Berber family, whose mother had made this carpet shortly before she died forty years ago. Here they could feel the wool from the family's own sheep. This story was real; its heritage was not an interpretation of some symbols but a real life, something that could be told to friends who visited them in their Italian home, a real slice of Morocco that could be cherished long after the holiday had ended.

I finished my spiel, which prompted a totally unintelligible discussion in Italian. I felt powerless to influence any further this monumental decision, one that could release me from my torture. 'Buy the rug!' I thought over and over, whilst continuing to smile and nod reassuringly. From the debate, it was clear that it was all the wife's decision, but I continued to show her husband pictures of the family home from where I'd bought the carpet in some vain hope that he'd make the first interior décor decision of his marriage, and possibly his life. Eventually, my translator reverted to English: he was delivering the verdict. They understood, they agreed, they liked the pattern, could they keep the wool, could they keep the photos, how much was I asking, they'd like to buy the carpet for the asking price, €600.

It happened in a flash. One moment this carpet was the apple of my eye and I'd focused all my energies on acquiring it, the next it had become a millstone round my neck and my entire focus was on getting rid of it. Now, it belongs to someone else and I have a bundle of cash in its place. In a sense I actually miss it. As soon as I saw it, I liked it, I wanted it, I had to have it; but then once I had it, I needed to get rid of it, to sell it. A trader cannot afford to get attached to what he sells; yes, it's important that he covets good products as these are the things he can be confident of selling, but he has to be careful not to develop what economists call an endowment effect – a feeling that something is worth more than its monetary value simply because you own it. It's yet another lesson I'm going to have to learn if I'm going to make a habit of this.

Two

THE CAMEL CRUNCH

INVESTMENTS: $0
IN THE BANK: $50,000

I have a friend. Let's call her Sarah. Sarah wouldn't mind me telling you that she is simply the most disorganized person I know. Sarah is someone who once turned up late for a flight only to discover that in fact she was a day early. When she returned home, she found that she'd left her iron on. That's Sarah's luck. If she'd caught the flight as she meant to then her flat would probably have burnt down. And if Sarah were Sudanese, they'd probably make her minister for planning, or possibly even president. Well, maybe not president. You're not allowed to be president if you're a woman in Sudan.

There are lots of other things you're not allowed to do in Sudan. Lots. I have been aware of this for some time, since I met a Sudanese man back in England who had been recommended to me by a well-travelled friend. My contact explained that it is impossible to organize anything in Sudan unless you are there. After I told him about my intention to trade my way around the world beginning in Sudan, he convinced me that the best plan would be to pay him to go to Sudan ahead of me to arrange the necessary permits and licences for trading. It is a bit disappointing, then, when I arrive in Sudan and he is not there.

I'm back in North Africa to pick up where I left off in Morocco but a few things have happened in the meantime that I should explain. First, I've sold my flat. I've put all my belongings in storage, taken £25,000 of the profit from the sale and come up with a plan. Morocco was a test, a challenge, an exercise even, which proved to me that it is possible to make some money in new markets in foreign climes. But it only served to whet my appetite for a bigger challenge. You could say that I'm now raising the stakes.

I've decided to back myself to trade my way around the globe. I have £25,000, which I've converted to $50,000, to invest in any products that I think I can turn a profit on and I've booked a round-the-world plane ticket. I have a schedule that kicks off from northern to southern Africa then up through India, Central Asia, across China to Taiwan and Japan then over the Pacific, down through Mexico to Brazil and then home. I've picked these countries because, with the exception of Japan, they are all former developing countries that are now flourishing. These so-called Newly Industrialized Countries (NICs) are where I think I'll find the best opportunities for new business. I'm looking for places where people have disposable income, which rules out the poorest countries, but at the same time I want to avoid the more sophisticated economies of the world where opportunities are all sewn up.

Leaving aside travel costs, I reckon that I can make it round the globe in five months, double my money along the way and return with $100,000 in the bank. The countries I'll be going to are set, when I'm going there is set, but what I'm going to trade is still up for grabs because, if I'm right, new opportunities will present themselves along the way. I'm going to start here in Sudan and then my rough plan is to find things to trade between each of the countries along the route. I've already done a bit of research and have had a few ideas. The first half of my plan after trading camels in Sudan is to head south, picking up some African coffee en route to Cape Town, and then possibly to export frozen curries from Cape Town to India. From there, who knows? Nothing is locked down and I'm not entirely sure myself whether any of this is going to work. All I know right now is that I've begun. First stop: Khartoum.

I have to hand it to my friend's Sudanese contact. It would seem that his insight was spot on. It really is impossible to organize anything in Sudan unless you are there. At least, he's not here and nothing has been organized. I am allowed into the country but I will need to present myself to the Ministry of Information in the morning to get permission to be a journalist in Sudan. I try to explain that I am not a journalist, but as far as they are concerned I am, so I need to present myself to the Ministry in the morning. On a more personal note, the twenty-year-old bottle of Bowmore single malt that I have brought with me because I've heard that Sudan is a 'dry' country is impounded at customs because, again, what I've heard was right: Sudan is a dry country.

Khartoum is the capital of Sudan. Its skyline is a curious blend of minarets and satellite dishes pushing religion in the form of Islam, and European football. Driving around, it strikes me that every single vehicle on its dry, dusty streets is white. The temperature is a stifling 48° Celsius and there is no breeze. A smog hangs over the city like a blanket, pushing the temperature even higher. A car that was any other colour would simply be a human oven.

This is the place where the White Nile and the Blue Nile meet, which is why Khartoum is the capital, or at least why it was originally. Now it remains the capital because it's the place where most Sudanese feel safe. It's this need for safety that must have driven one in three Sudanese to join the army and the other two to join the police. They keep an oppressive eye on each other day and night, matched only by the ever-watchful eye of Allah.

Sudan is becoming increasingly Arabized. Arabs have been in north-east Africa for over a thousand years but their influence is becoming increasingly pervasive. The streets of Khartoum today are full of impromptu markets: blankets thrown down in the dust displaying goods for sale. People go about their daily lives, some dressed in long, white Arab *jallabiyas*, others dressed in more modern Western dress; jeans and T-shirts are not uncommon. There is a clear move towards Islam, although not everyone here has fully embraced it. You could easily believe that there are two separate races inhabiting Khartoum, but in fact they are all Sudanese.

My Arabic is a little rusty but one expression that any new arrival in Sudan will pick up before long is *insh'Allah*. This translates approximately as: nothing is certain about tomorrow, something will only happen tomorrow if it is God's will, and that is if you manage not to get arrested.

The day after I arrive in Khartoum is Tuesday. My plan is to head to the south of the country to embark on a camel trade. The market in El Obeid is where many of the camels from the south (including the war-torn region of Darfur) are sold on to traders, who transport them north to sell in the Birqash camel market in Cairo, Egypt. From my initial research back home, I have a rough idea of the economics of the trade. A good camel down south will fetch $300–600, but by the time it reaches Cairo, the same animal will be worth $700–1,000. This is a journey of over a thousand miles that has historically been known as the Forty-Day Road on account of the length of time it takes to walk it. That seems a little optimistic to me, given that it's 48° outside and the last time I walked 25 miles in a day (the Birmingham Walkathon, aged 13), I certainly wasn't up for doing it again the next day, or indeed every day for the next month and a half, and I'm a lot less sprightly now. So my plan is to hire a camel truck and drive the thousand miles in four days instead. The transport costs can be kept low as I'm a cash buyer.

A bit like our own banking sector in the West, there's a degree of credit crunch going on in the Sudanese camel trade at the moment. The way it usually works is that I buy your camel from you but I don't give you any money, yet. I take the camel to a market up the road and sell it to a man who doesn't give me any money for it, yet. And so it goes until the last man sells it at the big market in Egypt and gets paid. He then goes home and pays the man he got the camel from who then goes home and pays the man he got it from. So it goes until the first man gets paid and then pays me. Sometimes the money never makes it all the way back.

The parallel with banks in the global financial system is uncanny. Banks make loans to each other all the time, and make profits from the interest. The lending bank makes a profit from the loan to the borrowing bank, which then makes a profit from lending on to someone else, maybe to you as a mortgage lender. Everyone is lending to everyone else, and as long as the second bank can count on you paying your mortgage payments every month, the first bank can expect that their loan will be repaid too. The system works like a well-oiled machine, where money takes the part of the oil. The problem is that once the expectation changes, once the belief that the loan can be repaid is undermined, people become nervous and less willing to lend; the oil dries up and the machine breaks down. Whether it's camels or credit, the system depends on trust that the next man in the chain will pay up.

Back on the Forty-Day Road, the obvious solution would be for the Sudanese traders to take their camels all the way to Cairo themselves, but this is not the Sudanese way. There is no culture of travel here, and it is still regarded as unusual for people to do so. Camels are mostly transported on foot and so a man must leave his wife and family to take them to market. Time limits the distance that he is able to travel and so limits the profit that he is able to make. This inherent delay at best, bad debt at worst, is what I hope to use to my advantage by employing an old technique called 'cash up front'. I'll miss out all the middlemen, as if I was the first bank lending straight to the mortgage lender myself. I'll take the camels all the way to Cairo, and as long as I can hold my own at the negotiation end of things then I stand to make a few quid out of the deal.

If the figures that my original contact and I were knocking around are anything to go by (a big 'if', in the circumstances) then I'm looking to blow $4,000 on eight camels in El Obeid, and another $1,000 for transport and food takes the total to $5,000. If I get all the camels to Cairo in one piece then they could be worth $8,000. I've got a total of £25,000 to invest on this whole journey, which right now is equivalent to $50,000. This isn't just pretend money, it's money that I should be putting aside for my future. I should really be reinvesting it in property or a pension or something sensible but instead I'm investing it in camels.

I'm taking the first step cautiously – camels are not really my area of expertise. Camel trading is a risky enterprise and I need to be prepared for something going wrong. If it does then I still want to have enough money left to carry on with the trip. Of course, if everything goes well, I'll have made a good start. Ideally, I want to leave Egypt with a few extra quid in the bank and a bag full of confidence.

Unfortunately the plan is going awry. Tuesday is taken up with visiting the Ministry of Information and securing permission to be in Sudan. The building looks more like a car park in mid-construction than an important seat of government. Outside, the unfinished concrete fascia is still punctured by steel rods, and inside I have to dodge several stepladders in the corridors as the walls are being painted that shade of pale blue gloss that we haven't seen in the UK since the seventies. Note to self: next time I'm in Sudan, bring lorry load of paint.

I am ushered into the minister's office. Osma has a very big desk. There's nothing on it, but it's very big. It's almost as big as his moustache, which in turn is almost as big as the enormous right hand that he crushes mine with as he says hello. The television in the corner is playing the latest from the Sudanese hit parade on some Arabic MTV-esque channel, and in the opposite corner is a pasty, tired-looking American man who tells me that he works for the *LA Times*. He has been to see Osma every day now for three weeks and I'm guessing this isn't because they like 'hanging out' together. I'm sorry for the American guy but fortunately I don't have to suffer the same fate; I have Adam.

Adam is a small man with a large moustache and a cherubic face that dimples when he smiles. I've employed him ro replace my original Sudanese guide. His English is terrible and he knows as much about camels as the average Sudanese knows about whisky, but at least he's here. I am able (slowly) to translate my frustrations into Arabic and Osma seems a lot more interested in me than in the forlorn-looking American watching MTV in the corner.

In a mere four hours we overcome the issues surrounding the misunderstanding at the airport. I am assured the problem was because the requirements for visas in Sudan have changed in the last three days and the embassy in London must not have known. I am issued with a 'Journalist' pass that Osma stamps before sending me down the corridor so that someone else can stamp it. Another man behind a big desk eventually does just this, only to point to yet another office down the hall. After it has been stamped many times by various people sitting behind large, empty desks, I am invited to go back to see Osma. I'm developing a suspicion that no one in Sudan is actually working. It's as though everyone is pretending to work under the false illusion that everyone else is working, and if they don't appear to be working too they'll be given some paperwork to fill in. And believe me, that is not a road you want to go down in Sudan.

Osma gives his own stamp a counter-stamp and explains that this now entitles me to be a 'Journalist' trading camels in all areas of the country. I am given carte blanche to trade camels and write whatever I like about it wherever I please. The key to Sudan is mine. All I need to do is go to the Ministry of Movement to get the permission to go to these places before I trade there. I must do this tomorrow, as it is now shut for today.

As the day draws to a disappointing end I find out another, more disappointing, piece of news. Adam informs me that the camel market in El Obeid is only held on Tuesdays and Saturdays. Not Thursdays, as I was told originally. Now, you may think this is something I could have checked for myself before I got here, or verified easily from another source in Khartoum, but you'd be wrong. There is no substitute for on-the-ground experience in most situations and in Sudan this is doubly true. The problem is that people here don't travel much, so they have only a very shady knowledge of what happens in other parts of the country. Me asking someone in Khartoum what the market is doing in El Obeid is a bit like asking a pre-Industrial Revolution Briton in London what the price of eggs is in Derby.

The problem is that my route is now firmly set. I have already booked my ticket out of Cairo for a week's time so I simply can't wait another week here in Sudan. I have to buy my camels and get across the border by Tuesday at the latest. Already the delicate house of cards on which my final flight from Rio rests is in danger of being blown over by the first gust of hot desert wind.

The next day Adam and I head over to the Ministry of Movement. The Ministry requires that I have a sponsor in Sudan, whom they can torture on my behalf if I do anything wrong, such as be a spy. I wish I was joking but I'm not. When we arrive, Adam has forgotten his documentation, which he needs in order to sponsor me, and so he arranges for a friend of his to come down instead. His friend will be here in one hour.

While we wait, a helpful official asks to see my journalist pass and asks where I intend to go. I explain to him the disappointment over the southern camel market and he suggests that instead I go to the Khartoum camel market. It's not quite as cheap but it's a good market and my transport costs will be lower. This is the best news I've had since I arrived. But he also points out that my journalist pass doesn't cover the part of Khartoum where the camel market is, so I need to go back to the Ministry of Information and get this permission before I get my documents from the Ministry of Movement. Well, of course I do.

Adam and I dash back across town to see Osma, who is still busy at his big desk. The American journalist from the *LA Times* is back in position, the desk is still empty; it's as though I'd never left. I explain hurriedly the situation and Osma concurs that the Khartoum camel market would be a good Plan B. He takes my journalist pass and scrutinizes it. It does cover the area where the market is. He insists it does. He insists that I wait while his secretary writes me a covering letter specifically mentioning this area and the fact that I have permission to go there. Meanwhile, my new sponsor calls Adam from the Ministry of Movement: where are we? He's come all the way down to sponsor me and we're not even there. He's understandably furious. I try to leave to go straight there but Osma is not for moving until my letter is written. My sponsor cannot wait. He can come back again after lunchtime. Another morning wasted.

The next six hours are filled with more waiting, more to-ing and fro-ing, more people suspecting me of spying, more men behind big empty desks making me sit and wait while they adjust their desk fans. My passport goes on a magical mystery tour of the inner sanctums of the Ministry and finally returns certified, stamped and authorized. I have permission to move, write, buy, transport and sell camels in Sudan, and I am free to get on with what is left of my plan.

With El Obeid out of the plan, Khartoum camel market seems to be the next best option. Adam is confident that I can source good camels there and although it is late in the day we have enough time for an initial scout around. The market is a little way outside the town and we set off, for the first time since my arrival, optimistic of achieving something.

It would be easy to see all this as a tale of doom and gloom. It would be easy to feel that there was no happy ending in sight, to give up, get out of Sudan and try to start again somewhere else. But to do any of these things would have meant missing out on an important lesson that I was about to learn – when we eventually found the camel market.

Unfortunately we are hopelessly lost. Even five miles off his own patch, Adam is totally clueless as to where to go. Very quickly after leaving the outskirts of town we are driving in what can only be described as barren desert. Small collections of walled sandstone houses make for the only landmarks, so to be fair to Adam there is little to go on. Eventually, after many stops to ask for directions, we come to what Adam confidently proclaims is the camel market. It certainly looks like a market; there are hundreds of cars parked in the middle of the desert. I assume this must be the car park but wonder how on earth you get your camel home in your car after you've bought it. It's hardly going to fit in the boot. Once we get out of our car and ask around it transpires that this is in fact Khartoum's largest second-hand car market. The camel market is five miles away.

Strange as it seems, in a second-hand car market in the Western

Desert, Adam has bumped into two people he knows. They are adorned in white, flowing robes, fully turbaned and look like extras straight from the set of *Lawrence of Arabia*. They are from his village in Darfur and they are livestock traders. Adam explains to them how we are looking for the camel market and, not content with simply giving us directions, they jump in our car and come along for the spin. They certainly look the part and as we all head off into the desert I start to feel like we might actually get to a camel market today, *insh'Allah*.

There is no car park at Khartoum camel market. There is a massive clearing in the desert and there are lots of camels in it. Even at this late hour there are a handful of traders showing off their beasts. Our friends from Darfur explain that in the morning there are many more camels here but now most people have gone home. It seems likely that I can come again tomorrow but while I'm here I want to get as much information as I can about prices and how they change with age, sex and size. The crucial thing is that I don't let the traders know what I'm planning to do, so I have a strategy meeting with Adam where I had hoped to explain the importance of 'keeping one's cards close to one's chest'. With Adam briefed, we walk over to where a group of traders are sitting.

There may have been situations where I've stood out more in my lifetime, but I can't think of one offhand. Maybe it has been a long day, maybe sales are slow at this time of year but every – *every* – trader in the market immediately comes over to find out what I am up to. A gaggle of men all shouting in Arabic engulfs us and Adam starts shouting back to them. I'm initially flattered by the attention but very quickly become concerned by what Adam could possibly be shouting about for so long. I force my way over to where he is standing and, after calling his name several times, manage to make him stop. I ask him what is going on. 'They are curious what you are doing here,' he explains. And what are you shouting about,

Adam? 'I am explaining to them that you have come from England, and that you want to buy camels to take to Egypt.' As he tells me this I can see all my cards being prised from my chest one by one and flung on to the desert sand for all to see. What chance do I have now?

The first camel I enquire about is a four- to five-year-old male, the kind of camel that my research suggested I could sell in Cairo for around the $1,000 mark. To make a profit on it, including transport and food, I would need to buy this camel in Sudan for around $500–550. This is the price I have been told that camels of a similar size and shape sell for in the south. After discussions in Arabic with his closest associates, the trader informs Adam to tell me that the price of this camel is $900. What chance? No chance. My cover is completely blown. Even if I come back tomorrow, word will have spread that there's a funny-looking guy from out of town who's made of money and looking to be ripped off as much as possible.

I've missed out on El Obeid market and now Khartoum camel market is blown too, so I'm a little deflated. I start to wonder if I'll ever find a reasonably priced camel in Sudan. The crucial thing is to find someone whom I can trust to guide me in the right direction. Adam is similarly deflated, having realized that his poker play is a little rusty, but he can offer a suggestion. His friends have a contact in Dongola in the north-west of Sudan who they say is a very well-respected man. He is responsible for organizing all the export papers for camels crossing the border to Egypt so in any case I would need to contact him to pass along my intended route. There is apparently another camel market in Dongola and their contact, Mohammed Emieri, would be the ideal person to help.

I put a call in to Mr Emieri. I particularly want to know if there is actually a camel market in Dongola and, if so, how does it compare to Khartoum in terms of selection and price? Now, let's face facts: the man is going to be extremely confused as to why he's getting a phone call like this. What do you mean you've come from London and you're interested in buying a job lot of camels? But he seems happy enough that there is indeed a camel market in Dongola, and the really good news is that it is almost identical in size and the prices are pretty much the same. He goes so far as to say that if it were him then he'd just buy them in Khartoum, seeing as we're here already. Easy for him to say; if it were him he wouldn't have Adam to contend with.

Three

INSH'ALLAH

INVESTMENTS: $0
IN THE BANK: $50,000

That night in Khartoum, I had a call from a friend in London who had been at a wedding in Zimbabwe and met an American living in Cape Town. He called me because, he said, I should check out a bizarre research project that the American was running which he thought was in danger of becoming a really innovative new business idea. The American's name was Loki and the project involved saving elephants.

I was still trying to get my head around camels, so the idea of elephants was a little out of left field, but this was exactly the kind of thing I wanted to stay open to on this journey. Fortunately he wasn't talking about me buying any. There are elephants all over the place in southern Africa in countries like Zambia and Botswana. I'd heard about them being a menace to farmers in the region. This seemed sad to me because I'm sure there are many parts of the world that would gladly have taken a few elephants off their hands. I'm sure that Dartmoor or the Peak District could be enhanced no end by having a few elephants roaming around. What is also sad is that the current solution to the problem is simply to shoot them.

If you're a southern African farmer living on a subsistence farm growing maize or fruit and a troop of elephants decides that it wants to pass over your land, there aren't many ways to stop them. It is also safe to say that once they've let themselves in they'll eat every last inch of vegetation you have. What they don't eat they will trample. Either way, elephants aren't going to command such a dear place in your heart as they do in the average safari tourist's. So I could empathize with the farmer who felt he had no choice but to shoot the elephants; it was entirely understandable in a dog-eat-dog kind of way.

However understandable, there seemed to be one glaring problem in all this: aren't elephants an internationally protected species? Aren't they endangered? Isn't there an embargo on ivory trading in order to protect them? Well, no. Apparently not. There are loads of these pesky elephants all over southern Africa trashing farms, and the governments sanction culls all the time.

Fortunately, there are still a few people who continue to see them as magnificent beasts, who believe that the elephants must be cherished, and among this bunch of liberal-hearted lunatics are clever people like Loki. Loki had come up with an even more ingenious means of protecting them than deportation to Dartmoor. He'd actually found a way of making money out of his idea and he was looking for new people to do business with. My friend thought I might be just the man.

I got Loki on the telephone from Khartoum to ask if we could meet up and talk about his idea when I finally made it to Zambia. I had a flight booked from Cairo in just under a week's time. Loki was in Mozambique but he told me that his business partner, Mick, would be back in Zambia in a few days and would be happy to meet and fill me in. If I had more questions after that then he'd be back in Cape Town in a couple of weeks. This all sounded great – a little surreal after spending the day in a camel market, but great nonetheless. I said I'd call Mick and set up a meeting. In the meantime I had some camels to find.

*

Bright and early, we're up and ready for Adam to arrive with the car we arranged the previous night to take us to Dongola: a Land Rover, negotiated at the competitive rate of $100. The Land Rover will come with a driver thrown in for free. Eventually Adam turns up but without the driver, or indeed the Land Rover, which is apparently being fixed. Did an alarm bell just ring in your head? It should have rung in mine, but it didn't. So we get a taxi across town, wait outside the garage for a few hours while the vehicle is fixed and eventually get on the road at 3 p.m. Not to worry, the car-hire man reassures us, it's only a five-hour drive. We should still be there in time for tea, *insh'Allah*.

Full of beans, finally on the way, we leave Khartoum far behind and head along the road towards Dongola that passes through the eastern edge of the Sahara. The journey is frequently interrupted at either police or army checkpoints where they check and recheck my passport, presumably in case the last twenty people who checked and rechecked it missed the page that said SPY in big capital letters. I am, like most Sudanese, becoming desensitized to it. Suspicion has become something I am used to living with. It's a bit like being back at school.

The road is straight and flat. The landscape is a barren, flat, brown vastness, broken only by the occasional outcrop of rock on the horizon. Mile after mile passes without so much as a tree to look at; a journey made for the iPod or a good book. I have neither.

We seem to be making such good time and I'm so bored by the monotony of the scenery that when I notice a camel breeder leading a group of camels through the desert beside the road, I ask our driver, Dahil, to pull over. I want to conduct a bit of market research. The man is leading his eight camels to a water trough across the road.

Let's be clear; there's no way in the world that I can buy a camel

33

yet. I have no transport for it. But he's not to know that, and I want to gauge the price of his beasts. So I ask him, how much? He explains to me that they're not for sale but I take a punt and offer him $200 for one. Heaven help me if he says yes. He doesn't; instead he explains that they're worth at least $300 each at market, if he were buying them he'd want to pay nearer to $275 for them, and if he were ever to consider selling one to me he wouldn't accept a penny under $400 on a point of principle because I am a foreigner. Charming, yet informative.

Back in the vehicle, Dahil and Adam are discussing my exchange with the camel herder as the sun begins to set. The vaulting desert sky takes on shades of first orange and then pink. Dahil noticed that all the herder's camels were female. He says that females are cheaper, so I should expect to pay more than $300 if I want males. The sky gets dark and a million stars come out. I've never been anywhere with so little light pollution before; there actually seems to be more white than black overhead.

We pull over at a truck stop for some gristle stew and stale bread. I have no idea what type of meat is in the gristle stew and I am thankful that the tables are so badly lit that I can't see to hazard a guess. What I can see, however, are trucks. Camel trucks, to be precise.

Up until now the idea of buying camels, hiring a truck to transport them to Egypt and selling them there was still a notional plan, but finally here was hard evidence that such activity was more than notional; it was actually happening. Again, I want to find out as many details about this trade as I can. It's all very well planning to miss out the middlemen, but many of them eke out their living by exploiting a vital piece of information in the chain. If I'm going to replace them I need to know what they know, like how much a truck costs and how to book one.

As a truck readies to pull off, I run after it and hop up into the cab. The driver is a little stunned when I jump up beside him. I want to know where he's heading. He explains that he's going to Dongola to drop off his load and then he's looking to pick up a consignment of camels that he'll drive to the Egyptian border at Argeen. Bingo. I ask him how long this drive takes and how much he charges. It takes around eighteen hours and it would cost $500 all in for me and any camels I might have. It sounds expensive but I take his number just in case and let him get on with his journey.

According to the man from whom we hired the car, Dongola should only be another hour away, so we are all a little tired when three hours later we are still in the middle of the dark desert. Dahil looked so cool this morning when he arrived in a crisp, white linen shirt and wrap-around shades; now, after several hours behind the wheel, his driving is starting to concern me.

I notice that Dahil has developed a routine. First, his speed slows to around 30 miles per hour. Then he starts to lurch onto the other side of the road. Next he reaches into a small plastic bag in his pocket and takes out a pinch of khat, which he rolls and tucks into his cheek. Khat is a sort of herbal amphetamine used by men all over Africa as a stimulant. The leaves are rolled and then popped inside the cheek. It creates a buzz that lasts for an hour or so, and bad breath that lasts far longer. After another good mouthful, Dahil picks up speed to around 80 miles per hour; then the buzz wears off and the lurching starts again.

Every country has its own etiquette for how best to use head-lights at night. The technique in the Sudanese desert seems to be to turn them off until you are just about to pass another car, at which point you turn them up full and blind the oncoming driver. Why they do this is totally beyond me. What I do know is that, in light of this, Dahil's lurching onto the other side of the road is going to get us killed.

I drive. It's not long before I get the hang of 'blind the oncoming driver', or whatever it's called in Arabic, and I start to understand the reason for doing it. It's fun. Unfortunately, as the time passes I start to run out of oncoming traffic to blind and soon there is not another car on the road. That is because it is 3 a.m. There is still no sign of Dongola. When I notice that the temperature dial of the Land Rover is in the red zone, I ask Adam to wake Dahil and ask him if it is broken. I can't remember noticing it before and I am a bit worried. Dahil is also worried. We pull over so that he can put some more water in the radiator, then carry on our way for another few miles before the Land Rover starts overheating again and finally conks out altogether. We wait, let it cool and then push-start it a few times, but to no avail. It is dead. Nobody has any mobile phone reception, and in any case, whom would we call? Now, remember those alarm bells? I can still hear them so clearly.

Sleeping in the desert sounds a lot more glamorous than it is. The reality is that I am emptying my bag of every soft piece of clothing I own to make a lumpy bed on top of some rocks on the side of the road. Yes, the desert sky is truly breathtaking, you can see stars along the horizon and all that, but this is not a romantic moment for Adam and I to share. In fact, this is the most animated I've seen Adam since I met him. He is genuinely annoyed at this inconvenience and is actually berating the car-rental man for hiring us such a lemon. Tomorrow, if we ever get out of here, *insh'Allah*, Adam is going to phone him and demand he either give our money back or send a replacement car. In the meantime, we get a few hours' sleep.

In the morning Adam walks down the desert road to where his mobile phone can pick up a signal. A phone call to Mr Emieri reveals that we are now only an hour from Dongola and he even offers to come and rescue us. I am beginning to like him already. Perhaps this is the turning point of the trip. I feel like it can't get any worse. And I'm all the more determined to make this crucial opening trade work. Failure is not an option. Somehow I will get some camels to take to Egypt. I haven't come this far to be beaten.

I've also had time to take stock of the situation. Take, for instance, the car-hire man's claim that the drive was five hours – when the reality is that it's more like thirteen hours – and what it means. One interpretation is that he wanted us off his back so we wouldn't make too much fuss about the delay with the Land Rover. Another is that he simply didn't know, so instead he made something up. I think both are true. Certainly it got us out of his hair, so by the time we realized, he was far enough away not to have to hear our complaints. It also seems to hold with the lack of reliable information here in Sudan. He's probably never been to Dongola and he doesn't know anyone who has, so he made something up.

Mr Emieri arrives in a shiny new Toyota Land Cruiser. His right-hand man is a six-foot-three Nubian who appears to be mute. The Nubian may well be the strongest man I have ever seen as he takes two 40-litre tubs of diesel from the roof of the Land Rover and throws them onto the roof of the Land Cruiser. We all pile into the back and head off for Dongola. Mr Emieri says that the market is the day after tomorrow, so tonight we can just settle down and get some rest in town. Tomorrow we can have a powwow about strategy in preparation for the market.

*

The town of Dongola, like all Sudanese towns, is kept secure by the military. There is no city wall, so anyone could walk in from the desert side, but if you come in on the road your path is blocked by a security barrier. It's the kind of arm barrier that you often encounter at the entrance to a car park; in the UK they're usually painted red and white, in Sudan it's made from the branch of a tree. Next to the barrier is a tent where the soldiers sit to keep out of the hot sun. We are invited to step out of the car and into the tent.

The soldiers have military uniforms but budgets don't stretch to boots, so they wear ordinary shoes. It's hard to tell who the senior officer is as they are all in their teens and none of their uniforms match, but one of them has a rifle slung over his shoulder so I assume it is him. They stare at me with suspicion and yet also terrifying innocence. The boy sitting at a wooden table checks my passport, not really looking at it, and without a word passes it back to me. We step back out of the tent and into the Land Rover. One of them lifts the barrier and we proceed.

We only proceed as far as 'registration'. Inside a single-storey concrete building with no door a young man is asleep behind another big desk. I say, 'Knock knock' out loud, to stir him. He sits up quickly to emphasize his importance and holds out his hand, I presume for my passport. His job requires him to take down my details but the drawers of his big desk are empty so I lend him a pen. He goes next door to the shop to borrow a scrap of paper and jots down my name and passport number. He gives me back my pen and places the scrap of paper in one of the empty drawers in the desk. He closes it carefully and then reminds me to inform him before I leave town. Presumably, this is to enable him to update his filing system.

With a day spare in Dongola I decide to go for a run. I like to run when I have time as it helps me relax and sometimes helps stir up my mind to generate a few fresh ideas. In 48° heat it also helps me to sweat out every last drop of moisture in my body. Dongola is a no-horse town. There are four streets arranged like a noughts and crosses board. The buildings are all single-storey and residential, although there is a solitary restaurant in the centre. In the oppressive heat I begin to stagger through town and it is clear that I am fascinating to the Dongolese. People come out of their homes to gawp at me. Obviously, jogging is not popular here. As I turn for home I run past a diesel pump where some camel trucks just like the one I saw on the desert road are queuing for fuel.

It's time for my first negotiation in Sudan. If I don't organize transport in advance then I'll be stuck once I do actually have some camels in tow, not to mention in a weaker position from which to negotiate. The truck driver on the desert road quoted me $500 for a round trip from here to the border, so I want to get a better price than that. I ask a few of the drivers who owns which truck and who might be free to drive me and a load of camels to Dongola tomorrow. One says he'll take me but he wants $400, already cheaper than the last offer, but I tell him it's too expensive. He says that the diesel alone will cost $150 and he has to drive back as well. I offer him $200 on the basis that $50 for two days of his time is a lot of money in this part of the world. He explains that it will take him three days so $300 would be a better price. I can see where this is going; so can he. We shake on $250 and I agree to meet him tomorrow when I will have some camels for him to transport, *insh'Allah*.

The next morning the Nubian man comes to collect me from my guest house. I wanted to ask his name but how would he tell me? Arabic sign language? My excitement finally to be buying camels is now becoming unsettling and I find myself repeatedly clapping and rubbing my hands together, which the Nubian finds endlessly, if silently, amusing. With Mr Emieri's help I believe I should be able to find a clutch of camels by midday, when I've arranged to meet the truck. If we load up quickly we could make the border by nightfall tomorrow. This will give us a whole day's contingency for the crossing on Tuesday.

The Nubian and I happily bounce along together in the back of Mr Emieri's pickup truck with another man, who introduces himself as Mr Sayeed. He is a big, fat, cheery man dressed in a white *jallabiya* and turban, who is getting a lift with us to his camels outside town. Once we've dropped him off we'll head to the market.

The drive to Mr Sayeed's drop-off takes us out to a clearing in the desert where there are two large groups of around one hundred camels. One of the groups belongs to Mr Sayeed. I'm a bit envious when he starts telling me how he bought them cheaply in the south, as this is exactly what I had originally planned to do. I wonder if he means to sell any at the market in Dongola, but he's not interested; he's going to take them all to Egypt to sell them there for meat. He explains to me that the price is much higher in Egypt. He's only stopped in Dongola to get the paperwork stamped by Mr Emieri.

There's a certain satisfaction in finding out that one of your hunches is right. A voice inside you wants to scream, 'I told you so!' at all the people who smirked or raised an eyebrow or tutted disapprovingly when you first shared your idea with them. Now take that satisfaction, magnify it and reverse it, and call it anti-satisfaction. It is more powerful than satisfaction; it is a destructive voice that screams inside your head, 'Bollocks!' Over and over. It is a rueful voice, embittered by missed opportunity, and it is deafening. As Mr Sayeed gleefully explains to me how much profit he is going to make in Egypt, this is the only voice I can hear.

While Mr Emieri and Mr Sayeed are doing their paperwork, one of Mr Sayeed's camels breaks away. The herders are supposed to tie up one leg of each camel to stop this happening but this one has broken free and is making a dash for it. Dahil is quickest to react, and rather nonchalantly picks up one of the herder's sticks and trots off after the camel. He's back with it a couple of minutes later, much to the amusement of the whole group. A few words of explanation are called for and Dahil obliges by explaining that his father was a herder, and so was he, until he left Darfur for Khartoum to become a Land Rover driver. It seems that I have been travelling the whole time with an expert. Seeing as he doesn't have any driving to do now that the Land Rover has exploded, I ask him if he wouldn't mind being my adviser in the market. He's flattered to oblige.

We head off to the market. I am full of determination to make this work. I want to be like Mr Sayeed. I want to share in his success. I want to drive my camels all the way to Egypt, over the border, and sell them for a big, fat, juicy profit. I don't care that they are going to be sold for meat. I justify to myself that it is no different to cows and lambs being sold for steaks and chops back home. I want some camels and I want to have them slaughtered.

We seem to make an unscheduled stop when Mr Emieri's pickup pulls over in the centre of town at a walled-off pen full of animals. There are four or five very sorry-looking, mangy camels in one corner and forty or so goats looking similarly dishevelled. I hop down to stretch my legs and to see what Mr Emieri is up to. I'm looking at my watch because I want to get to the market and get my camels in time to meet the truck tonight, and it is already nearly 11 a.m. Emieri turns to me and asks how many camels I want to buy. I explain somewhere between six and eight, but I won't be sure until I see what the camels in the market look like. Then it hits me. This is the market.

Mr Emieri has brought me halfway across the desert for this! My head is spinning. I'm trying to think and Adam keeps asking me what I want to do now. I try to explain to him that I want to rip Mr Emieri's head off. He sensibly counsels against this course of action on the grounds that no one can export camels from Dongola without the paperwork that Mr Emieri has to approve. I ask Mr Emieri why he told me that the camel market here was the same as the camel market in Khartoum. He offers no explanation to this but asks me if I am interested in any of the camels that are on display here.

Not really, no.

I have a thought. I swallow my frustration, politely thank

Mohammed Emieri for taking the time to 'help' and decline the offer of his geriatric camels. I then hightail it back to where I'd left Mr Sayeed.

Back in the clearing, Mr Sayeed has gone. His camels are still there, and now so are another three or four hundred belonging to other traders. I approach one of the men who has arrived with the new groups. He explains to me that, like Mr Sayeed, he has no camels to sell as he is taking them all to Egypt tomorrow. Over the next twenty-four hours many, many traders will come here with their camels. There will be some buying and some selling until the time comes to leave and then they will all go to the border together. This is the safest way to travel in the desert as there are bandits in the areas north of here that prey on small herds. What's more, he estimates that by tomorrow there will be over one thousand camels here. Then I have a thought. Well, two thoughts. First, it seems that the reputation camel traders have made for themselves the world over as ruthless cut-throats is not unwarranted. Second, I know I've said this before, but it seems that, at last, I may have found somewhere to buy myself some camels.

I'm back in the clearing at dawn and already the large herds I was promised have begun to arrive. There are a thousand or so camels and more are coming all the time. I remind Adam of our 'cards close to the chest' strategy but he seems distracted. His phone is ringing repeatedly and he has to keep going off to answer it. Dahil, too, is getting calls and is wandering off all the time. I have to sort this out before we start negotiating so I get them both together to find out what the problem is.

The man from whom Adam rented the Land Rover is not being very helpful. Adam, not unreasonably, after a night sleeping on the hard, cold desert floor, put it to him that he would be best advised to return the money that had been paid for the car. The car-hire man, though reluctant at first, agreed to pay the money back to a friend of Adam's in Khartoum. But it seems he failed to show up with the money. It seems that Adam has been arguing with the man for the last twenty-four hours about this. The car-hire man has now decided that he only wants to pay half of what is owed. I, however, still have the key to the Land Rover in my pocket and he has no spare. For once in this country I have the upper hand so I'm in a position to dig my heels in. Pay the money over; get the key. I'm actually enjoying the situation so I tell Adam to just relax; eventually the guy will have to give in and pay up, or we'll take his key to Egypt with us.

In most other places I know, the reaction of a man running a car hire operation to the breakdown of one of his vehicles would be to apologize, offer a refund, provide a replacement, do whatever he could to keep the customer happy to ensure that his reputation and future business would not be adversely affected. But this man must feel that there is more value in keeping the money he has now than counting on making any more money tomorrow. This, I fear, is the consequence of living in a state where there is no trust, no faith in tomorrow. His behaviour is completely rational if indeed he believes that there is no chance of any more business tomorrow; after all, life here generally is punctuated with the phrase *insh'Allah*. It seems to me that there is a genuine reluctance to put too much faith in anybody knowing with any certainty what is likely to happen tomorrow. It is presumptuous of you to make firm plans, since it is not up to you, it is the divine will of Allah. I wonder whether this devout faith is at odds with a flourishing economy generally – if no one is accountable for not delivering tomorrow what they promise today, as they always have the perfect excuse that Allah simply didn't will it that way. I have been in Muslim countries before, but never have I felt this deferment of the future to a higher order so acutely as here in Sudan.

The car rental refund situation at a stalemate, and the clock forever ticking, Adam and I approach a man standing with a group of camels. I ask him first of all if these are his camels and if they are for sale. He confirms not only that they are his camels, but also that for the right price he wouldn't mind selling a few of them, so he could buy food for himself and the remaining camels along the route to Egypt. Dahil and I move among the camels picking out the ones that his expert eye thinks will fetch the highest prices in Egypt. Once we have five or six likely candidates, I return to the man to commence the inevitable haggle over price. In Sudan, they say that a negotiation over a camel should begin at dawn and end at dusk, so I know I'm in for a long haul to sort out a price for six of them. As I have to get on the road tonight, it seems to be the best use of time to try to agree a price for six in one go.

So begins the first camel haggle. I learned a thing or two about north African negotiation while I was in Morocco so I'm keen to put some of that knowledge to good use. When I'd been negotiating for a carpet in the Atlas mountains the carpet owner had opened with an asking price of nearly twice what he really wanted for it, so of course when the camel owner opens with a ridiculous price, a price in excess of what he could sell them for in Egypt, I offer him less than half. He takes this in his stride and counters with a price only slightly lower than his first.

So it goes up and down, stop for tea, up and down some more and then more tea, until we seem to be reaching somewhere close to a deal. At which point Mr Sayeed reappears. Now, I'm usually more than happy to see Mr Sayeed, but right now he's shouting – a lot. The trader with whom I'm doing business, Adam and Mr Sayeed are soon all shouting. This is the crucial stage of a very long negotiation and my first thought is that Mr Sayeed is somehow trying to muscle in on the action, steal the deal from under me after my skilful negotiating has reduced the price so low. So I start shouting. Then I realize no one actually understands what I'm shouting about, so this is a bad tactic. I change course. I ask Adam to ask Mr Sayeed to stop shouting. This works much better. 'What is he shouting about, anyway?' I ask Adam. 'He says that these camels do not belong to this man. This man is only a herder paid to look after these camels.'

That's it. I have wasted the best part of an hour negotiating with a shepherd over the cost of his boss's camels, which he has no authority to sell. I have been lied to face-to-face once again. I am on the edge. Where is the man who actually owns these camels? He is not here. These camels are not for sale. These camels are going to Egypt, but not on my truck.

I ask about what feels like each and every one of the thousand or so camels in the clearing, but none are for sale. One by one, I approach the men minding the camels around the clearing, and they admit that they are merely handlers paid by the owners to lead the camels to Egypt. The owners are in town, in Khartoum, in Egypt, anywhere but here. No one can contact them and no one can sell me a camel without them. How can this be? How can I have $5,000 worth of hard Sudanese currency in my pocket and yet find no one to sell me even as much as a hoof or a fetlock or whatever a bloody camel's foot is called? I take the hump (sorry). 'Somebody, sell me some bloody camels!' I can still hear myself screaming in vain into the desert sky.

Adam's phone rings for the hundredth time. Again, it is our friend the car-hire man. This time Adam puts it on speaker phone so that I can hear. I am truly shocked by the venomous tones of the voice on the other end of the line. I don't need to be able to understand Arabic to hear his scorn and his rage. Adam listens intently, trying again and again to interrupt, but to no avail, and eventually he hangs up. Not for the first time, Adam looks like a little boy who has been scolded for being naughty. But I quickly realize that it is more serious than that. The man has told him that he is going to inform the authorities that he suspects that I am operating as a spy and that Adam is acting as my accomplice. To me, this is simply ridiculous, but Adam has lived here longer and knows better the consequences of such an accusation.

Adam explains to me that he now expects us to be arrested. He expects that my government will secure my release without too much trouble but that he will be held, tortured or worse. I have no doubt from the tone of his voice that he believes this completely. I tell him to phone the man back and tell him to keep the money.

Desperately trying to come up with a new plan, I wonder if maybe we can still find one of the camel owners in town, buy some camels quick and make our way straight to Egypt and not look back. Adam looks at me with total disbelief. 'Nobody really believes that you are in Sudan to buy camels, nobody!' he hisses at me.

In that moment I realize that I have failed, fallen at the first hurdle. I have come to Sudan to take on the toughest traders in the world. I had hoped to transport camels along one of the oldest trade routes in history. Instead of travelling triumphantly up the Nile like thousands of traders since the time of the Pharaohs, I have found myself paralysed by lies and deceit and even my own naivety. Sudan is a police state where the government has managed to create an economic environment full of people who have no faith in any concept of return business and no interest in developing relation-ships that might bear fruit tomorrow as well as today. In opting instead to meet their short-term ends, they propagate an environ-ment where information is unreliable at best, deliberately misleading at worst.

There are certain fundamentals that must be in place for an economy to flourish, and reliable or at least verifiable information is one. Accountability is another. I have been plied so much unreliable information on this journey that I have ended up in this ridiculous situation where I am surrounded by a thousand camels, all nominally 'for sale', but not actually for sale to me. I have $5,000 in currency to spend but no one who actually believes sufficiently that I am serious about spending to do a deal with me. The paranoia is so acute that those with whom I came to trade would rather believe I am a spy than a serious customer. It is time for me to leave.

The camel truck I organized yesterday arrives as if it's been cued up by a director waiting in the wings. It drives right into the mêlée and the cheery driver hops out expectantly. His expression says it all: 'Right then, where are your camels?' What could I say? I can't find any? What camels? No, I am clearly a man who has no need of a camel truck. All I can do is apologize for wasting his day and offer him $50 as compensation. I reason that as he would have made $100 profit for four days' work this is a reasonable pay-off for half a day of sitting around.

I know I shouldn't be surprised and I should have expected it, but it still makes me laugh when he turns to me and says, '$150'.

Four

WHO'S IN CHARGE ROUND HERE?

LAST TRADE:
— Transport for non-existent camels: $150 loss
INVESTMENTS: $0
IN THE BANK: $49,850

Making money in Africa was never going to be easy but I remained convinced that there were opportunities here for the adventurous investor. I hadn't exactly put a pin in a map and decided that Zambia was somewhere I would go after Sudan (or, as I had originally planned, Egypt) but I had read a few articles about how the southern African region had received generous aid from the EU recently and that money had been invested wisely in infrastructure and education.

Now I had an interesting idea involving elephants to check out, and another lead that had come out of a conversation with a friend, Grant Rattray, a coffee broker at a big London firm to whom I'd put the idea of trading African coffee. I was proposing a relatively small-scale trade, say five or ten grand sterling. At first I'd had to convince Grant that I hadn't gone totally gaga. After that it was just a simple case of making him stop saying, 'You'll lose all your money.' Eventually, I persuaded him to have a serious think about where there might be opportunities for this kind of trade. And he came back to me with one word: Zambia.

Zambian coffee is beginning to develop an international reputation as a genuine competitor for its neighbours Tanzania and Kenya but, being less well known, it comes much cheaper. Once I'd dusted the Sudanese desert sand from my shoes and resolved to continue with the project, I called Grant again to ask him where the quality growers were in the country. He suggested a particular estate just a couple of hours outside Lusaka, called Chulumenda. 'But,' he said, 'be careful; coffee traders don't take any prisoners.'

'Yeah, right,' I thought. 'I should introduce you to some camel traders.'

If you ever find yourself in the unusual situation of taking a flight from Sudan to Zambia, the first thing you'll notice on arrival is that it is a good 15° cooler. This immediately struck me as a good start by Zambia, so I already liked the place a lot more than Sudan before I'd even cleared customs. The second difference was that the airport was full of smiling faces. I hadn't exactly known what to expect from Zambia but I had assumed it might be one of those hard, scary, sub-Saharan African states full of crime, violence and disease. Wrong. Instead I found an airport full of young, vibrant people whose smiles suggested an optimism that was the complete opposite. And, if you're lucky enough to be travelling on an Irish passport, you don't even need a visa. Why? Nobody knows. Right away in the airport at Lusaka I had a warm feeling that, after the smoke and mirrors of Sudan, I might be among people who could do business in a civilized way.

The next morning I sat outside a café in Lusaka drinking a cup of Nescafé. I despise instant coffee but it was all they had. Lusaka is a small, flat city, bustling during the day. There were bicycles everywhere and many of the men of the town wore formal suits. Women dressed garishly and even with a baby over a hip would cart the weekly shopping around the streets in pots and baskets on top of their heads. I watched a young girl try a couple of times to scoop up a watermelon in a sarong and sling it round her back. Each time the melon shot out and bounced off down the street into the drain. You won't see any Mothercare papooses in Zambia; instead women carry their children in sarongs. They gather up their babies in the material and gracefully swish them over a hip or round their backs so that the child is held securely and comfortably next to them while they go about their business. It looked easy but, watching the young girl practising for the day when her watermelon was a real baby, it clearly wasn't.

Fuelled somewhat by my noxious brew, I drove out to the Chulumenda estate to meet its owner, Craig Shiel. It took no time at all to get out of town and into the Zambian countryside. Either side of the road there was a big sky covering a million acres of long, dry, golden grassland and only the odd tree. I turned off the main road at the sign for the Chulumenda farm but still had another three or four miles to go before I reached Craig's front gate. The fields became clearer as I drove up, fences marked out areas where cattle were grazing and a huge system of black pipes ran at head height over acres of ground. Water sprayed out from them onto lush green bushes below, creating a fine mist that shone in little rainbows when the sunlight caught it from the right angle.

A large, steel five-bar gate marked the farm entrance. Razor wire ran along the top and across the mesh fence that marked the perimeter. Inside the courtyard there was the usual mix of farm buildings, tractors and four-wheel-drive vehicles, and the sound of a noisy mechanical process going on somewhere. A large, smiling man in a peaked cap came out of the house to greet me.

Craig is a typical Zambian coffee farmer: he's strong, and he's white. He's taken investment from a Danish company who want to sell his coffee into Denmark and has transformed a crumbling old coffee farm into a modern, 500-acre, fully irrigated coffee estate. The rest of his 1,000 acres of cleared land he uses to grow some wheat, maize and soya and then there's a beef and dairy herd on the side.

Growing coffee is Craig's passion. A bit like growing wine, there's more sophistication to it than growing wheat. Craig has to oversee the growing, processing, roasting and selling of his coffee. Each stage is an intellectual battle that any farmer would relish. A field of wheat doesn't pose the same challenges nor offer the same rewards to Craig. But if the price of wheat continues to soar on the world's food markets, he's fully aware that the time may come when he has to let go of his baby and make a hard commercial decision. For the time being though, like many Zambian coffee growers, he's sticking with it.

Craig greeted me in his Chulumenda farm hat, shirt and shorts. If he was selling burgers in McDonald's he couldn't have had more company logos on. He's rightly proud of what he's built here and I was treated to the full guided tour of the dams, the irrigated fields and the new processing plant where beans are graded by size, shape and density. The plant had only been up and running a couple of months and Craig was training everybody himself. Everybody, from the men operating each of the selection machines to the ladies who individually hand-pick the best beans after the machines have done their best. Craig explained to me that he only let women do this part of the operation because only the women on the farm are able to talk and sort at the same time; any time he let men have a go they all started talking and stopped sorting. Though while he was telling me this, he chatted away merrily and hand-picked faster than any of the women sitting around him!

This kind of farming would be impossible in Europe. Even if you could find somewhere that had the climate to grow good quality coffee beans, you would never be able to find cheap enough labour to pick it and then sift through it. This picking out of the defective ones is vital because even the most sophisticated industrial machines miss some. If Africa were to develop overnight into the economic tiger that we all want to see it become, we'd have to drink something else in the morning before work.

The Holy Grail that Craig's looking for with all this new processing machinery and the hand-picking is consistency. One bad bean in a bag can throw the whole flavour off. Any roaster who wants to buy Craig's coffee must like the taste of it but, more than that, he must be sure that it will taste the same next time he drinks it. This is a massive challenge to someone manufacturing a natural product, as nature tends to operate in the opposite way, diversifying as much as possible. It's nothing short of miraculous that when I take two handfuls of Craig's AA coffee beans from two separate bags they do actually look identical.

The problem that Craig has is similar to that of so many people like him. He has to be here to supervise 24/7. As with many owner-managed businesses, the person in charge often spends all their time running the business at every level. Craig is occupied with training staff, managing the accounts, quality control, distribution and logistics; the list goes on and on. All these things require him to be on the farm. The question that occurred to me as I walked around with him was, who is going out and finding new customers? The business is getting better from the inside, but how is it growing on the outside when the one person best placed to go and tell the world about it is so bloody busy all the time?

I started to explain to Craig what I was thinking while we walked and talked. He's too busy running and managing his farm to have any time to devote to marketing his coffee. He has good links with northern Europe but as yet no penetration to the South African market, in particular the Cape Town region, where a rash of coffee shops are springing up to meet growing demand for coffee from its young, urbane and sophisticated residents. I wanted to make him an offer. For the right price I would take a couple of tonnes of the best grade he had, the AA grade coffee that's processed and ready, and I would organize to transport it to Cape Town and find a buyer for it. Craig had 1.8 tonnes ready to go. When the deal was done and I'd taken my profit, I would put him straight in touch with the buyer so that the repeat business would go directly to him.

As I explained it to him, I wondered, what's going through Craig's mind? On one hand here was a complete stranger with no background in the coffee trade trying to wrestle 1.8 tonnes of his top-grade coffee from him at a knock-down price. If this deal went nowhere he was down in cash and short of his best stock which he used to entice new customers. On the other hand, here was someone seemingly willing to hand deliver and market his coffee to much-needed new customers in an unexplored market. For a man whose time was taken up 100 per cent by the demands of running a farm, it must have been a real temptation.

There are traders all over the African coffee market looking to broker deals for people like Craig. They have links with roasters in the developed world and they scour the developing world look-ing for new opportunities, hoping to discover the next big thing, the next Kenyan Blue Mountain. Fortunately for me, Africa is a big place and, thanks largely to Grant's tip-off, I'd gotten to Craig soon after he had installed his new plant and before any of the established players in the market.

I had an idea from the research I'd done that I could sell a good AA grade coffee in Cape Town for a maximum of $6.50 per kilo but I should be prepared to have to drop that price to nearer $5.50 or even $5 if the quality wasn't consistent. As long as I could get a good deal on transport, buying at anything below $4.25 per kilo should give me a good margin, possibly as much at $2 per kilo. After missing out in Sudan, it was important that I make some money here if I was going to make any inroads into my $100,000 target. To make a success out of the African leg of my journey, then, I had to make sure I got a good price here.

Craig and I sat down to business across the big old table in the middle of his office. I had the feeling that he was looking forward to this. He'd made another strong pot of his great coffee and I realized that I'd probably had too much of it because I was starting to feel a little jittery. He was clear as a bell.

'To be quite frank, we have been selling this coffee for between $4.70 and $6 per kilo.' He wiped the sweat from his face as he said it. I always find it interesting when people offer you a range of prices because if you're the buyer then you only hear the lowest one. From now on I knew that Craig had sold this coffee for $4.70. Never mind $6, I knew that he'd sold it for $4.70 so that was the benchmark.

The negotiation was about to enter full swing. I had two prices to keep an eye on. First, my worst case scenario selling price was in the $5 region and I'd need to allow for costs. Second was the all-important cost price: $4.70 would allow me to make a profit, but only peanuts. If this was going to be worth it at all then I needed to knock him down lower, and the lower the better; remember anything below $4.25 would give me every chance in Cape Town.

I ignored the reference to $6 and simply repeated, '$4.70'. I looked unimpressed and tried to seem a little concerned even. I explained that there was no way I could make this work for me. Even if I were to get the transport costs for free, I'd still have no room to manoeuvre when I came to sell it. I pointed out that this was maybe going to involve him taking a small hit this time, but he had to remember that I'd make it worth it for him in the long run.

Craig was laughing to himself. One of those laughs that says, 'What am I doing?' I was definitely wearing him down and, right enough, he admitted that he was prepared to take a risk on me and sell me the coffee, but he wanted at least $4.40 per kilo. I had him on the run, he was dropping below his minimum price, so I pitched in with a suggestion: 'How about $3.50?' I was delighted that he'd opened negotiations so low so I was duty bound to see how low I could push him. Of course, I couldn't let him see but inside I was smiling a big smile.

I explained to him that a cost of $3.50 was more what I had in mind. This was ridiculously low so it was a good way to test how valuable he saw my involvement. If he went for this price then he really believed in me enough to forgo any profit for himself. I suspected that this wasn't going to be the case but it was worth a try.

Right again; not valuable at all as it turned out. In fact Craig seemed to change, as though he snapped out of whatever madness had taken hold of him. He visibly perked up in front of me.

'OK, you want to do some real horse trading.' He now seemed genuinely excited and he even leapt up to grab his calculator like a gladiator to his sword, except he had only one calculator so it was more like two gladiators sharing a sword.

He started to tap the buttons, half saying numbers under his breath while he thought. I didn't really want to get into a protracted negotiation with him. We both knew now what the score was so I suggested we save each other a lot of time and fast forward the haggling. I wanted $3.50 and he wanted $4.40, so why didn't we just settle at $3.90 per kilo? Craig paused for a moment; he took off his cap and wiped the sweat from his brow. I couldn't be sure but I reckon that $4 per kilo was probably the minimum price he had in mind before we started so I was giving him the perfect opportunity to save face and counter with an offer of $4. At this stage, I'd be happy with that, too. If he was thinking that he could out-negotiate with me and get more than $4 then I'd find out now. He pulled his cap back on and looked me up and down. I could feel him sizing me up a little.

'Well, I like round numbers.' He smirked at me while he said it. I could see we were getting close. 'So I'm happy to settle at $4 per kilo.'

Bingo. I was in. But he'd given me an idea. I had one more card to play. I did the maths out loud: '1.8 tonnes at $4 per kilo is $7,200. Such an ugly number. Seeing as you like round numbers, why don't we call it $7,000?' OK, I was pushing it, but he'd given me the material. Craig let out a loud laugh. I think he actually appreciated my cheek.

'Look, if there's a psychological problem with $4 then I'll drop to $3.95.' He sighed a little but he was still smiling. 'That's $7,110 total.'

'That's still an ugly number but, OK, I'm not going to haggle over $100.'

He shook his head. '$110, actually.'

He laughed again. We both did. We shook hands to seal the deal, and as we did I could feel the tension of the situation ebbing away. We'd reached an agreement. In our own little way we'd gone toe to toe, duked it out, and at the end we were both a little raw. Being able to share a joke afterwards was a sign that we had done a deal that we could both live with. In so many ways this encapsulated what my trip was all about. Two people from opposite sides of the world doing a deal to make a living, but remembering that making a living is about exactly that – living. It's so easy to become obsessed with the bottom line and simply forget to enjoy getting there. I hadn't had so much fun in as long as I could remember.

This negotiation had gone very differently to the Moroccan deal and my first thought was that this was because Craig and I spoke the same language. I had been able to 'fast forward' the negotiation by being funny and then to finesse the deal at the very last by throwing the 'round numbers' back in his face. Both of these tricks relied heavily on the use of language. I hadn't been as quick in Morocco because I'd had to rely on translation. Having said that, I had only been able to bring Craig down 34 per cent from his top price ($6 to $3.95), whereas I had got the carpet for 41 per cent cheaper in Morocco ($600 to $350). It may have felt like I worked a better deal from Craig but in fact I'd got a slightly better deal in the mountains.

With the coffee bought, it was time to turn my attention to how I was going to transport it. This was the other major cost to be considered. Many coffee distributors will factor on spending anything up to $1 per kilo. For my consignment that would equate to around $1,800, which would eat heavily into the profit I hoped to make in South Africa. There is very little trade between South Africa and Zambia, but what there is runs largely in one direction: north. I contacted a South African transport company who routinely make deliveries of machine parts to Zambia from South Africa. By and large they return empty, so they were a bit surprised that I should want to take something in the opposite direction. I explained that I wanted to backload one of their trailers and they offered to take the job for a mere $250. This gave me a total cost including freight of $4.14 per kilo. If I could hit the $6.50 target, this would give me a massive $4,250 profit.

True to form, Craig refused to delegate even the packing of the coffee to anyone else, insisting on doing it all himself. He really takes no chances where his reputation is concerned. I met the coffee and its driver at a small town near where I'd stayed for the night. Martin, a white Afrikaner from Johannesburg, would drive the coffee and me all the way to South Africa. Because of the unrest in Zimbabwe our route would have to detour through Botswana, past his home town 1,200 miles away, and from there another 900 miles to Cape Town. Martin hoped to reach Jo'burg by tomorrow evening. I wondered how we could possibly cover 1,200 miles in only a day and a half in a pickup truck with a two-tonne trailer, through Botswanan roads that are famous for having big potholes and big wildlife to avoid. There's a joke among South African overland drivers: if you see two eyes in the middle of the road while driving through Botswana at night, chances are it's a giraffe standing in a pothole.

Martin is a man of few words but, as we intended to spend the next two days together with only each other for company, I was keen to find out a little about him. Unfortunately, Martin's accent was so strong that at times I struggled to follow what he was saying. For a while, say 300 miles or so, we had a fundamental problem that began to bother me before I worked out what it was. For example, I saw that Martin was wearing a Jo'burg Sharks rugby shirt, so I struck up a conversation.

'Do you follow the rugby, Martin?'

'Nyah.'

Taking this as a firm 'nah', as in 'no', I thought to myself, OK then, fair enough, that conversation isn't going anywhere. Maybe he just borrowed the shirt from a friend who likes the Sharks. But then, after a couple of minutes' silence:

'I like the Sharks.'

I took this to mean that Martin was either a fool or a complete psychopath. I sat there contemplating the next sixteen hours in a cab with a nutter, when I had a thought. I knew for sure that the route we were taking would go through Francistown in Botswana, so I tried again.

'Do we go through Francistown?'

'Nyah.'

OK. The penny dropped: 'nyah' means 'yeah'. I'm glad I got that one straight because we had another 900 miles to go.

Five

ICE TO ESKIMOS

INVESTMENTS:
— **Coffee (including fees and transport): $7,400**
IN THE BANK: $42,450

The phrase 'selling ice to Eskimos' is often used in sales and marketing. I have always been unclear as to whether it is supposed to be a good thing or a bad thing, and still am to this day. On the one hand, the suggestion is that Eskimos live in a cold place where there is no need for ice, and therefore trying to sell them ice is a rather foolish pursuit. On the other, anyone who can sell ice to Eskimos must be a brilliant salesperson for the same reasons. So, you have a challenge that you are stupid to start but brilliant if you finish.

Of course, once you start to think about selling ice to Eskimos as a challenge it can throw up all kinds of possibilities. Let's begin by turning this preconception about Eskimos and their ice on its head for a minute. What if Eskimos actually need ice? They do build their houses from it, after all. Yes, there's lots of it around the Arctic already, but there's always room for more as long as you can find a variation with an angle: stronger, colder, harder, coloured ice, whatever it is. Eskimos don't have a monopoly on ice. Identifying a new market needn't be revolutionary; just subtly different is sufficient. An Eskimo needs ice; you just need to convince him that it's your ice he wants, that somehow your ice is better than the ice he's already using. At least you know he already has a need for it. It would be a lot harder to convince someone who wasn't an Eskimo to buy ice from you, just as it would be a lot harder to sell another building material to an Eskimo.

For 'ice' read 'chilli sauce' and for 'Eskimos' read 'Indians'. Surely the Indian market has as much hot chilli sauce as it could ever want? Let's find out.

I arrived in the early evening at a bar on the eastern bank of the Zambezi River, at which I had arranged to meet a friend of the elephant-loving American that I had spoken to back in Khartoum, Loki. I sat outside waiting for Loki's business partner, Mick, while monkeys played in the trees overhead. The sun was bathing them in golden light as it set across the water. A few miles away, the enormous Victoria Falls was in full flow and I could hear its echoing roar in the distance. 'Cool place for a meeting,' I thought.

A man arrived on a motorbike and pulled up next to where I was sitting. He took off his helmet and greeted me with: 'G'day, mate, you must be Conor.' I was surprised to find that Mick was Australian. He explained to me that he'd been passing through Zambia around eight years ago as a backpacker and simply got stuck here. He had come to meet me straight from a barbecue and he struck me as someone who didn't mind mixing business and pleasure, which was fine by me.

Mick's colleague Loki had come over to Africa ten or so years ago as a researcher with a passion for conservation. He discovered in his research that elephants have a particular distaste for chillies. Mick was giving me his sales spiel and I was learning. Elephants have particularly sensitive mucous membranes and when they encounter a chilli bush they tend to simply turn tail and head off in the other direction. Loki seized on this as a great way for farmers to dissuade elephants from roaming onto their land and began a campaign to encourage farmers to plant chilli bushes around their boundaries as an elephant deterrent. The project proved very successful and the number of elephants being shot by farmers dropped as a result. Isn't that a great story? It gets better.

As the project expanded, and more and more farmers began to adopt the chilli prevention strategy, Loki started to think about what he could do with all the chillies. He struck on the idea of harvesting them and making them into a bottled chilli sauce, which he went on to call Elephant Pepper sauce. The idea was that he could then sell the sauces and put the profits back into educating more farmers in how to use chillies, not guns, to control elephants. This is where Mick got involved. It was Mick's job to help on the business side of things, as Loki's background was essentially academic and Mick had worked in marketing before he'd decided to pack it all in and bugger off to Africa.

The project was now entering a new phase. The company that Loki and Mick had set up was ready to begin exporting. The hope was that this would generate new sales and also raise international awareness. I could immediately see its potential as a product to sell. It is always a challenge to find a unique selling point for a new product, and here was a great idea that could cash in on the ever-expanding 'green dollar'.

Mick had brought samples with him that we tasted over a packet of crisps and a couple of beers. By the end of our meeting he had taken to repeating the phrase: 'It's a conservation project with a commercial sustainability link,' like a kind of marketing mantra. I did like the product. It tasted great. In fact it was just as good as the idea behind it, so I put it to Mick that I would be interested in taking a shipment with me on the next leg of my journey to India. He nearly fell off his chair, although so did I, after all the beers we'd had to go with the tasting. Either way, he hadn't heard my 'ice to Eskimos' theory yet.

Mick and Loki own a chilli farm. I've never been on a chilli farm before and I had no idea what to expect when I arrived next morning. I was utterly flabbergasted, speechless, lost for words when I pulled into simply the most colourful expanse of vegetation I have ever seen. I thought for a minute that I had arrived at Willy Wonka's factory where all the sweets grow on trees: fifty acres of verdant green bushes, laden with bright orange, red and yellow sweets, like Skittle trees. Of course if you ate any of these sweets they'd give you third-degree burns of the tongue.

Mick was looking a little sore from last night but this didn't dampen his enthusiasm for showing me around his farm. He was happy to be living the relative high life that even a meagre income can afford you in Africa. 'White people don't come to Africa to live in mud huts,' he explained.

'Don't they?' I felt there was a pearl of wisdom on its way.

'We come here because we can afford to do things we can't afford to do back home, like polo.'

Now, I reckoned the only polo he'd ever seen in his life had a VW sign on the front of it, but I took his point that the cost of living was probably a lot cheaper here and, like him, a lot of 'Western' folk came here to take advantage of that.

The chilli farm was his idea. When plans for the expansion of the business had been limited by slow uptake of the scheme by farmers, they faced a hard economic decision. To get enough chillies together to produce the volume required by international wholesalers, the chilli quota had to be supplemented. Of course, it would be ideal to make all their sauce from chillies sourced 100 per cent from the project, but the economic reality was that they wouldn't be able to produce enough sauce. So they decided to supplement their chilli production with a farm.

The Elephant Pepper production line was now fuelled partly by these farmed chillis and partly by those from the conservation project. But that's not the point; the point is that it could be marketed on the chillies that do help to conserve elephants. I looked again at all the chillies in this colourful field and understood exactly what Mick meant. This wasn't about mud huts; it was about polo.

Mick and I discussed the terms of our proposed deal in the field as the women he employs picked chillies all around us. They were dressed in sarongs and T-shirts and they had their hair tied up in colourful printed headscarves to avoid getting any noxious chilli in their hair. They shuffled up and down the rows around us, carefully selecting and filling their baskets with the bright chillies. I wondered how they felt about elephants.

I wanted to take a couple of thousand bottles of sauce to India with me. I had done some preliminary research and was confident that 125ml bottles of chilli sauce could sell for 160 rupees (Rs) in India ($4 per bottle). The standard retail mark-up there is 30 per cent and, factoring in VAT at 4 per cent, this meant my selling price to retailers would have to be around the Rs 115 mark ($2.88 per bottle).

I'd worked on a couple of retail projects when I was still in finance so I knew a little about how the pricing works. It is pretty standard for retailers to put a flat percentage mark-up on everything. If you go into your local convenience store and ask the owner how he prices the hundreds of items in his shop, he'll tell you that's what he does. That way, he doesn't really care what he's selling, as he's making the same rate of profit on it all. He probably also won't mind telling you what the mark-up is – retail is quite straightforward like that – and it is probably around 30 per cent.

So, continuing to work backwards, I wanted to make a mark-up of 30–50 per cent, in which case I needed to have the sauce landed in India after all transport and taxes for at most Rs 80 ($2 per bottle). We can assume that transport and taxes would be 100 per cent of cost, as India is a particularly fierce country to export to, so I needed Mick to sell the bottles of sauce to me for no more than $1 per bottle.

This was apparently a little more than Mick's cost of production so he'd still be making a small profit, although not as much as he was currently making from his US distributor. I had two things in my favour: first, unlike his US agent, my offer was cash upfront; second, as I reassured him, my intention was only to broker this first deal, and thereafter his negotiation would be directly with the Indian customers. I would be trying my utmost to establish Elephant Pepper at the highest price possible in the market. It was, I thought, a win-win situation for him.

I left Mick deliberating on the deal. He would still need to discuss the price with Loki, but if they decided to go for it I could pick up the bottles when I arrived in Cape Town. This seemed like a good start to me. I believed in the product, I liked the story and the more I thought about selling chilli sauce in India, the more I thought I was on to something with this 'ice to Eskimos' idea.

The numbers stacked up well. Southern Africa still has very low production costs and India's emerging middle classes have a new disposable income with which to buy imported goods. If there's one thing people in India believe, it's that anything made overseas is better than anything made in India. India is a tough market to break into but the branding and the story of the elephants might just be able to crack the ice.

Six

ROAD TRIP

INVESTMENTS:
— Coffee: $7,400
IN THE BANK: $42,450

The great Zambezi River separates Zambia and Botswana, a natural border no more than 275 yards across. The crossing is a vital trade link for both sides. Goods are cheaper in Botswana and people cross the river to buy staples such as maize and rice. On the Zambian side there were people milling around, waiting for the next ferry. Children sold baskets of bananas and packets of cookies from vehicle to vehicle as we all waited for our turn to make the short crossing to Botswana.

One side of the road leading up to the port was lined with parked lorries going back about two miles. There is no bridge. The river can only be crossed by ferry and the ferry can only carry one lorry at a time. The driver at the front of the queue told me that he had been waiting three weeks to get a space on the boat.

There were so many people here that a small roadside community had formed. There were open fires barbecuing meat, and even a bar and a small restaurant. Nobody I speak to thinks it is unusual; it's widely accepted that this has become part and parcel of the journey from central Africa to southern Africa. I decided to grab a beer and some barbecued chicken while I waited for Martin to sort out our paperwork at customs. On a small wooden deck I sat with a noisy crowd of drivers and local girls; the next ferry provided us all with live entertainment.

When the ferry landed on the Zambian side, a hundred or so foot passengers coming from Botswana, laden with bags of blankets, beers and food, jumped down from the boat. Many of them started sprinting into the nearby jungle, deciding that, rather than declare their goods at customs, they would pick the 'green' channel. They scampered off clutching their contraband while a solitary and rather irate guard tried in vain to stop them. Unfortunately for him he was simply outnumbered, even more so if you counted the audience at the bar who were cheering on the smugglers. Every individual who escaped into the undergrowth was greeted with a loud round of applause, and Zambia lost another dollar or two in customs revenue. As I sat there among the revellers watching the chaos of this river border I had the feeling that I was doing just what I should be doing with my life: carrying two tonnes of coffee over the Zambezi River, trading like in the old days.

Given the situation in Zimbabwe, there is only one way from the ports of South Africa to the heart of Africa, and this is it. A bridge to span 275 yards of shallow, slow-flowing river would provide such a boom for trade here that I cannot understand why neither the Botswanan nor Zambian governments, nor any number of mining companies in the region, haven't collectively made this happen. If this were Europe, Asia or the Americas it would have been built a hundred years ago, and yet here I was queuing for my turn to board a one-lorry ferry over the river that for the foreseeable future represents the only viable trade route for the region.

Several hours were spent waiting in the bar before I started to get concerned about the state of the coffee out in the sun. To keep the value high, the coffee must be kept from getting too hot or, even worse, wet. This heat was losing me money and I had been sitting at the border control for long enough, watching lorry after lorry push its way through, while Martin was passed from one official to the next. Eventually I resorted to shouting at the border guard. I'm Mr Irate of Livingstone, my coffee is baking in the sun, I've been here for hours, no one is taking responsibility for our paperwork and all the time people are pushing in front of us. I got more and more incandescent but his face did not change. He stood patiently, listening to my rant, and when I was completely finished he responded calmly, 'No problem,' and waved me through, smiling as if to say, 'All you had to do was ask.'

The ferry pulled away, leaving Zambia behind. Two men in a dugout canoe paddled past as we crossed the short stretch of brown water to Botswana. People frequently get eaten by crocodiles on this part of the river so I was worried to see one of the men casually draping a leg over the side. Ten minutes later we had cleared Botswana customs with not so much as a by your leave; none of the dysfunctional chaos that I'd seen in Zambia here.

It was onward and upward and, with Martin at the helm, we rolled on full steam ahead through the border, round the barriers and straight off the road into a ditch. Eight yards into Botswana and we were stranded with two wheels in the air and two wheels halfway down a muddy bank. Thankfully, the trailer full of coffee was anchoring us to the road; otherwise we'd have slid into the river. Martin looked a little embarrassed.

We were quickly the centre of attention of a large crowd of foot passengers travelling the other way. With the strength of fifteen men and a bit of digging we got the car back on the road, reattached the trailer and, rather more cautiously, re-embarked on the Botswanan leg of the journey.

Besides a passion for rugby, Martin's great pleasure in life was getting out of Jo'burg with his 'chick', a schoolteacher in the city. They liked to head up to some hot springs, kick back in the hot water and forget about the drive from Jo'burg to Lusaka. I got the impression that Martin liked the simple things in life and the path of least resistance.

Beautiful Botswana passed in a bit of a blur; all 650 miles of it. I'd been told before I left by others who had been here to enjoy it as the 'jewel of Africa', and in particular to look out for the wildlife. Martin's view of the wildlife was rather different. It was by no means beautiful, in fact it was a bloody nuisance; elephants, zebras, giraffes and donkeys were merely obstacles to be avoided, as hitting any one of them would write the vehicle off. 'Effing Donkeys!' became a common utterance that punctuated many a conversation. While I cooed at every sighting (not so much the donkeys), Martin simply tutted at having narrowly avoided another potential collision that would have crushed his radiator or seen a couple of tonnes of coffee spilt all over the road. It was fair to say that donkeys in particular were the bane of this man's life.

By midnight, I reckoned we'd been on the road for seventeen hours, and Martin was starting to go hoarse from all the donkeys. He made the call that it was time for a rest so we pulled into the car park of a shopping mall outside Francistown, rolled the seats back, threw a blanket over and slept for three hours. Three hours. I thought I'd repeat it as I can still feel the pain that I felt when Martin prodded me awake. I have never been so affronted or so tired. I decided that this would be the ideal time to break into the gargantuan stock of caffeine that we were carrying, so I fished the gas stove out of the back of the truck and boiled up a pot of the coffee that Craig had ground for me before we left. It couldn't have come at a better time.

The sun came up over the bush as we made our way towards the South African border. We'd covered seven hundred miles in just over a day and seen at least a hundred 'effing donkeys' along the way. It was an epic journey happening in fast forward. The coffee had left the farm, crossed southern Zambia and the whole of

Botswana, and arrived at the border by 9 a.m., twenty-eight hours later. If we had a clear run through customs we could make it to Jo'burg before the rush hour.

I don't want this story to get bogged down with descriptions of border crossings and customs bureaucracy, so bear with me while I just say that in my humble opinion, South African customs made Sudanese customs look positively dynamic.

I arrived in Jo'burg long after dark.

The next morning, keen to get to Cape Town, I headed down to the depot where I found Martin repacking the coffee onto another trailer. From here I would be with another driver, Doopie. Martin was technically on his day off, but he'd taken the time before heading off for a break at the springs to come and say goodbye and good luck. It was a touching end to our journey. If I hadn't made this trip I could possibly have gone my whole life without meeting anyone like him.

With the coffee repacked in a light tarpaulin, I started for Cape Town with one stop-off to make along the way. Jo'burg is not known for its sophisticated coffee-drinking culture, but there is a company that has started to retail and distribute some single origin coffee in the city. I thought this would be a good opportunity to practise my sales technique, maybe even offload a few bags and also, more importantly, get an expert opinion on the coffee. All I had to go on so far was Martin's typically brief critique that it had 'a good kick'.

Iris and Lee run the Green Bean coffee franchise that shares an idyllic setting with an Italian restaurant on the outskirts of Jo'burg. Iris used to fly relief planes for the Red Cross into disaster areas, including the Sudan, so she laughed long and hard when I relayed my own experiences there. It seems not much has changed. Now, though, Iris has the job of running the roaster in the shop.

First perusal of the green beans was favourable. The things to watch out for are defective beans that look different to all the rest. Lee thought that the bean bore a resemblance to an Ethiopian coffee. It's this kind of attention to detail that a roaster must have to ensure that they aren't selling any old rubbish. They make a few cups in various forms: black, white, with and without sugar are all put to the test. It's a massive relief when they both agree that the coffee is 'excellent'. It's even more of a relief that Lee is a bit of a pushover when it comes to negotiation. I chance my arm a little and ask for a whopping $7 per kilo. Lee haggles a little, and I am happy to settle on $6.50 for two 60-kilo bags. If I can flog the rest at that price in Cape Town then I'm set for a very satisfactory $4,000 profit from this trade.

Happy with the early indications that Iris and Lee had given me, I set off again on the last leg of the journey to cosmopolitan Cape Town. I hoped to find that Cape Town was more European in its taste and style, and if it was anything like the European cities I'd visited lately then it would be full of coffee shops and people paying exorbitant prices by the cup. My Plan A was to hit a very stylish outlet, Origin Roasters, who were doing a great job of publicizing themselves as a stand-out, top-quality roaster. A quick call to Grant confirmed that they were very fussy but, if they liked the coffee, they would happily pay top whack for it.

Seven

MARZIPAN?

LAST TRADE:
— Two Bags of Coffee: $287 profit
INVESTMENTS:
— Coffee (less 2 bags): $6,926
IN THE BANK: $43,230

I set up a meeting with the Origin boss, David, for the next morning and spent the night doing a bit of background research. On their website, David proclaimed himself to be a 'coffee evangelist'. All over the site were rather scary statements describing coffee with a similarly religious zeal. So I was a little apprehensive when I arrived at Origin Roasting, the cathedral of coffee, with a sample bag of Chulumenda green beans under my arm.

Inside, the cathedral resembled many coffee shops I'd been in before. In fact, it was a coffee shop. I met David, the evangelist, and thought he seemed more like a bloke who ran a coffee shop. This is the problem with evangelists these days; they rarely deliver all that they promise. David wasted no time in getting my beans ground and into the cup. He made an espresso and a white coffee and described them as 'exquisite'. It was time, he said, to go upstairs and meet Joel.

I imagine that if your business is making whisky, you probably end up drinking too much of it and alcoholism becomes an occupational hazard. In Joel's case, there's definitely too much coffee in his life and verbal diarrhoea is the result. Joel is a Canadian; not a race particularly known for their verbosity. I think this is because Joel rounded up all the words in Canada and took them with him when he moved to Cape Town. When he tasted the coffee, he began talking, but it was very difficult to make any sense of the stream of words that were coming out of his mouth: 'Very interestingly, classic issue in coffee is Brazilian. Coffee tastes like coffee. All coffee tastes like coffee. The subtleties of flavour are layered over the top of an overwhelming coffeeness, put it that way.' Well, put it that way.

Fortunately, David was on hand to translate Joel's stream of consciousness into English: they were interested. The next step in the process was for Joel to take a 60-kilo bag from me and try different roasts and blends to work out how Origin could best use the Chulumenda beans. If they found the right combination then David thought the price tag of $6.50 per kilo was a reasonable starting point for any negotiation. A lot was going to rest on the events of the next twenty-four hours; if my beans stood up to Joel's rigorous examination, tomorrow I could be banking a fairly tidy $4,000 profit.

*

I was keen to keep up the momentum of the last few days and it was time to finalize the price on the bottles of Elephant Pepper. I met Loki at his house, a gated mansion on one of the hills overlooking Cape Town; not the kind of residence you'd find the average British academic living in. Loki came down his drive to greet me, a tall, good-looking man of around forty-five, with a full head of blond hair. He wasted no time in leading me down to his garage where he said I could see the stock I'd come for.

The garage doors lifted to reveal what looked like far fewer bottles than I was after. 'What's this?' I asked. I needed around

2,000 bottles to make this deal worth my while and Mick had seemed confident that they would be available. 'This is all we have,' said Loki and, to make matters worse, 'We could let you have them for around $1.75 per bottle.' I was beginning to realize that there had been some sort of misunderstanding. Loki seemed genuinely in the dark and when I asked him where the bottles that Mick had discussed with me in Zambia were, he looked puzzled. Apparently they didn't have that quantity of sauce in stock and to make the full amount for me could take weeks, weeks which I simply didn't have.

As I think Craig's situation showed, there is a problem faced by any business run by a single person. It can be difficult to market your product when all your time is taken up with running the business. What we had here was a new problem: it is difficult for a two-person partnership to run a business unless communication between them is extremely clear, especially when they are so far apart and have such different roles. I had travelled 2,500 miles and come away empty-handed.

There was no point in wasting any more precious time on this caper; I still had to sell the coffee and the flights in and out of Delhi were already booked. I wished Loki all the best with his project. I still thought it was a great idea and did genuinely want to get involved, but it clearly wasn't to be. However, the idea of selling chilli sauce to India was now firmly planted in my head. Could I find another chilli sauce here in Cape Town with as good a marketing angle, stock in hand and at a price that I could afford?

Go to any bar or restaurant in Cape Town and the chances are they'll present you with your food and a tray of condiments; they love condiments in South Africa. On that tray there will almost certainly be a bottle of at least one of the Bushman's chilli range. You can recognize the bottles immediately because they have a picture of an African bushman firing his bow and arrow on the label, only the arrow is actually a chilli. It's generally regarded as being the best chilli sauce around.

I set off to meet the owner, Eddie Kloerte. There's a warm sense of safety that I get when I'm dealing with someone who is passionate about their business; there's always a danger that passion overtakes the commercial senses and keeping the business going becomes a rather fruitless labour of love, but if the passion can be harnessed there's the potential for someone to make money and have a lot of fun doing so. This is the category that Eddie Kloerte falls into. Eddie lives for chillies.

I met Eddie at his warehouse on the outskirts of Cape Town. It is a typically ugly new brick building on an industrial estate and, this being South Africa, it's surrounded by a heavy security fence and gate. The whole Bushman's operation is run from here: office, warehouse and factory all neatly housed in a one-stop shop. This allows Eddie to have a hand in all areas of the business, but luckily he has his dad (accounts) and mum (admin) to look after the aspects that he finds least interesting. What Eddie really wants is to be in the factory working on new recipes and getting out and finding new customers. With his mother and father taking on much of the time-consuming administration, this is exactly what he has been able to do. By peddling his sauces bar to bar, he now controls over 50 per cent of the whole restaurant sector of the market. In terms of brand awareness, Bushman's chilli sauce is one of the top players.

I rang a friend in Delhi and asking her to go to Tesco. She rang me back from the pickles and sauces aisle and read out the prices on the various bottles. Sauces that traditionally weren't available in India, such as peri-peri sauce and really, really hot sauces, were clearly popular. Eddie had a range of fifteen sauces in his warehouse and, after I shared my thoughts with him about what would sell well in India, we settled on four: peri-peri, smoked jalapeño, original chilli and his tongue-ulcerating Hot az Hell, which Eddie likes to put on his ice-cream.

Eddie and I retired to the office to negotiate a price for 4,000 bottles. I particularly liked the Hot az Hell, with its chilli rating of twelve out of ten. Eddie and I sat at his desk and he produced two plastic spoons from his drawer. We had a dollop of Hot az Hell each and I tentatively tasted it, like a sick child with an icky medicine. After a brief taste of beautiful, sweet chilli, I started to feel as though my tongue was being stripped of its taste buds. Eddie watched me carefully and even looked a little impressed. I had given a good account of myself as I hadn't gone red or cried like a baby. 'We could even be friends,' he said, in his deep, rasping, chilli-damaged voice. I took this as the highest of compliments.

Eddie's sauces may have lacked the elephant conservation uniqueness but they had two other qualities that I thought would do well in India. First, Eddie's was a family business; I'd met his mum and dad. This is very important, as in India a family-run business is regarded as being more stable and reliable. Second was Eddie's passion about the high chilli content of his sauce.

The sales pitch was simple: his chilli sauce is made from chillies. It sounded basic, but if you look at the bottle of most chilli sauces you'll find vinegar listed as the first ingredient. Not so with Bushman's. These sauces were nearly 100 per cent chilli and that's why they tasted so good. Well, that was a good selling point, but the price had to work too. I was keen to find out what price he could drop to.

What followed was the fastest negotiation of all time. Eddie wanted $1.10 for the sauces, I said I had more like 80¢ in mind, we settled quickly on 90¢ per bottle, for a total of 3,840 bottles (960 of each of the four flavours). In total the deal came to around $3,500. We shook hands and I left, sure that I would never meet anyone again in my life who could be so passionate about chillies. If I could replicate even a fraction of that passion in India then I'd have no problem selling them on.

I now had $7,000 worth of coffee and another $7,000 ($3,500 plus $3,500 for taxes and shipping) invested in chilli sauce. I needed to start putting some money back in the bank and that meant selling the coffee. I couldn't sleep that night for thinking about what decision the Origin Roasters had come to.

*

Back at Origin the next morning, the sun was shining and I had a spring in my step. The cool cats of Cape Town like to stand outside Origin in all their finery: flat caps on backwards and tartan waistcoats seem to be the de rigueur dress code for the discerning coffee drinker here. I'd become caught up in the Origin brand. I wanted my coffee to be on the menu for the beautiful people too, I wanted Chulumenda to be the coffee of choice for the new generation. I couldn't wait to see David and Joel's faces and judge how much they loved the coffee they'd been cupping all morning. This would be the best way to evaluate how hard to bargain with them once we got down to the nitty-gritty.

Inside Origin, one of the baristas scuttled off to find David while I sipped on a black Americano from somewhere in Kenya. I imagined it tasted like summer meadows sprinkled with peanuts and toffee to the discerning palate. Actually it just tasted like coffee, but good coffee. I've decided that, to me, coffee falls into one of two categories: coffee I like, and coffee I don't like. That'll do. But, as David bounced down the stairs to shake my hand and invite me up to the tasting chamber, I had a feeling it would be more complicated than that.

Joel was waiting upstairs for us in his usual cupping regalia: hat and apron. I supposed this was in case a coffee-tasting went so badly that he had some uncontrollable reflex to spit it out all over himself. I was sure that wouldn't happen to me; I had just come from Sudan, where the coffee was so bad that if Joel were ever to go there he would probably be forced to cut out his own tongue and bury it somewhere it could never be found. He was clutching three pieces of paper, one of which he handed to me.

You may not have seen a coffee scorecard. You may feel it was never necessary to score a cup of coffee for dry fragrance, acidity and mouthfeel, but apparently this is what you do if you take your coffee seriously, and these boys certainly fell into that category. The coffee had been roasted in three different ways: light, medium and dark. An exact, weighed amount of each is laid out in front of five cups, fifteen cups in total. Joel started the stopwatch – yes, that's right: the stopwatch – and the frantic process of grinding each pile of beans, putting it in the cup, adding water and setting the timer began.

David was explaining while Joel was doing. Once roasted, the coffee beans should ideally be left for twenty-four hours to maximize the flavour – something about letting the carbon dioxide escape – but I haven't given them time to do this so the results won't be ideal. Once ground, they have to be used immediately as the flavour begins to deteriorate (so that coffee you've had sitting in your fridge for the last two weeks is off). Joel threw the ground coffee into the cups one by one and added hot water. David explained that they should be left to sit for exactly four minutes. Exactly four minutes for every coffee is what has been decided is the optimum brewing time and it is imperative that all coffees are compared on this basis. So all fifteen cups of coffee are timed for exactly four minutes before the cupping and scoring begins.

Now, David said what we were looking for was quality but also consistency. It's one thing for a coffee to taste great but the crucial thing is that it tastes great in the same ways time and time again. So if the flavour of one cup is of peanuts or rose petals then it needs to be peanuts or rose petals every time. Got it? Joel and David ran their spoons, their noses and their palates over every one. I followed them along for the craic as much as anything else. Every cup just tasted like a cup of black coffee to me. I didn't get it.

'Marzipan,' David became exasperated all of a sudden, 'marzipan, Joel!' He bounced up and down and pointed his spoon accusingly at one of the cups. 'This one has a distinct taste of marzipan that none of the others have, Conor,' he said as though I had ground up a load of almonds and dropped them in the cup while he wasn't looking. 'That sounds nice,' I replied and tried a sip, which just tasted like coffee. 'Well there's nothing wrong with marzipan,' David started to explain – this is open to debate, personally I can't stand the stuff – 'but it's not good that this one cup has a marzipan flavour when all the others don't.'

Now you don't need to be an expert in coffee to know that things weren't ideal. Joel continued to bounce from cup to cup, scribbling his thoughts onto his scorecard. David put down his scorecard altogether. I asked Joel what was going on. 'This very much gets in our way with regard to the ability to produce the cup at the level we need to produce it,' he replied. I should really have known better. David?

David translated: 'Where we stand now there's just absolutely no way. It's not a coffee for us. So you're looking at the New York C market price at best and I think you're going to be trading this coffee in the $2–3 range. Sorry, but you've got a little challenge ahead of you here.' He wasn't messing around. He was deadly serious.

It was a real kick in the balls, I was totally knocked sideways. The coffee was the same coffee that I'd sampled in Joburg with Iris and Lee. They really liked it. It tasted great to me and I drink loads of coffee. OK, I don't necessarily pick up on the potentially lethal hint of marzipan in every cup but I know that this coffee is drinkable and yet here was David standing in front of me telling me that I was going to struggle to sell this coffee in Cape Town and that I should prepare myself for the possibility that I'd only get $3 or less for it. If David's valuation was right then I stood to lose over $2,000. That was, if I could sell it at all.

I left Origin in a daze and got back in the car. I'd now have to scramble to find other potential buyers. Fortunately, Cape Town is a big town full of coffee drinkers and there are several other roasters. My problem was that Origin had been Plan A and I hadn't really thought through Plan B, let alone C, D or E. It took quite a few phone calls and some very useful local contacts but eventually I turned to a wholesaler that supplied many of the smaller roasters in town.

Gourmet Coffee sounds like it should be a coffee house next to a five-star restaurant. In fact, it's a large brick warehouse on an industrial estate on the outskirts of Cape Town. The car park has a skip in it and the shop is up a staircase that starts downstairs in the warehouse. At the top of the stairs I found John Lear busy selling one of the hundreds of coffee-making gadgets that were on show. He stocks everything from coffee to roasting machines, filters to grinding machines. There's no retail side to his operation as he sells wholesale to the smaller shops. He does, however, have a coffee bar where he makes coffee for customers.

I was immediately drawn to John as a potential buyer, as much because he stocks the kind of volume that means he could easily take the whole lot from me as the fact that he was the one person David and Joel told me not to visit. I wanted to see for myself why they were so sure he couldn't be sold Chulumenda coffee. By the time I saw John I had the sales pitch down pat. I gave it to him with both barrels and sparked the same kind of interest that Lee, Iris, David and everyone had shown initially, although this time I wasn't getting my hopes up. How quickly one can become a cynical old hand at something so new.

John has a giant roaster downstairs that's capable of processing high volumes of beans but he doesn't have the kind of machine that I saw at Chulumenda or Green Bean for roasting samples. John, being a seller of coffee kit, has a small automatic roaster that does a sample bag in under five minutes. He uses this when he wants to test a coffee that he's interested in, and he seemed interested enough in my coffee to plug it in. I was now on unfamiliar ground. Where were the timers, the scorecards, the dry fragrance indicators? Was John blind to the marzipan risk? I certainly wasn't going to bring it up, but I did wonder.

John Lear told me the best way to decide if you like a type of coffee is to make a cup of it the way you like it, and then drink it. This sounded like crazy talk to me and I sincerely hoped that Joel never got wind of it. John knows how he likes his coffee and, in his experience, the way he likes it is the same way most of his customers like it. I asked him if that was to wait for it to go cold and he just laughed. I started to think John was playing with me.

Once the roaster had finished its cycle, John took his newly roasted beans, ground them, put them in the filter machine and made a pot of coffee. He had his with milk and one sugar. I repeated the now-familiar ritual of waiting and watching and waiting until he pouted, nodded, sipped again to make sure, and then congratulated me: 'That's good coffee.' That's all well and good, but I needed to know how he would feel after he'd made another fifteen cups of it, batted it round with the spoon and scored it for mouthfeel. John reiterated that that wasn't going to happen. He was interested in a second opinion so he called over his business partner, Casper.

The misery continued. I could see it happening before it happened: Casper was going to taste the coffee and wish he'd put an apron on. He would spit it right out and run for the nearest tap screaming, 'Marzipan!' all the way. I could hardly bear to watch him raise the cup to his mouth and sip it down, I felt sick as he swallowed and considered the taste and I had to ask him to repeat himself after he concluded, 'That's really good, where's it from?' I repeated the Chulumenda story to Casper and he seemed genuinely surprised. He and John thought most African coffees had an undesirable bitterness to them that was missing in this one. They were sold. This was something that they could take on. Now if the price was right then we had a deal.

John and I retired to the office for the usual duel over price and quantity. The quantity side went pretty smoothly; he would take it all. How much did I want for it? I admit I was taken aback and had to think quick. The $6.50 price tag was way too much and I'd do better to start with a sensible opener, so I grabbed a number out of the air: $5.50 per kilo. This was still a really good 40 per cent mark-up on what I'd paid but John was straight on to it. He had a figure more like $4.50 in mind and told me that was still at the top end of what he would usually pay for a Zambian coffee.

Now, I had three things going for me. First, I could guarantee that the quality of the coffee matched the sample John was drinking because I'd transported it myself, which reduced his risk considerably from the levels that he would usually be exposed to with a new coffee. Second, I had found him a new product that none of his competitors in Cape Town had access to; I could leave him with that access as part of the deal and in future he could have a direct relationship with the estate without needing me or anyone like me to be an intermediary. Third, I had taken all the risk so far; I had acted as a trailblazer, found supplier and buyer without guarantee or support from either and in my mind that warranted a premium on the price. I'm still not sure which of the three reasons persuaded him but we agreed to settle the difference and I sold the remaining stock of Chulumenda coffee for $5 per kilo. Although he did make me promise not to tell anyone!

I'd made my first big sale and it felt pretty good. With the profit from the deals in Jo'burg and Cape Town, I was up nearly $2,000. Not bad, considering how close I'd come to total failure. At one point it had seemed I might even have to sell it for a loss. What felt even better was that I'd tested my theory that there was a market for Craig's coffee in South Africa, and I had been right. Craig simply didn't have time to make this trip because he was too busy running the farm; but I did. That I had made a success of it this time meant there was no reason why Craig and John couldn't do business together in the future. I had taken four days to make the journey and find a buyer and now the potential return to Craig could run into thousands of dollars. It just shows how important it is to get out there and sell a product. It doesn't matter how good it is; if you don't tell everyone, they'll never know.

Eight

OUT OF AFRICA

LAST TRADE:
— Remaining 1.8 tonnes of coffee: $1,515 profit
INVESTMENTS:
— Chilli sauce (including taxes and shipping): $6,989
IN THE BANK: $44,663

Another fast-emerging market that I can't ignore while I'm in South Africa is China. The middle class in China is now estimated at over 300 million people and the disposable income of this population is set to make a massive dent in the global economy; if everyone in China had a car, the demand for petrol alone would drain the remaining oil reserves in just a few years. Unlike the Indian middle class, the Chinese have a patriotic loyalty to goods made in China, but there are products which they believe are better made elsewhere. These goods tend to be found at the luxury end of the market. One that has received much media attention of late is French red wine. It is not uncommon for a bottle of Lafite '96 to fetch a couple of thousand dollars more at auction in China than it would in Europe. Many Chinese enjoy the showmanship of presenting important guests with this kind of celebrity wine, and my favourite aspect of it all is that many prefer to take it with a splash of Coke. Well, they laugh at us putting milk in our tea.

As I'm passing through the Cape region of South Africa to sell my coffee and follow up on an opportunity to purchase some chilli sauce, it seems like a great chance to seek out a wine that might sell well in China. It's not everyone that can afford the Lafites and Latours; there are also many people trying cheaper wines and gradually the market is starting to broaden out. Undoubtedly, the preference is for French wine, however a quick call to an import agent in Shanghai reveals a few recent trends.

Tony Wang helps foreign companies import goods to China. For a fee, he can handle all the paperwork necessary to get a shipment of wine into Shanghai. He is also a prime example of the kind of middle-class Chinese that are beginning to enjoy a glass of wine while relaxing after a hard day's work. I chat with him on the phone about his preferences and the wines that are selling well in China today. There is a clear theme: simple, sweet, fruity red wines are what the market is demanding.

Many Chinese have been turned on to red wine as the colour red is lucky and is perceived to have health benefits (no point in bringing white, then). Merlots and Cabernets are known and trusted. A Pinotage is not a good bet; they don't know it and, in any case, the tannins wouldn't be well received by the relatively unsophisticated Chinese palate. This is all clear enough. Find a wine that tastes a bit like Ribena.

My friend Dave Azam is a very successful wine trader in the UK and he imports wine for the London restaurant trade from all over the world, including South Africa. I have on occasion even tasted a bottle or two with him. A quick call to explain the kind of wine I'm looking for and his encyclopaedic knowledge of South African wine kicks into action. He recommends a smallish estate on the coastal end of the Stellenbosch region of the Cape called Rozier Bay. If it's good enough for Dave then it's good enough for me. I call to set up a meeting with the owner, Adam Mauerberger.

Adam is a handsome man in his late thirties, refined, slick, sophisticated; perhaps not what the world thinks of as the typical

South African farmer. He's confident that he is ready to take on the international wine market. The estate at Rozier Bay was initially a syndicate investment, but when the other buyers wanted to take the brand in a different direction, Adam simply bought them out. He's pretty passionate about the wine that he wants to make here. The estate is rare in that it overlooks the sea. This would be quite unworkable in many wine-growing countries but here in Gordon's Bay there is a unique microclimate that means Adam can enjoy stunning views over the ocean while he tends to his vines.

From his uppermost field, Adam visibly delights in showing me views of the mountains and the picturesque bay below. As far as I'm concerned this is part of the brand. Wine, like everything else, needs to have a unique selling point; buyers like to identify with the product, and with wine in particular people like to know where it comes from. I can use the fact that I've been to the vineyard to paint a picture to potential buyers as a way of helping to market the wine. If it tastes half as good as it looks from up here, we have a winner. As long as the price is right.

Back down the hill, Adam lives out the South African summers in a large, white-washed farmhouse, then during the winter he heads back to Britain to enjoy the summer again there. He has developed the estate to include holiday cottages and a riding centre. Today there are children from the local school taking riding lessons. Next door is a swanky new office and vault complex into which Adam has built his own private, glass-fronted wine bar that wouldn't look out of place down a quiet side street in Kensington.

Adam has a suite of wines to show me, including one of South Africa's most decorated wines: his Mount Rozier Cabernet. Like a war veteran who has survived umpteen campaigns in Europe and beyond, it is decorated with so many medals that you can barely see the label beneath. At 145 rand (R), or $19 per bottle I think it's still a little rich for the Chinese market: they might pay this for a French wine, but South African wine is still fairly new.

I'm after something a little more accessible; the kind of wine that I could buy in Sainsbury's for £4.99 ($10) per bottle would be perfect. Adam has just the thing. From his Reef Bay range he pulls out a light, sweet and fruity Merlot. The wine has a big, juicy flavour, full of cherries and raspberries and even a hint of chocolate. This would be ideal to bring to China and the price is a mere R30 ($4 per bottle). Unfortunately, there's a big problem with this wine – or rather with the bottle. The Chinese market is still new to the concept of wine and there's a fair degree of snobbery that permeates it. Included in that is the preconception that a bottle of wine should have a cork and the wine that Adam was selling me was screw cap. Most experienced wine drinkers will scoff at this, and will right now be shouting: 'Don't be ridiculous!' or something similar, and rightly so, but I wasn't about to go and re-educate the whole Chinese wine market about the merits of screw caps, so put a cork in it!

This presented us with a bit of a problem. Adam has wine that he prices at three points. You have probably seen on the shelves in most wine retailers that some wine brands come in both cheaper and more expensive versions. Sometimes they call the better one Reserve or Reserva, or they'll have a subtly different variation on the brand name that differentiates between wines of a different quality. In Adam's case, his cheaper range is Reef Bay, mid range is Rozier Bay and then his war hero range is Mount Rozier. Subtle? Yes; but important. To the wine producer with a brand to build, it's vital that the cheaper wine never undermines the better wine by being sold at a higher price. So they sell at 'price points' to ensure that retailers and restaurateurs sell the wine on at the correct level. I wanted a wine at the Reef Bay price point but, as I needed one with a cork, it would have to be from the Rozier Bay range.

I wasn't entirely sure what I would find in China so I was being very demanding; I wanted to have my cake and eat it. I was asking

I want to be like Mr Sayeed.

'Is that the fourth emergency service?'

...very, very long way from the chilli sauce in your Saturday night kebab.

Craig's search for the perfect coffee bean.

If the wine tastes half as good as it looks...

Which way is China?

Hold on to your hats!

Anyone for a game of Ulak Tartysh?

A bad day at the races.

This is going very badly.

Skimming stones on the river.

Needles and haystacks.

Adam for a wine that was easy to drink but wasn't going to look cheap next to a French wine on the shelf. I also wanted it cheap in case I got there, found that there wasn't a market for it and had to offload it cheap. I believed in this trade as a real money spinner and I was preparing to throw at least $15,000 at it. If the price was right, I was in the market for a few thousand bottles.

As we worked our way through the wine tasting, I had no doubt that the best wine for China would have been the screw cap Merlot, but not to worry – the Rozier Bay Cabernet was a good, fruity wine that had won lots of awards in South Africa. It had a rich plum colour to it and the taste was a wonderful mix of blackberries and cassis, not too much tannin and perhaps just a hint of spice. If anything, it was a little too complex for China, but I thought I could work with it. I would be tapping into a new market that knows very little about wine from South Africa, so would be selling the whole idea of South African wine, not just Rozier Bay. At least this is what I'd convinced myself by my third glass of the stuff at 11.30 a.m.

Adam wanted R45 (nearly $6) per bottle. I couldn't really see myself being able to sell any wine from South Africa into the Chinese market for any more than around $12 per bottle, especially for a non-French wine. With taxes and transport taken into consideration I needed to be buying nearer to the R31 ($4) price point. I was happy to be open with Adam: 'I need this wine at near to the R26 or R27 mark,' I lied.

'That's going to be very difficult for me, Conor.' I could see him squirming a little as though I had insulted him. 'But, as I like round numbers, I'll come down to R30 [$3.95] per bottle. But you must assure me that you will respect that it must be sold in the Chinese market at the higher price point.' So, he was happy to give me a massive 30 per cent off his initial price and in return I had to promise to sell it as though it cost me more; in other words, he wanted me to make more profit.

This was too good to be true; I should have bitten his hand off. However, if you don't ask, you don't get: 'R29 per bottle and you have yourself a deal.' I'd chosen to ignore his round number plea. I'd heard that old trick before! Adam paused for a moment and looked slightly broken; he was trying his hardest to accommodate me, and in return I was taking the piss. He sighed and then held out his hand. 'OK, Conor.' Unbelievably, we were shaking hands and I'd picked up a cracking wine for a snip of its value – only $3.80. At this price I could sell it in China and make 50 per cent, 60 per cent, even 70 per cent profit on it.

I bought 1,500 bottles of Adam's wine for around $5,725 and decided to pick up another 1,500 bottles of a cheaper wine called Arniston Bay from a stack 'em high, sell 'em cheap discount place down the road for another $3,150. I was now over $10,000 on my wine investment and I still had taxes and shipping costs to factor in.

The shippers in Cape Town needed thirty days to make delivery to Shanghai and another $1,460 for their trouble. In four weeks' time, Tony Wang should have customs cleared and the wine ready for me to collect from a downtown warehouse at a further cost of $4,448 for import duties. At over $15,000 all in, this was my biggest outlay so far and potentially my biggest profit. If I could have a slice, or even a slice of a slice, of the Chinese wine market then I could make some serious money. This could be a $25,000 deal when I arrived in Shanghai. I couldn't wait to get there, but in the mean time I had four weeks to kill and four thousand miles to cover. It was time to leave Africa.

*

I had expected India to be all shanty towns and abject poverty but as I drive in from Delhi airport to the new town I don't see any evidence of this. The main road is busy with traffic and there are more than the odd Mercedes on show. The overwhelming sense in this part of Delhi, with its mansions and gardens, is of opulence and, crucially for me, disposable income.

It is May, and only 8 a.m., but already the temperature is 44°. Summer is on its way. My first thought is that this is probably the worst time to be trying to sell a twelve out of ten, Hot az Hell chilli sauce. In the taxi from the airport I do a quick bit of consumer research. I explain to the driver that I am here selling chilli sauce but I'm a bit worried that nobody will be eating chilli when it is so bloody hot. He quickly puts me right: 'No, sir. When you are hot, you must eat more chilli. Chilli makes you sweat and sweating cools you down.' I could argue, but I won't.

When you import new goods into a foreign country it is a good idea to use the services of someone who has done something similar before. All over the world there are agencies that provide this kind of service – known as freight forwarders – and for a fee they handle the paperwork, including local customs clearing and duties; all the boring stuff. I've used a man called Puneet Gupta to do this for me but unfortunately when I arrive the sauces are still stuck in the quagmire of Delhi customs. When I get hold of Gupta on the phone, he tells me that it might be a day or two before they reach his warehouse. Fortunately, I have a selection of sample bottles in my luggage with which to entice new customers and so I start straight away with the business of cold-calling likely retailers in the more middle-class parts of town. I have to become a cold-calling salesman.

Coming as I have from the more formal world of finance, I've never done cold-calling before. I have no idea what the requisite skills are. I know I have a product that tastes good and hot and I can vaguely remember how Eddie sold it to me. He focused heavily on how the main ingredient was chilli and not vinegar, so I decide to borrow as heavily from that as I can and just give it a whirl.

My first stop is at a very well-known shop called Jimmy'z, in the Noida district, one of the suburbs of Delhi in which there are many leafy squares lined with shops. Outside Jimmy'z is an array of executive cars, Mercedes and BMWs parked by wealthy-looking Indian housewives doing their shopping. They look to be exactly the clientele that I'm targeting with my imported product. Having said that, from the outside Jimmy'z store looks much like any Indian grocer that you might find on any British street corner; hardly Fortnum and Mason.

Jimmy is a rakish-looking man in his early thirties, dressed in a smart shirt and chinos. He's one of the new breed of young, dynamic traders that are emerging in a blossoming Indian economy. Inside, his shop is an Aladdin's cave of imported goods stacked high on shelves that reach from floor to ceiling. Even Jimmy's till is hidden behind a counter that is stacked high with hessian sacks of Colombian coffee beans and boxes of American sweeteners. It's the kind of shop that can safely claim to sell everything.

While I'm waiting for Jimmy to finish with a customer, I give the sauces section a quick perusal and I'm pleased with what I find: chilli-based sauces from the US and the Caribbean are already on the shelves and they're priced in the range I anticipated, Rs 150–260 ($3.75–6.50 per bottle). As long as Jimmy likes the Bushman's sauce then he should be able to afford my Rs 115 ($2.88) asking price, still make his standard mark-up and be able to sell at the bottom end of the price range.

Jimmy is of course sceptical as to what a South African sauce can offer the Indian market. I manage, however, to persuade him to give the range a go and we open a bag of imported crisps over a pile of boxes in a quiet corner of the shop. Every inch of this shop is taken up with stock so there's nowhere else to go. One by one, I load up a crisp with each of the sauces for Jimmy to taste, and straight off the bat he is impressed with the flavour of the peri-peri and the jalapeño sauces. But he turns his nose up at the suggestion that Hot az Hell sauce can really be hot enough to engage the Indian palate. Now this tickles my wicked sense of humour enough to encourage him to load his crisp with a double dollop of it before he pops it into his mouth. He has me in stitches when his eyes nearly pop out of his head. 'Oh my God, that is HOT!' Gotcha. Jimmy is sold. The price of Rs 115 is fine with him, as I guessed; he can be confident of selling it at around Rs 155 per bottle so will easily make his standard mark-up of 30 per cent. As I landed the bottles in Delhi for Rs 76 ($1.98), I'll be making a whopping 90¢ per bottle! If I sell them all that's a great profit of nearly $3,500. Jimmy says he'll take 18 bottles of each.

How many? That is only 72 bottles in total. Less than 2 per cent of my total shipment. This is a great endorsement of the sauces but it's next to useless in terms of helping me to shift all this stock in four days. Nevertheless, it's better than nothing and I promise Jimmy a delivery as soon as I have the stock through customs. I pack up my samples and head down the road, hoping for a slightly bigger order from another retailer.

Alas not. Four retailers later and I have total orders for 200 bottles of sauce: just over 5 per cent sold – albeit at a great mark-up – but I simply haven't time to hang around and wait for these retailers to sell the first order and place another, nor do I have time to be traipsing around every retailer in Delhi and beyond. At this rate of selling it would take me a month or more, and I have to be in Shanghai before that. I need to come up with another route to market.

Puneet Gupta is a jolly, rotund sort of fellow. He is part of the Brahman caste, which means he is a trader by nurture as well as nature. He has charged me around $1,500 to get my sauces through customs. Puneet knows how the system works and knows how to work the system.

Puneet is pretty well connected as he imports goods from all over the world and sells to the retail sector. He could be just the man to talk to about maybe taking over this trade from me. The way I see it, I could provide him with the stock and a list of the retailers who have already placed orders, he could target other retailers that he already does business with and then over time he could realize the $2,500 profit. Who knows? He may even decide to order more stock directly from Eddie in the future. Obviously, we'd have to come up with some way of dividing the profit this time, but in the future I'm happy for him to go directly to Eddie.

I meet up with Puneet in his Delhi office to put my plan to him. We do the usual tasting and the sauces impress him. He's impressed enough to be interested but not convinced. It's a big commitment and he would need to take advice. He suggests that tomorrow we go to meet the man who knows the market best, Mr Singh. Puneet will collect me from my hotel and we'll take it from there.

Next morning, Puneet is waiting for me outside in his air-conditioned Mercedes. He doesn't drive himself; he has his own driver. I always wonder at what point in life you decide that you'll spend a load of money on a really great car but then decide that you can't be bothered to drive it yourself. I suppose that comes sooner in Delhi than most other cities, because driving in this city is scary. They say that unless you're born here, you cannot ever drive here. Puneet laughs at this.

'Yes, but I am from Mumbai,' he tells me.

'Ah, so you drive yourself when you are in Mumbai?'

'No.'

Oh well, there goes that theory.

We arrive at a grubby, falling-down concrete warehouse and head into the basement where Mr Singh has his office. In fact it is where Messrs Singh have their office, because sitting behind a desk in the corner are two bearded Sikh gentlemen who I would bet ten to one are father and son. At least, their beards look very similar.

Right again. Mr Singh introduces his son, Mr Singh, and together they present a very formidable front. Puneet introduces me and explains that I have brought an interesting new product to India that he thinks has potential to sell well here. I do a quick sales pitch and for the hundredth time in three days I tuck into a feed of crisps covered in fiercely hot chilli sauce. Before I know it I'm into a selling pitch. As I start to explain that Bushman's is the only sauce made with 100 per cent chilli and how most sauces are vinegar based, I can almost feel Eddie sitting next to me, egging me on. I throw in a good bit of 'family-run business' stuff too, for the Singhs' benefit. They like that a lot. It's going great and there's lots of beard–stroking, and a fair bit of head–nodding, too.

Of course they like the sauce, and everything else I've said seems to have convinced them, but they want to try it out on a few retailers. They have a good customer in town called Jimmy'z. Oh, really! Jimmy apparently stocks this kind of thing, and if he says it's good then that would encourage them to go in with Puneet on a deal. They favour simply buying me out completely, for a price to be agreed. They would rather take it on themselves from there. I'm happy; I have a hunch Jimmy will like it. Tomorrow Puneet will call me to deliver his verdict and, if all goes well, we could negotiate a price for the whole lot then.

After a restless night's sleep from wondering what the hell I'm going to do with 4,000 bottles of chilli sauce if Puneet and the Singhs decide not to buy it, I'm a little sluggish over my Judgement Day breakfast. My flight leaves from Delhi tonight. One bit of good news is that I had a message from Puneet overnight to say that the sauces had finally cleared customs and were in his warehouse. He went on to suggest that we meet there today at lunchtime. There's no point in doing any more selling; all my eggs are in Puneet's basket.

It takes over an hour of driving around to eventually find Puneet's warehouse, another ramshackle old concrete two-storey building in a maze of similar buildings on the outskirts of the north of the city. The roads that divide them are merely labelled with letters and numbers in what seems like a random order, and E42 is helpfully placed between E14 and A6. The street is paved but there are piles of rubbish on either side. Camden Council obviously has a branch in Delhi.

Inside the warehouse, Puneet is waiting to show me the sauces. They're piled high in a dark corner in boxes of six. It is only now that the sheer size of the job in hand fully strikes me. It's now obvious that without Puneet I have no chance of selling all this and making my money back, let alone making a profit. Only someone stationed permanently here in India could access enough retailers to move all this chilli sauce; someone like Puneet. It's important, though, to act cool.

There's an old Japanese business trick whereby you are invited to Japan to do business, and when you arrive they lay on entertainment and generally show you a good time. The trick is that they continue to show you a good time right up to the last day before you leave. Every time you try to bring up the business that you are there to do, they just show you an even better time, which makes you forget because you're having such a good time. Then, on the day you're about to leave, they get down to it. With no time left to negotiate the deal, you're forced to accept terms less favourable than you would have liked. I am now in this situation, although Puneet doesn't know it; my bags are packed in the boot of my car.

Puneet and the Singhs have had positive feedback from their customers and think they can market the sauces both here and in Mumbai. They will have to undercut the market a little at first to get a foothold but Puneet could afford to offer me Rs 88 ($2.20) per bottle. I try a little haggling to get him up to Rs 90 but he only goes as far as Rs 89 ($2.23). I'm happy. At this stage I'm lucky to be getting out of this with my money back, so I should be over the moon to be leaving with $1,500 profit.

All that remains is to give Puneet my bank details. He'll pay 50 per cent now and 50 per cent in 45 days. This is a small concession but I think I'll live with it. I shake his hand and have to turn down his offer of a celebratory meal tonight as I'm off to the airport. He must know the old Japanese trick because he looks very disappointed to find out that today was my last day in Delhi.

Nine

GREAT WALLS OF CHINA

LAST TRADE:
— Chilli sauce: $1,555 profit
INVESTMENTS:
— Wine (including taxes and shipping): $15,218
IN THE BANK: $37,989

'Barriers to entry' is a common term in business and economics. Anything that makes it difficult to set up a new business or get into a new market can be a barrier. It could be something formal such as requiring a licence to operate in that market, for example if you wanted to start a new airline, or it could be something more informal, say if you wanted to start exporting to a country where you didn't speak the language. Rarely does it represent a physical barrier literally blocking your path.

I still had three more weeks before the wine I'd bought in South Africa would be landing in Shanghai dock, three thousand miles east of Delhi. I was keeping my eyes open, as always, for another trade but I had to press on with the journey. Unfortunately, there was a bloody great big mountain range in the way and only a few specific passes where you could cross.

The uprising in Tibet had meant that all its borders had been shut to outsiders so the Chinese could have a quiet word with those responsible. My original plan had been to cross over the newly opened Nathu La pass, and I had high hopes of being able to find a good Darjeeling tea to bring with me to Tibet (hoping to build on the 'ice to Eskimos' momentum). This unforeseeable political development forced a rethink.

The other obvious route was the main pass through Karakoram in Pakistan but this was still shut due to bad weather. Kashmir had a war going on, so that pass was off limits too. Afghanistan, well, doesn't really need an explanation, does it? So the next point on the map was a pass at Irkeshtam in the former Soviet republic of Kyrgyzstan, not somewhere I'd even considered going to before I left.

Fortunately a friend of mine, Paul Wilson, had. Paul had not only walked the route but had actually written books about it, so I gave him a call to ask his advice. I was interested in the options I had for goods to trade and possibly even transport into western China from Kyrgyzstan. With my map book open in front of me while I chatted to him, I started to familiarize myself with the layout of Central Asia. Paul was sure there was only one trade to take on in Kyrgyzstan, and that was horses. The Central Asian states produce some of the world's finest; the Fergana valley was famous for producing the 'Heavenly Horses' that were so coveted by the Han emperors of China two thousand years ago that they even went to war to ensure a constant supply. I began to imagine how I could re establish this ancient trade route and even drive horses over the Pamir mountain range to trade at the world's largest livestock market in the ancient silk road town of Kashgar.

I was now almost a quarter of the way round the world and over a month into the journey. My total profit was running at just over $3,000 so I was still a long way short of reaching $100,000. I did have $15,000 invested in wine though, so if I could squeeze another couple of grand out of a deal along the way, and sell the wine for a decent mark-up, I could feasibly be halfway there by the time I left China. This still all seemed like a long way off. For now, I decided to just concentrate on getting myself to Kyrgyzstan, sorting out a visa for the Irkeshtam pass and sourcing a truck full of horses to sell when I got to China.

So, deciding that this kind of back-of-a-fag-packet, half-arsed scheme was enough, I jumped on a flight from Delhi to Almaty in Kazakhstan and then hitched a lift south over the border and into the Kyrgyzstani capital, Bishkek. Bishkek was unbelievably clean for a modern city. It's not a pretty city by any means, although its architecture does have a strong brutal quality; everything is concrete and boxy. But it was clean like someone had taken a toothbrush to it. In the centre of town was the main government building, which looked like a large incinerator in the middle of a vast square. In the square was a colossal bronze statue of the hero Manas, the spiritual grandfather of Kyrgyzstan. He was only put here in 1992 when the statue of cantankerous uncle Lenin was usurped and moved to a less salubrious spot round the back.

The people of Bishkek were as ethnically diverse as any place I'd seen. This was a place where East really met West. The mountains to the east were formed when the two continents collided, and Bishkek is the result of thousands of years of migration over them ever since. Walking round the streets I could see Caucasian faces, Mongol faces, southern Indian and Chinese faces, and a spectrum of variations in between; there was clearly little discrimination here between groups when people decided whom to marry. It was a beautiful rainbow of cultures.

Although considerably poorer than towns in its oil-rich neighbour Kazakhstan, Bishkek was still a modern commercial city. The streets were busy with traffic made up mostly of imported German cars. There were bars and restaurants popping up all over the place and the weather was a perfect, sunny 25°. In summer at least, it's a very pleasant place to be.

Although the Kyrgyz have their own language, the lingua franca in this part of the world is still Russian, an enduring legacy from the old Soviet days, and so I had to find myself a Russian-speaking translator and guide. Slava came to my hotel to meet me. He was an enterprising twenty-eight-year-old ethnic Russian Kyrgyz. He was wearing jeans and a North Face fleece and spoke perfect English; he wouldn't have been at all out of place in London. He was also a tremendous translator.

Slava was keen to get going but from the off he wanted to make it clear that he was not a horseman. In the UK this would mean that he didn't know about horses; in Kyrgyzstan, it meant he still knew more about horses than just about anyone in the whole of the UK, just not as much as the average Kyrgyz, most of whom know so much about horses that Horse Whispering is listed as the third official national language after Kyrgyz and Russian.

The plan was to leave Bishkek and drive 200 or so miles south-west, up and over the Tian Shan mountains that run through the heart of the country, to the town of Toktogul. A heavily clouded sky was almost indistinguishable from the snow-capped mountains as we climbed steadily upwards. The roadsides were still covered in snow even though it was now May. Once over the top, we dropped down to where the weather was better and soon the clouds broke to reveal clear blue skies. The lush green valleys were covered with herds of grazing horses and acres of red poppies. The landscape divided into neat horizontal bands of blue, white, red and green. It was easy to see why Kyrgyzstan has often been referred to as the Switzerland of the East.

At one of the passes we saw a sign for a ski resort. I had no idea that Kyrgyzstan had a skiing industry so I was curious to stop for a look. Could I maybe even squeeze in an hour or two on the piste? We were right on the snow line so there was no more than an outside chance that it would still be open, but it was worth a short detour from the main road. Unfortunately, the resort was closed;

there were only a couple of Portakabins, two old lift stations and four bare ski runs. The Portakabins were there to serve coffee and food to a small team of builders who had started to build a hotel on the site. They were happy to share their coffee with me and explain what they were up to.

The resort had been bought by a Kyrgyz millionaire. The hotel was to be a five-star development, with another ten lift stations planned to open up the other side of the mountain. The temperatures here can be below zero for weeks on end but it does offer guaranteed snow for over eight months of the year. That's twice the length of the alpine season, and skiing here is only a fraction of the cost in the Alps. It occurred to me that maybe it wouldn't be too long, as more outsiders began to explore Central Asia, that someone would call Switzerland the Kyrgyzstan of the West.

*

Slava had contacted a horseman on the other side of the pass who lived outside of Toktogul, a small town of around 15,000 people built on the north shore of a large reservoir that supplied the west of Kyrgyzstan with water. The reservoir was enormous and crystal clear and it gave Toktogul a certain lakeside charm, *à la* St Moritz two hundred years ago. The streets were empty save for the occasional donkey and cart, yet all the houses were hidden behind high walls and gates. We arrived at the homestay of the man we'd come to meet just in time for supper.

Munarbek had been breeding horses and taking foreigners on tours of the Kyrgyz mountains for many years and he had offered to show me some horses he had for sale. He was ethnically Kyrgyz, a round-faced, slightly chubby, friendly-looking man with a tendency to frown deeply when he was thinking. He must have been thinking, 'What the hell is this bloke up to?' because he spent most of dinner with his forehead squished up between his eyebrows.

While I regaled him with tales of the unfortunate events of my Sudanese camel trade, his mother served up plate after plate of meat and vegetables. For the first time in my life I was confronted with a plate of an unusual-looking dark meat that I suspected was other than it seemed. 'Beef?' I asked, hopefully.

'*Non*,' she replied. '*Pas bouef. Viande chevaline.*' Munarbek's mother was the French teacher at the local school.

OK, let's get it over and done with: they ate horses. They bred them, rode them, their national sports all revolved around them, so it's safe to say that they loved them, BUT they also ate them. In fact, they really enjoyed eating them. I'm not sure how I felt about eating them but it's such a great insult not to eat all that's put in front of you in Kyrgyzstan that I just made up my mind to not make up my mind about how I felt about eating them. I haven't eaten any since, so it's fair to assume that I must have not really enjoyed eating them.

I was keen to get on with the business at hand but Munarbek explained to me that nothing would happen the next day, as 9 May was Veterans Day in all former Soviet Bloc countries. Back home we have a day of sombre remembrance, a time to take stock of the horror of war and respectfully turn our thoughts to what our dead sacrificed for us. In the former Soviet states it's a big party, a celebration of how they gave Jerry a damn good beating. Everyone who survived is heralded by the family, who come with gifts of hats, and there's a large feast. It was a great honour, therefore, to be invited to Munarbek's friend Bopong's house to meet his grandfather, a real veteran, on his big day. Of course I, too, would have to bring a hat.

The veteran lived in a dark timber farmhouse at the foot of a wooded hillside a few miles outside the town. Next to the house were a corral and half a dozen open stables. In total I counted five horses. On a covered deck in the garden the whole family were sitting on the floor around a low, square table drinking tea, or *chi* as they call it in Kyrgyzstan. *Chi* means 'tea' and *na* means 'land', so in Kyrgyz Chi-na is, literally, 'land of tea'.

For an eighty-five-year-old, the veteran still looked incredibly strong. When I arrived he watched me carefully with his dark, glassy eyes and I was a little nervous because I didn't want to do the wrong thing and cause offence. Straight away I presented him with the traditional *kapoc*, a high, peaked cap a bit like an embroidered French kepi. Judging from the size of his family, this must have been at least his twentieth hat of the day but he accepted it gladly and shook me by the hand. At first I wondered if he'd mistaken me for a Mason but when I looked down I could see that his hand was actually missing two fingers. The only reason the old boy was still with us was that his rifle backfired some time in 1942, removing the central digits of his right hand. On the one hand this might have seemed like bad news (sorry!) but on the other it got him sent home from the front line the week before the battle of Stalingrad kicked off, and so undoubtedly saved his life. It didn't stop him becoming a horse breeder or a champion at Ulak Tartysh.

There are many games across the world that take place atop a horse. In the UK we have our own dear polo: sunny afternoons, cucumber sandwiches, stomping the divots at half-time with a glass of champagne in hand, and all that. In Kyrgyzstan they have Ulak Tartysh, a game that starts with the beheading of a goat that then becomes the ball. The two teams aim to get the carcass of the goat into the opposition's 'goal', a kind of concrete bin at the other end of the field. The rules are a little like rugby after that, but on horses; it is very, very physical and people often get badly hurt as they deliberately crash their horses into the goat carrier to try to unbalance and then wrestle the goat-ball from him. Hard enough to play with all your fingers. As I listened to the family's tales of how good my host was in his day despite his disability, I knew that I was in the presence of a true horseman.

I probed with questions about just how the horse trade worked, how to eke out a profit, where to source and where to sell. I was slightly dismayed when the answer was: 'Take them to Kazakhstan, they always pay over the odds there.' This was not what I wanted to hear as I'd just come from there, I'd used up my visa already and I'd committed to heading in the other direction, towards the southern pass at Irkeshtam, en route to China. The crossing was already arranged.

I tried another angle: 'How would you take horses in the other direction – where are the markets in the south?'

He laughed. 'This would be foolish; horses are cheaper in the south. Traders in the south are taking their horses north to Kazakhstan, they always pay over the odds there.'

I'd heard this last bit before. I could see it was going to be difficult to make any profit from horses that way. 'What about China?' I asked him.

He didn't know about China. 'People don't trade horses with the Chinese any more.'

This is what I thought, and that might be an opportunity.

Unfortunately, when I got back to the homestay there was bad news waiting for me in my emails: a friend in China alerting me to a news story saying that the Chinese were rethinking their quarantine rules. A recent outbreak of equine flu meant that now all horses entering China would be required to spend up to fourteen days in quarantine in the country of origin before then spending forty-five days in Chinese quarantine on the other side of the border. Added to this, all certification would now have to go through Beijing rather than local administrative centres, further delaying the process. My plan was in tatters; there was no way my schedule would allow me to take horses over the border to China the following week.

I was disheartened, but not ready to give up yet. Munarbek was still keen to show me the region and had already arranged some horses for a trip up into the mountains. I could see that he was disappointed. I'd come such a long way to leave empty-handed, and this would be a blow to his sense of hospitality. He persuaded me to take the trip; in any case, my visa to cross into China wasn't valid until next week, so I couldn't leave before then. I agreed to ride out with him at first light.

Ten

HACKING IT

INVESTMENTS:
— Wine: $15,218
IN THE BANK: $37,989

Today, Munarbek, Bopong and I will ride up into the mountains above Toktogul on horses that Bopong is already saddling up for us when I arrive just before dawn. We ride off while it is still dark, up an old dirt track that runs from the back of his yard. I am riding a medium-sized, black, eight-year-old gelding with a short, hurried stride that, worryingly, according to Munarbek is called Speedy. Like most horses trained to be ridden in Kyrgyzstan, this horse wants to run. Given the slightest chance, he pulls forward out of a walk, bypasses trot and canter and heads straight into a gallop. This is because he has been trained to play Ulak Tartysh.

We're heading for the high meadow where the horses are being tended to by a shepherd. When spring arrives, the snows gradually retreat and his job is to lead the horses higher and higher in search of fresh grass. Munarbek takes us along a gorge and upstream. The water is running fast and fresh with last year's melted snow. Eventually we begin a climb so steep that Speedy and I have to traverse the slope from side to side just to reach the top. From the summit I can see a breathtaking span of snow-capped mountains stretching far into the distance, the pretty town of Toktogul next to the lake behind us and a small farm way down below in the steep valley. No vehicle, 4 x 4 or otherwise, could access this land. This is why horses are so valuable in Kyrgyzstan; there is simply no other way to access these lands, or to work them.

The horses carry us down and through the farm. There is no sign of any people, only a barking dog that runs out to greet us and see us off. The horses aren't bothered and we plod through the farm and back up into another tortuous climb. From the next summit we can see down into another long valley where Munarbek says the shepherd sometimes makes camp. He has arranged for him to bring the horses down later in the day.

I am interested in whether Munarbek and Slava agree with the old man's assessment of the lack of opportunity to make a profit down south. There is a market in Uzgen where the population is mostly comprised of Uzbek people. There, they will pay more for bigger horses. The part of the country we are in now is mountainous and the people are mostly Kyrgyz. The Kyrgyz people like small horses because they are good in the mountains. Uzbeks prefer a larger horse because in Uzgen the landscape is flatter. If I were to find horses up here that were too large to be good mountain horses, I could buy them cheap and then sell them for more in Uzgen. The margins would only be small, and making a profit would depend on my ability to negotiate with the Uzbek horse traders at the market.

Now, I can see the challenge: ride up into the mountains, rustle up some good horses and then drive them to market. I'm still smarting a little from the failure in Sudan with the camels and this seems like a great opportunity to have another go at what I so clearly failed to do there: practise the dark art of negotiation with some of the world's most notorious traders. We all use the term 'horse-trading' when we want to emphasize tough negotiation but do any of us really know why? I was going to test myself and go toe-to-toe with real horse traders. If nothing else, I might learn a thing or two.

After over three hours in the saddle, we come to the end of the valley where the land opens out into a wide meadow. The shepherd has his winter camp another couple of miles away and I can tell that Speedy knows it. He's champing at the bit to get there so Munarbek suggests a race. With no warning, he gives Speedy a hard slap on the arse, kicks his own horse into gear and we're off galloping across the open meadow. It's all I can do just to hang on and obviously there's no way I'm going to get in front of Munarbek, who is beaming with delight at me as we tear across the mountain pasture. As we come around the edge of the valley I can see a man watching us from the hillside. He is sitting on top of a fine-looking steed, wearing a bright red bobble hat, and is laughing at my attempts to keep up with Munarbek. He rides down to greet us as we pull the horses up alongside a stream where they drink long and thirsty gulps of cooling water. He welcomes me with a firm handshake and a genuinely warm smile. He is the shepherd's son; the shepherd will be along later with the best horses from the high mountain pasture.

We pitch our tents across the stream from the shepherd as a way of both staying close and, symbolically at least, giving him his space. His wife has been inside the tent busily preparing food and appears to invite us in for hot cups of tea, bread, cheese and sausages. We remove our shoes and sit on the floor of the tent, happy to receive the warm brew. Already the sun is beginning to disappear behind the high mountains on the western side of the valley, taking its warmth with it. Every day the mountains steal precious hours from either end of the day and both dawn and dusk are simply lost.

The shepherd's son tells us it is now unlikely that the shepherd will return tonight. Every day he looks to take the horses higher and higher and the weather of late has been warm for the season. It's likely that he has been able to go higher than expected and so it will take him longer to return back to the lower pastures. He will most likely stop and sleep as descending in the dark is dangerous; a stray horse could easily be lost and there are wolves that would happily take a new foal for an easy meal. So he will return here in the morning. It is barely 8 p.m., but after the long ride and without any electricity there is nothing else to do but turn in for an early night.

I wake soon after dawn, before everyone else in camp and before the sun has made it high enough to be seen over the mountains. There is just enough light to make out where I'm stepping so I decide to hike to the top of one of the ridges running up the hillside. From there I'll be able to see further up the valley and maybe catch a glimpse of the shepherd as he arrives. It's hard going up very steep, rocky ground and it takes me over half an hour of speedy climbing and clambering to reach the top, around the same time as I get first sight of the sun. First it lights only the uppermost rim of the western peaks, then slowly pours itself over the edge and down their sides until the whole valley is drenched in golden light. From the highest point I can see a single rider appear in the distance, herding maybe twenty horses. Damn it! I'd hoped to catch my breath before I had to head back down but if I'm going to arrive back at camp before them, I'll have to hurry up. I jump and bump and almost break my neck scrambling back down the hill to meet them.

I survey the horses as they make their way down the valley. The shepherd moves either side of the group, mopping up any strays and guiding them back in line. I'm looking to see whether any stand out as being larger than the rest. There are certainly a few big ones but there are also many younger foals in the group. I wonder if they might be a good investment. The shepherd is a small man with faintly eastern features and dark, leathery skin. Some of these horses are his but most belong to others who pay him to keep them over the winter months. One of those people is Munarbek, another is Munarbek's friend Bopong. I can see a potential conflict of interest, as Munarbek becomes both adviser and vendor.

I decide to start with one of the shepherd's horses that he's indicated is for sale. A three-year-old male, already bigger than the other three-year-olds and, according to Munarbek, the foal of one of the largest mares on the mountain. This horse will be no good for this terrain and will most likely be sold for meat. I ask Munarbek what he thinks the real value is and he tells me around 32,000 som (around $800). This is a good test of whose side Munarbek is on.

Overall, I'd ideally like to buy no more than four horses. I've got to remember that the point of this exercise is to make money, and the way to do that is negotiate hard, but the problem is that I don't know what the real price of a horse here is other than what Munarbek has told me. I'm going to have to use this negotiation as an experiment and reassess the situation from there.

I decide to test Munarbek's valuation and dive straight in: 'How much for that horse?' The shepherd seems confused. Why do I want to buy his horse? He must be wondering what on earth I plan to do with it; it hasn't even been broken in. It's not as though I could even ride it. Maybe he thinks I'm going to eat it. In any case, some reassurance from Slava is required that my request in genuine, and then he's offering me the horse for 35,000 som. I counter with an offer of 25,000 som but he's not impressed. After a pause he says I can have it for 32,000. I offer 30,000 as my last price. Immediately I regret this: too high too quickly. I should have offered 26,000, or 25,500 even; I've let the moment get the better of me. Of course, he asks for 31,000 and my last option is only to split the difference and pay him 30,500 som ($763). He agrees. I've paid over the odds, I'm sure of that, but I have just bought my first ever horse. I'll call him Charlie because that's what I've just been: a right charlie.

Time to reflect. A bad trade, but it is only one horse. The main thing is that my opinion of Munarbek has changed. I certainly won't be taking his advice again in a hurry. In fact, I may as well just see him as another horse trader – someone to haggle with. So, I ask him, which of his horses are for sale? He starts to point them out but it's hard to see when they are scattered all over the field so I ask him to gather the bigger ones that are for sale together and we'll start a negotiation from there. This, it turns out, is much easier said than done.

The process of catching wild horses is not one that gets any easier with experience, it seems. Bopong is a horseman, no doubt. He fashions a lasso on a stick in no time at all and shows me how simple it is to use: toss, lift, pull and, hey presto, you have yourself a wild horse. The reality is toss, miss and toss again. And again. And again.

Munarbek has chosen one horse that he thinks will sell well in Uzgen even though it is only two years old and unbroken. He thinks it will be a very large horse, just the sort of horse the Uzbeks love. Unfortunately it seems rather reluctant to accept its own suitability for life in the south and actually seems to me extremely adept at manoeuvring the mountain. At least well enough to avoid Bopong's lasso. Time and time again Bopong lifts the lasso only to find no horse attached to the end of it and in doing so, at one point propels himself head first into the mountain mud. I decide that, should this horse ever be mine, I shall name him Steve after Steve McQueen in *The Great Escape*.

Eventually the horses are lined up in front of me in a kind of four-legged beauty pageant. I decide there are three others beside Charlie that fit the bill for Uzgen. Two of them belong to Munarbek and the fourth is the horse that Bopong rode up on, a beautiful skewbald stallion with an acute attitude problem; none of the other horses is able to get within ten feet of him without receiving a good, firm hoof. I've already bought one horse so I need to buy more if I'm going to make this work. Transportation won't be cheap so I'll need at least four horses to spread the cost if I'm going to make a profit.

I decide to start with Munarbek's biggest horse: a large, black stallion with a huge fringe that makes him look a little like Liam Gallagher. Let's call him Liam. Liam is going to cost me 50,000 som ($1,250). He's a strong horse and certainly the largest of the group, but I'm wary of Munarbek now after the experience with Charlie. It's difficult for me to know how much he's worth so I come up with a plan. One thing I can do is compare the horses I can see, so I leave the negotiation with Munarbek to one side and turn to Bopong. How much for the skewbald stallion? Bopong is not a wheeler-dealer in the same way that Munarbek is, and I'm delighted when he comes up with a starting price of 50,000 som. This is probably a fair price for this horse, and what's even better is that it puts Munarbek's opening price for Liam to shame. If this great horse is worth 50,000 som then Liam can't be worth more than 40,000 som.

I try to push Bopong lower. How about 45,000? A 10 per cent reduction from his asking price. No; 50,000 som is his price. I am now even more convinced that he's not trying to exploit me. Maybe I'm naive, but I think I can spot a good man when I meet one, and Bopong is a good man. How about 48,000? No. Alright, Bopong, good man or not you have to give me something here! How about 49,000? There's a long pause before a reluctant Bopong extends his huge shovel of a hand. Deal. As soon as he has finished crushing my much smaller hand, I own the best horse on the mountain, the seven-year-old, piebald stallion for the knock-down price of 49,000 som ($1,225). I'm going to call him Martin. I only hope I can convince Bopong to ride him back down again for me.

Time to go back to Munarbek. If Martin only cost 49,000 som, then his asking price for Liam is starting to look untenable. I put this to him and he shoots Bopong a sharp look. Bopong looks unmoved. I offer Munarbek 40,000 for Liam and 25,000 for the evasive Steve McQueen. He laughs. 'Shall we talk about the real price?' he asks. Now it's my turn to laugh; the games are over, it seems, Bopong has set the tone and we cut to the chase. He wants 75,000 som ($1,875) for the pair, real price. This is a cheap trick. As far as I'm concerned this man is out to get as much as he can for his horses, real price or not. I offer 70,000 for the pair as my final offer and he shakes his head: 72,500? I am unmoved; it's time to stick to my guns: 70,000 som. Final offer. Munarbek looks pensive. I can tell he's happy with the amount but I suspect he doesn't want to lose face in front of Bopong. To be diplomatic I offer him an olive branch: in return for his help returning the horses to Toktogul and finding me a truck to transport them to Uzgen, I will pay 71,000 som ($1,775). Munarbek smiles the broadest smile. He'll go one better: he and Bopong will come all the way to Uzgen with me, just in case I need help. We have a deal and I have four horses for a total price of just under $4,000.

We sit to eat and seal the deal. A plate of horse meat and potatoes is enhanced no end by a jar of Bushman's peri-peri sauce. The shepherd in particular is very curious as to how this flavour has changed the taste of his food. The same food he eats every single day. In fact, he's so enthralled by it that I feel obliged to leave it with him as a gift. Frankly, given how crushingly terrible the flavour of food is generally in Kyrgyzstan, I'm sure it's only a matter of time before Eddie Bushman comes riding up here on a horse with a saddlebag full of the stuff and cleans up.

After a breakfast of noodles, porridge and the obligatory fifteen cups of *chi*, we round up the horses a little more easily than the previous day and discuss who will ride whom back to Toktogul. It is decided that I shall ride Martin and no one will even listen to my protestations. He can obviously sense my hesitancy as I mount him as he immediately turns sharply to test me. I hang on, a little relieved, and resolve to show him who's boss. I do own him now, therefore I am, after all, his boss. Once everyone, including the shepherd's son, has saddled up, we're off again: all cowboys together. I suggest another race to Munarbek but this time I have the advantage. As Martin opens up I feel like I am flying low above the ground. Munarbek is now back on Speedy and is struggling to keep up. I have bought a cracking horse. I start thinking about how I can take him home with me.

Eventually we reach a point on the path where the shepherd's son announces that he has to leave us, and so it falls to me to lead Steve McQueen the rest of the way back to Toktogul. We ride for six hours up and over the two mountain passes back to Bopong's house, where the horses will be washed down and stabled overnight. When we arrive, I suddenly feel the effects of the sun and the saddle and a profound tiredness hits me that I know will take a few good nights' sleep to make up. Unfortunately, I also know that this is not going to happen any time soon. I hit the hay to grab what I can, but the alarm is set for 4.30 a.m.

Eleven

YOU CAN LEAD A HORSE TO . . .

INVESTMENTS:
— **Wine:** $15,218
— **Horses (including transport):** $4,250
IN THE BANK: $33,739

Even before the sun has come up, Bopong and I are leading the horses out from their stables. As we fetch the last horse, the truck comes up the lane, a wheezing, spluttering old Kamaz, a ten-ton relic from the Soviet days. The Soviet Union stopped making these around eighteen years ago so it's at least as old as that. As it backs into the field it lets out a black, tarry belch of smoke that engulfs the horses and me. When the smoke clears, I notice that Martin in particular looks unimpressed with my choice of transport for him.

The driver, a dead ringer for Richard Gere, hops out and takes the $500 I've agreed to pay him for transport to Uzgen. After he's counted the cash (twice), he lowers the ramp at the back so we can begin loading. Unsurprisingly, none of the horses seem at all keen to jump on board so a mixture of blindfolds, disorientation techniques, sticks and carrots are needed to get them in. I'm happy I'm only transporting four horses; the norm is to squeeze fifteen in. That would be entirely unpleasant.

The 300-mile drive to Uzgen takes us through some of the most beautiful countryside I've ever seen: vast green meadows, streaks of red poppies stretching out to meet snow-capped mountains and a crystal blue sky. As we near Uzbekistan the road flattens out and we pass enclaves that, even though they are within the Kyrgyz border, are almost entirely ethnically Uzbek. Even the road signs are in the Uzbek language. This is a strange leftover from Stalin's division of the Central Asian states. He divided the ethnic groupings to reduce their threat to the Soviet regime. There is still unrest here periodically but for now, at least, it is calm.

We stop occasionally for document checks and the police nose around the truck. This is another hangover from the Soviet era. On one stop we get out to stretch our legs while the police have a good look at Mr Gere's papers. This is a good opportunity to check that the horses are doing alright. My one priority at the moment is to ensure that they arrive safe and sound in Uzgen. I can see through a crack in the back that my four beasts have produced four fresh piles of dung. On the basis that you only go when you're comfortable, I'll take it as a good omen.

We get back in the cab only to discover that we have a problem: the truck won't start. Incredibly, Mr Gere decides we should give it a push start; more incredibly still, a group of local bystanders help us; and most incredibly of all, between us we manage to push-start a ten-ton truck with four horses in it, and continue on to Uzgen.

The truck pulls into a large common on the outskirts of the town, opposite the market, just before sunset. My plan is to unload the horses and find somewhere to feed and water them and after that I'll find somewhere for us to sleep. The truck's arrival has drawn quite a crowd and people gather round to inspect the cargo. I've not even unloaded the second horse before questions start firing in about how much I want for the first one. The crowd are all men and they remind me strangely of the farmers who used to come into my grandfather's pharmacy in the west of Ireland when I was a child helping out in the holidays. I've read before how much shared DNA there is between Central Asian and Celtic peoples, and as I look at these all-too-familiar faces I can easily believe it.

Common ancestry or not, it isn't long before the throng is growing rowdy and demanding prices from me. I try to restore some order and I select one of the horses. Martin is the clear star of the troop so I push him forward. A fat man in a white T-shirt steps up to the plate demanding to know how much I want to sell him for. It feels a bit strange selling this horse that I've only just bought. We haven't really had a chance to get to know each other yet.

I tell the man that I want 70,000 som ($1,750) for Martin but he offers me only 26,000 som. That's around half what I paid. These men are obviously speculators seeing what bargains can be picked up before market day. If they can convince me to sell cheap then they can make a quick profit tomorrow. I'm not playing this game; I've got four good horses and I'd rather hold out to take my chances tomorrow at the market. I ask Slava to explain to them that the horses are not for sale today and I'll see them tomorrow. The fat man is not happy. 'I'll buy that horse from you tomorrow for 25,000 som,' he gladly tells me, before he turns his back on me and walks away.

Munarbek and Bopong are not from this part of the country and are worried about the Uzbeks that we've encountered here. The town always hosts a fair on the eve of the horse market and tonight all these men will be drinking vodka. Lots of vodka. My plan is to sleep out here on the common with the horses but Bopong thinks this will only invite drunken visitors in the middle of the night who may even decide that it is time for a negotiation. With vodka inside them they may not take no for an answer. We agree that it would be better to find a more secluded spot, so we lead the horses further out of town to a field that is hidden behind a line of trees, away from the road. While Bopong feeds the horses, Munarbek and I collect wood and start a fire. Munarbek produces a bottle of vodka and we sit and drink while the horses stand by.

This is a good opportunity to pick the boys' brains and get some tips for how to do well in a horse market. Bopong says that there must be people who have made money on their first trip to the market, but so far he's yet to meet one. This isn't exactly the kind of constructive advice I'm looking for. Munarbek explains that the traders that I met earlier today will be there again tomorrow and they will gang up to try to break me. The horse market is a kind of Dutch auction in that the price of the horses will fall as the day goes by. The reason for this is that most business is done in the morning when the farmers come in to buy horses. The traders realize that if you are still there after midday then you must be desperate to sell and they'll take advantage of you. Munarbek is sure that the gangs will try to engage me in pointless negotiation to try to waste my time, keep me there until the real buyers have left and force me to sell cheap.

This all sounds fairly scary. Munarbek is worried for me, too. I must stay firm and hold my nerve. I must also respect the traditions of the market. There is a customary way that negotiation is conducted here that the locals will exploit to make things even more difficult for me. When a negotiation begins, both people take each other's hands in a firm handshake. Offer and counter-offer are made but it is considered rude to break off the handshake before a deal is reached. If I make you an offer then I try to make you shake on the deal. If you do not accept my offer then you let your arm go limp and therefore the handshake is no good. Instead, you make your counter-offer and try to shake my hand, and if I am not happy then I make my arm go limp. Whatever happens, you must not take your hand away. The result of this is that a negotiation can take a long time as offer and counter-offer go back and forth. The technique that the gangs will use is to pose as serious buyers but only offer me very low prices and then only slowly increase each offer until I either have to sell below fair value or am eventually given no choice but to lose face and break off the handshake. The killer in all this is that if there is a genuinely serious buyer standing by then he can't interrupt our negotiation; he must wait until the conclusion of the first negotiation, by which point he may have already left. This is how they waste time and this is how you can be left with unsold horses in the afternoon. It all sounds very daunting.

I am utterly knackered. I thought I was knackered yesterday, but after driving halfway across Kyrgyzstan to come here, being battered by today's confrontation with all those traders and now sleeping by the side of the road in a field next to a farting horse – I've got to say it's getting about as tough as it can get. But tomorrow at dawn I will find out whether I can hack it as a horse trader.

*

Despite Martin's farting and in some small part thanks to Munarbek's vodka, I sleep well for the four hours before it is time to get up and head down to the market. It is important to arrive early in order to secure a good spot. It is barely 5 a.m. and already the street is alive not just with horses but all manner of livestock. As I lead Martin and the others up the road I am passed by an estate car containing half a dozen goats. Already the speculators from yesterday are here and even before I reach the walls of the market area they are trying to weaken my resolve with their offers of derisory prices for the horses. The market square, walled on all sides, feels every inch like a gladiatorial arena as I enter and tether my four horses to a railing near the centre.

Time to make sure I've got all my figures straight in my head. I'll need to be able to work out profit margins on each horse quickly once the market is under way. I've paid a total of $3,750 for four horses, which breaks down as follows:

MARTIN: 49,000 som ($1,225)

LIAM: 45,000 som ($1,125)

STEVE: 26,000 som ($650)

CHARLIE: 30,500 som ($763)

If I can make a decent mark-up on this lot, even a normal retail 30 per cent (after absorbing transport costs), then I could walk away with a tidy $1,500 profit in my pocket. Not bad for a couple of days' work.

The first hour passes with a flurry of speculators coming and checking the horses. The offers fly in and, as with yesterday, they are low. I'm beginning to fear that prices here in Uzgen may actually be even lower than in the mountains near Toktogul. I decide that advertising Steve McQueen may draw in some business so I untether him and lead him around the market area. It works. There's interest from a man I haven't seen before and he takes my hand. I give him my asking price of 34,000 som ($850), 30 per cent more than I paid. The offer comes back as 16,000 som ($400). I counter with a small reduction to 33,000 som but the counter comes back only 16,100. I notice the man is now being advised by two of the men whom I met in the field when I arrived yesterday: speculators. This is exactly what Munarbek warned me about. It may be taken as poor form but I have no qualms in breaking off the handshake with this timewaster and getting back to the other horses.

A crowd has started to gather around my star horse, Martin. There's no doubt he's a draw and, as long as I have him here, I can use him to bring in potential punters. Any request for a price on him I refuse: 'He's not for sale,' I announce. One of the men enquires about Liam. His friend points out that Liam clearly has a problem with his rear left leg. I hadn't noticed it on the mountain but now he does look a little stiff. I've no idea if this is serious or not. The man offers me 20,000 som, half of what I paid. Slava counsels me not to ask for too much as I will scare him off. I'm stuck, what am I going to do? The clock is ticking, I haven't sold any horses yet and here's an opportunity to offload one that may have a serious problem with its leg. Even if I have to take a hit on this horse, I can make the money back on the others. The main thing now is to start selling. I go for a break-even asking price of 45,000 som. The man takes me by the hand and grins at me with the two teeth that he still has. He knows he's got me in a corner; it's just a question of how bad he's going to make it for me.

We begin the process of offer and counter-offer. Each time he makes an offer I let my arm go limp and he nearly tears it from its socket. Every time I ask him for more, he makes a huge theatrical gesture of walking away but at the same time keeping his handshake in position. So it goes until the distance between his offers and my asks begins to narrow. By now a huge crowd has gathered and is pushing in so close I can feel the breath of at least five other men, and the noise of their cheers and laughs is deafening. They are all willing the deal to reach its conclusion; I can feel that there is no way they will let us leave now without reaching an agreement. One of the men actually reaches out and seals our handshake with his own hand; he joins in to encourage us to reach some middle ground. The bids are now only 1,000 som apart and we're arguing over pennies but it's still adversarial and I don't want to be the one who concedes the last offer. The argument over pennies draws more cries and hollers from the crowd than the bigger bids had earlier, and as we finally conclude our negotiation at 32,500 som ($813), we both firm up our arms for a final flamboyant handshake and the crowd are cheering like they would a last-minute goal at Cup Final. This is their entertainment, their theatre. I've put on a show for them and they appreciate it. I have sold a horse, I have lost around $312, and yet my heart is racing as though I have just made a fortune.

I'm still reeling from this experience when he comes back looking for a price on Charlie. I'm struggling through the tiredness to remember what I even paid for Charlie and that I probably paid over the odds for him. The crowd are following in tow and the man is taking my hand for another negotiation. Slava is translating for me all the time but the pressure is even taking its toll on him, as he keeps talking to me in Russian. Many of the traders are shouting in Uzbek, which Slava can't understand either. I'm trying to ensure that I get at least 25,000 som for Charlie, a moderate loss but probably fair in the circumstances. The handshakes go back and forth and I manage to get the price up from an opening offer of 15,000 som to a more respectable 22,000 som. I realize I'm being taken to the cleaners here, but what can I do? If I don't sell the horses it's not as though I can take them to China with me. I'm backed into a corner and I feel like I have no option but to accept 22,000 som ($550) for Charlie and free myself up to concentrate on the remaining two horses. Another $213 hit to the coffers; this is going very badly indeed.

The market is now reaching its busiest as the time approaches 10 a.m. This is when most of the serious buyers should be here and so it's time to introduce Martin to the market. The problem now is that I am no longer the best show in town. Other deals happening on the other side of the market have drawn the attention of the crowd and my patch has become very quiet. Munarbek approaches me and implores me to 'advertise' Martin. He wants me to get him saddled up and ride him up against the other horses in the pen in the way they do when they play Ulak Tartysh. Munarbek thinks this will impress the crowd and get them flooding back over here to bid for Martin. This seems like a coherent enough plan but I'm terrified at the prospect of riding a crazy stallion into a confrontational environment with my, let's be honest, moderate riding skills. My heart is telling me to stop being such a coward and just go for it, but my head is calculating that it will almost certainly result in serious personal injury.

Bopong steps up to the plate. He will ride Martin. As the horse used to be his, it seems logical that he's best placed to put on a good show. Up he gets, and begins to gallop Martin towards the crown before pulling him back hard. Martin raises onto his hind legs and spins back toward us taking only a step or two to reach a gallop again. There is immediate attention and new buyers whom I haven't seen before begin to move over to where Bopong is now climbing down from a very sweaty Martin. The veins along his neck and legs are pumping, his muscles are full of blood and the sweat is glistening on him; he is looking like a very fine horse indeed. The plan seems to have worked and one of the buyers is quick to take my hand.

Now let's rewind for a moment. Martin cost 49,000 som ($1,225) and as my best horse I would expect him to reach 60,000 som, although in the current situation I'd settle for 55,000. The offer I get for this fine-looking beast standing before me in his prime? 31,000 som. I break away, disgusted. I don't care about losing face, that's just rude. But straight away another man takes my hand, 32,000 som. So I do it again and a third man takes me into negotiation at 35,000 som. Now this is at least a starting point. I counter with a 55,000 but the negotiation never gets us beyond 37,000 som. It's dawning on me that I'm now seen as a soft touch and there is no way back. I am the outsider and, to everybody local, I'm easy prey.

Another potential buyer steps up to ask if he can try Martin out, like a test drive. I don't see why not. Slava reassures me that this is normal behaviour and possibly an indication that the man might be a serious buyer. The buyer jumps up onto Martin and delivers a sharp kick to the haunches. No surprise, then, when Martin takes off like a rocket. He spins him round again and back at full pace, right past where we are standing, towards another couple of riders.

He rides Martin straight into the side of one of the other riders' horses, forcing both to rear up. The other rider counters by spinning his horse round and urging him round the back of Martin and up onto his backside. The weight of the other horse forces Martin to check his step and then the third rider crashes into him, letting out a shrill, excited scream to incite the horses further. It is brutal to watch. I try to step in to put a stop to it but Slava grabs hold of me: I'll be hurt and, besides, this is their way. This is how Ulak Tartysh is played. This will help sell the horse. This may be true, but I can't bear to watch; it is too distressing. When it is eventually over, the man rather sheepishly disappears back into the crowd; he was no serious buyer. At least Martin looks unhurt, unmoved even. Maybe he even enjoyed it – who can tell?

There are no more serious offers and the time has moved past noon. A few of the speculators begin to come in with even lower offers than they had made yesterday. As promised, the fat man reappears offering to buy Martin for 25,000 som. I tell him he can have Steve McQueen for 25,000 som or he can just sling his hook. He hangs around like a vulture. I need to think through my options. One thing is sure: the market is over for me.

The first thing that has to be done is to load the remaining two horses up and head down the road to where a friend of Munarbek's lives. The horses can be fed and watered there and we'll have a bed for the night. I can honestly say that I have never been as tired as I am right now and the offer of some space and time to think is the best thing I've heard all day. So we load Martin and a sorry-looking Steve McQueen back onto the truck that they'd hoped never to see again and drive another 50 miles south to a farm on the outskirts of Osh. The horses are put out into the field and Munarbek, Bopong, Slava and I discuss what can be done over dinner.

I would love to keep Martin but the quarantine laws between the EU and Kyrgyzstan forbid it, so he has to stay here. I could send the horses back to Toktogul with Bopong and Munarbek and they could try to sell them at the market in the autumn when prices are higher. We are discussing how else we can manage the situation when one of the local farmers knocks at the gate. He wants to see the horses. He's heard that they are for sale. I saddle Martin up again and he gets a rather easier test drive this time, trotting up and down the street with a fat old farmer on his back.

The farmer is interested in both horses but the offer is only 45,000 som ($1,125) for the pair. I'm looking at another whopping loss of almost $750 but I think it's now my only option; I'll have to accept. He points at Steve McQueen and says something to Slava with a big laugh. Slava is reluctant to translate it but I force him to. 'This one is only good for meat,' is what he said. Now this is where I go soft. I was determined not to develop any emotional attachment to these beasts but I just can't sell Steve McQueen for meat, no matter the cost, I simply can't. The deal is off. The man is irate; he can't understand it, and is very disgruntled when he gets back in his car and drives off. Slava thinks I'm crazy as that was my last hope. We return to our dinner and eat in silence.

After dinner there is a second visitor to the house: another local farmer who has heard about the crazy stallion that is for sale. I take him out to show Martin and he takes him for a ride. It is clear that this is love at first sight. Before we start negotiating, I show him Steve McQueen as they come as a pair. He is less interested in Steve but says that he could turn out to be a fine big horse with a little feeding. He's happy to agree a price for the pair. He opens with an offer of 50,000; that is 5,000 more than the meat man. Now at this point in events I think Bopong must have decided that he has seen enough because he walks straight over to where I am in clenched handshake with the farmer, undoes my grip and takes the farmer's hand himself. They argue and laugh and argue some more in Kyrgyz for nearly an hour before the discussion concludes with the now familiar flamboyant shake of the hand. Bopong doesn't look happy. He takes me quietly to one side and explains with a pained expression that the best offer possible was 65,000 som ($1,625). This is what the man will pay as a maximum; he is sorry but this is as far as he could make him go.

I feel for Bopong. We have travelled a long way together and had some good fun along the way. He has made a profit while I have made a loss from the same horse but I respect the man who realized that, unless he stepped in, I was going to lose a whole lot more. He secured 65,000 som for the remaining two horses, maybe out of some sense of guilt, but I have no doubt that it was more than I would have been able to negotiate for myself. I have not taken on the horse traders and won by any means. I have been roundly beaten by them. There is a reason why horse traders have a formidable reputation and I have learnt the hard way what that reason is. It has cost me $1,263 to find out.

People often say that trading livestock is hard because one easily forms an attachment to the animal that is painful to break when the time comes to sell it. I have to admit that this was never a concern for me with any of these horses. Maybe, for a moment, I considered Martin as a potential pet, but not for long. As I stand and watch these last two beasts being led away while I clutch 65,000 som in my hand, I am profoundly relieved that they are no longer my concern. This trade has taught me a valuable lesson. Never allow yourself to be backed into a corner in a negotiation; try always to retain the option of a Plan B. If you can't walk away and your adversary knows it, your position is weak and you will always have the lower hand.

Twelve

A LITTLE JADED

LAST TRADE:
— Horses: $1,263 loss
INVESTMENTS:
— Wine: $15,218
IN THE BANK: $36,727

I press on from the failure in Kyrgyzstan and head over the Pamir mountains into western China. Very few vehicles pass along this dusty road other than a few Chinese trucks. They come loaded with scrap metal bound for Chinese factories; they return loaded with Chinese goods for European shops. I'm looking out at the landscape to the east and thinking ahead to what I might trade next on this journey. The mountains rise up high out of the flat tundra to over 16,000 feet and they are, as I suspect they always are, covered in snow; today, against a crisp, blue sky they are simply breathtaking. I think it is vital that the next thing I pick is something easy to transport, something I can always take with me. I can't put myself in the same position I was in with the horses ever again. The scenery goes a long way towards soothing my soul.

The border between China and Kyrgyzstan is a curious affair. The whole of China is on the same time zone, Beijing time. This makes absolutely no sense when you're 3,500 miles to the west of Beijing but this is how the Chinese government have decided to organize things. I suppose it makes organizing things a lot easier if you're in the business of organizing things, which the Chinese government definitely is. Unfortunately, it makes things a lot harder if you happen to be in the west of China, because every morning when you get up it is dark, and then it stays light until 11 p.m. To compensate for this, China's westernmost province, Xinjiang, operates an 'unofficial' time zone. Don't tell anyone in Beijing though, or there'll be trouble.

There are only two passes through the mountains and I am heading through the southernmost one at Irkeshtam. The two borders are separated by a two-and-a-half-mile stretch of no man's land. The road suddenly improves a great deal once we get to the part the Chinese are responsible for maintaining; a clear indication of the relative wealth of the two countries. The only vehicles allowed to cross the pass are trucks, so I have to hitch a lift with a Chinese truck driver. He doesn't really have much say in it as a Kyrgyz soldier forces him to stop. The soldier has a big rifle and he doesn't.

Treading a line between apology and gratitude, I climb up into his cab and we cross the Kyrgyz check point. Then we stop. The Chinese soldiers who man the Chinese side of the Irkeshtam pass operate on Beijing time, so they take their lunch between 1 p.m. and 3 p.m. Two and a half miles down the road where I am sitting, just over the Kyrgyz check point, the guards take their lunch between 1 p.m. and 3 p.m. Because of the ludicrous two-hour time difference between the two countries, this means that I find myself stranded in no man's land in the cab of a Chinese truck for four hours while everyone eats their lunch except me.

When, finally, the clock strikes three for the second time and the Chinese border reopens, we progress to customs. A troop of Chinese soldiers comes running towards the truck and I am nervous until I realize that they only want to help me with my bags. They quick-step to a small hut by the side of the road. Inside the hut, a Chinese officer checks my passport and visa. 'Ireland,' he says, in a way that suggests he might have heard of it before but never really believed it was a real place, like Narnia or Middle Earth. He turns it over in his hand a few times, stamps it and then hands it back to me.

'Ireland?' he asks me.

'Yes.' I'm not sure; am I confirming its existence as a real place, or just my association with it? Surely, I can't be the first Irish man to have crossed the western frontier of China? He nods an impressed kind of nod and smiles; as far as he's concerned, I am. And he saw me first. 'Ireland.' He repeats it again. I bet he can't wait to get home and tell his wife.

GUARD: You'll never guess what I saw today, love – an Irish fella.
WIFE: No, I don't believe you, you'll be telling me you saw an elf next.

The troop of Chinese soldiers quick-steps back to the truck and a couple of seconds later we're over the border into China. The road drops down out of the mountains and in no time we're passing through rocky brown desert. The Taklamakan desert is one of the largest in the world, covering nearly one hundred thousand square miles. Put it against the vast Pamir mountains that I've just crossed and it's easy to see why it took until the thirteenth century for east–west trade to really get going. It wasn't until travellers like Marco Polo first took on the physical challenge of taking goods across to sell that we knew what China had to offer us in Europe, and vice versa. Once this trade route became established, however, it provided the basis for the founding of an extraordinary market town, 50 miles over the border: Kashgar.

Kashgar is possibly the oldest market in the world. I say 'possibly' because it is entirely feasible that someone thousands of years ago established a trading post on the road between Babylon and Ur or Mesopotamia and claimed the title of first market, but you get the point: Kashgar has been here for a long time. So long that this is, in fact, the third Kashgar. The first one got destroyed in a flood; the second disappeared into the desert after some bright spark decided to divert the river; but number three seems to be doing alright. It even boasts the title of largest market in Central Asia. Not bad for a dead-end town in the middle of a desert.

My journey so far has brought me into contact with both new and ancient trade routes, but nowhere compares with Kashgar. Even the name has a mystery and magic about it in the same way that I think Ireland did to the Chinese border guard. Kashgar is the place people told tales about in the fourteenth century. It was, and is, a slice of 'old' China. I've come here to exploit an emerging Chinese middle class and sell them a new product: South African wine. But that's way over in Shanghai. I may be in the same country but it feels like I'm in a different century. This is the extraordinary aspect to China's potential right now. In the West, we're already amazed at its economic development in the last twenty years but, standing here, it strikes me how much more is yet to come.

Xinjiang is one of the few Chinese provinces where the majority of people are not of ethnic Han origin, although the Han are beginning to make some impact in the region. There are generous tax incentives offered to entrepreneurs from the large eastern cities to come out here and start up new businesses, and the outskirts of Kashgar are littered with shiny new factories and warehouses. In time the indigenous Uighur people and their culture will no doubt be squeezed out of existence as Xinjiang is modernized in the same way as Tibet. For now, though, things are in limbo, and Uighur people in the ancient market in Kashgar still sell Uighur products to other Uighurs.

Walking through the market I can see a cornucopia of products on sale. There are fur hats made from wild cats, hessian sacks overflowing with walnuts and whole carcasses of goats hanging from hooks. There are row upon row of boxes packed full of colourful spices: cardamom, turmeric, mustard seed to name a few. There is a stall selling Nike sports socks that stands right alongside another whose rail is draped with hundreds of Islamic prayer mats. Uighur men in brimless hats skirt the market on donkey-drawn traps, their wives adorned in colourful headscarves balanced precariously on the back. They pass along streets filled with sweet-smelling smoke that is drifting over from stalls barbecuing lamb and chicken kebabs. Every stall is covered with a red awning; red is a lucky colour in Chinese culture (it's why I picked red rather than white wine in South Africa) and this is a subtle reminder that, despite very Islamic appearances, these people are still Chinese.

I'm looking, as always, for something I can make money out of. China is in a rush to modernize but there are many aspects of ancient society that are still held dear. There's nothing in the market that strikes me as being valuable enough, though; nothing I can consider trying to make a margin on. The indigenous Uighurs don't appear to have sufficient disposable income to be worth targeting, either. It's the Han Chinese who have the cash in China and what I need to find here is something that's worth taking east. I don't have to look very far. On the outskirts of the market there are streets full of much fancier-looking shops and they're all selling one thing: Xingjian's most valuable resource, the hard, ornamental gemstone jade.

I don't know the first thing about jade so if I'm going to seriously consider investing some money in it I have to learn fast. How do you go about buying something you know nothing about? Get advice. I'd proved in Kyrgyzstan that it doesn't make sense to venture alone into an unknown market.

It's cheaper to pay upfront for good advice than to pay afterwards for investing badly. So I contact the only man I know in Kashgar, John Hu. When I had been thinking I was going to bring horses to China, I'd found John's café online. John helps tourists in this part of China get visas and organize logistics, so I'd emailed him for advice. The change in Chinese quarantine rules made bringing horses to China impossible but, as I'm in town, I thought it might be a good idea to look him up and ask him if he knows anything about jade.

John suggests that a good place to meet is his friend's jade shop. John is pretty tall for a Han Chinese at over six feet and, rarer still for a Han Chinese, he was born in Kashgar. This is probably what has enabled John to become a man of such influence here. Of course he knows lots about jade; he's Chinese and all Chinese people know about jade. His friend's shop is a small, glass-fronted shop much like a high-street jeweller's back home. There are all kinds of jade: different colours, some carved, some still in raw pebble form, all being displayed behind glass cabinets.

I suspect John's friend thinks I'm a genuine punter. He's very happy to spend an hour chatting and talking me through the various jades he has for sale. He explains to me the hundreds of ways that fraudsters will try to sell me fake jade. Too much red on the white jade makes it look too perfect so you can tell it's a fake. An acrid smell when you rub it against glass means it's a fake. A lack of translucency when you shine a bright white light on it means it's a fake. It quickly becomes clear that I have a problem. How am I going to avoid buying a fake?

John's friend does his best to convince me that this shop is a good solution to my predicament. I can't blame him for trying, but I am convinced that the fewer middlemen I go through, the better deal I will get. All the jade in Kashgar actually gets mined 300 miles away, across the desert in Hotan. John, unsurprisingly, knows someone there who can help me. I like John. He seems to think it very funny that I want to buy jade as I'm not Chinese, and at the same time he seems genuinely concerned that I might be ripped off. He makes me promise that I will meet up with his friend in Hotan before I buy anything there. He'll call him.

The drive from Kashgar to Hotan is an eight-hour dusty drive through the edge of the barren, brown, featureless Taklamakan desert. The only respite along the way is the town of Yarkand. Either side of Yarkand, the road is busy with hundreds of donkey carts carrying people and their goats to and from the market. The town itself is bustling with people trading; a smaller version of what I'd seen in Kashgar. Despite its remoteness, this is a trading society, and the Uighur farmers are busy buying and selling livestock. The scale of the trade that goes on here is small, but trade is prevalent nonetheless. There is little evidence of Han Chinese influence in this part of the Taklamakan but then a few miles down the road we see an enormous cement factory being built; the Han are coming. When I reach Hotan, I am reminded immediately of Kashgar and its modern, brutish architecture. There is money here.

I am meeting John's friend, Mr Chen, at 9 a.m., which really means 11 a.m., because everyone in Hotan is on the 'unofficial' time, two hours ahead. Tonight is the European Cup Final and this year, rather uniquely, it involves two English teams and my team, Manchester United, are one of them. There is one thing you can be absolutely sure about wherever you go in the world: there will be a bar, probably an Irish bar, showing the football. I am absolutely sure of this. Unfortunately, I am also absolutely wrong. There are no bars in Hotan.

Having tried every restaurant, shop and internet café in town without any success, I arrive back at the restaurant near my hotel, which I am disappointed all over again to find is still not showing the football. The restaurant is empty except for a private side room where a rowdy crowd of men are tucking into a feast of Chinese food and a couple of bottles of Johnnie Walker. A pre-football drink, perhaps? Actually no, and after a few whiskies my new friends convince me to give up the search. Not even they have satellite telly here, and if anyone is going to have it, they are.

These guys are the new breed of Han Chinese that are taking over Xinjiang. One is from Shanghai and owns a silk factory in town; another is from Beijing and is the vice-president of a digger manufacturer with a huge plant in town employing over five hundred people. They get together every week for a good old knees-up, and tonight's the night. While we polish off the last of the food and the whisky, a group of teenage Uighur boys come up to the window and bang loudly on the glass. Once they have our attention, they make a series of insulting hand gestures at us, and run off. This is a sign of how much the Han are liked here and I can't help but wonder why anyone would come to live in the middle of a desert where everyone hates you. Then the bill arrives. Twelve of us have eaten a feast of meat, fish, vegetables, rice and noodles, not to mention drunk our own body weight in whisky and beer, and the bill is still less than $6 per head. There, it seems, is my answer.

I wake in the morning with a dry mouth and a throbbing head, feeling every bit as though I have been up into the wee hours celebrating Manchester United winning their third European Cup. A quick check of text messages from friends and family back home reveals that in actual fact, albeit inadvertently, I have been doing exactly that. This goes some way to making me feel a little better, but not enough. My alarm clock goes off at 8.30 a.m. and I leap out of bed, have a rapid shower, run down, and grab a quick breakfast on my way out of my hotel to meet Mr Chen. It is not until I arrive at the meeting point, under the Mao statue in the main square, that I remember my clock is still working on 'official' Beijing time and I now have a two-hour wait.

Hotan's Mao statue is the largest in China and, so I suppose, the world. It's unlikely that anyone else has built a bigger one. Mao stands triumphantly, looking out over an enormous square. I'm standing right in the middle of it waiting for Mr Chen. After a while I'm accosted by a group of local youths with some shiny stones that they say is jade but I suspect isn't. To kill some time I start to practise a bit of haggling; at the very least I can find out what their prices are. I have, it seems, begun haggling with strangers for fun.

I'm happily amusing myself when over comes a middle-aged Chinese man in a red football shirt that looks like a Manchester United replica. While I'm wondering if he watched the match last night, he starts looking at the stones the boys are hawking. 'Fake. Fake. Fake.' He takes each stone, gives it the briefest of once-overs and hands it back to the boy with his rebuke. One stone makes him pause; he hands it to me. 'What do you think?'

I can't tell; it looks like jade, but what do I know? And who is he anyway?

'This one is good,' he says, taking it back and examining it carefully. 'How much?' He asks the boy.

The boy asks for $200 but with only minimal haggling from the man he drops to $20. 'Fake.' The stone is handed back to its owner. He turns back to me. 'If it was genuine, he would not have dropped his price so easily.' Wow! This guy knows his jade. This is Mr Chen.

'Come with me. Let's have tea and find out what you are looking for.' I follow Mr Chen to his car, a new, gold-coloured Toyota Corolla, and we drive to a café on the other side of town for a cup of tea. I tell him all about my journey so far, the trades and the countries visited, and I put it to him that I think there could be some profit in Hotan jade if I were to take it east with me. Mr Chen agrees. He offers his services for a couple of days to try to find me a piece of jade; $100 should cover his time and expenses. If last night's prices are anything to go by, around here that equates to fifteen nights out. Nevertheless, given the potential to get seriously burnt buying a fake, I'm happy with the deal.

Mr Chen suggests that the best place to start the search is as close to the source as possible, which means heading down to the river where the jade is mined. We drive off in his shiny new Toyota and in around twenty minutes we're turning off the road onto a rocky track that leads down to the riverside. The Toyota bumps and jumps over rocks and potholes, and piles of stones on either side of the road bear testament to earlier speculative diggings. Then the vast expanse of the 'river' comes into view ahead of us.

*

The Hotan River is nearly 1,000 feet across when at full flow, which is some time around July. The glacial melt from the Pamir mountain range comes crashing down and for two months either side of that it is a wide, fast-flowing river, but for the other eight months of the year there is no water at all. The long, cold winters hold the snow at the top of the mountains, so the river below completely dries up. What remains is what I can see today: a vast, flat expanse of dry stones. This is the cue for thousands of jade miners to get to work.

The miners work in collectives of around fifteen men to a mine. They pick a patch of river bed around 30 feet by 6 feet and they start digging with shovels and picks to a depth of around 6 feet. The digging involves four men in the hole turning over each rock individually and throwing it out to the next man, who passes it in turn to the next man. If a stone turns out to be jade it is kept to one side to be sold; this is rare. Most stones are worthless and simply get thrown on the discard pile.

Once the whole patch has been dug down 6 feet, the sides are reinforced with bigger rocks and the digging continues on the patch next door. This time they dig down 12 feet. The process continues like this, creating a series of large steps deep down into the ground of the river bed, and all the time the pile of discarded worthless stones gets even larger. As I'm standing on the edge of this particular dig and looking across the dusty expanse of river bed I can see a hundred similar mines and there are more out of sight up and down this particular three-mile stretch where jade is found.

Mr Chen leads me down into the mine to see if these men have found anything today. This mine is on its fourth step so the digging is happening around 30 feet below where we are standing. The stones are being passed up the human chain from man to man and are all finding their way onto the worthless pile. Mr Chen asks them if they have anything to sell, but they have nothing. The man at the top explains that they found a small stone last week which they've already sold. Before that, they had a three-week dry spell during which they found nothing. I ask him how they keep going when they find nothing and he laughs – one day they might find a big stone and they will all be rich.

This is the dream that keeps this town alive. Media reports suggest that the jade reserves of the Hotan River are entering their final phase and in five years' time there will be none left. This has pushed up the price of jade; it's now worth over ten times what it was five years ago. The knock-on effect is that more and more speculators come every year when the waters recede and the river offers up a fresh bed and the potential for new spoils.

Now, for the first time, diggers and machinery are being used, bankrolled by investors from Beijing and Shanghai. The price of jade is now so high that it's worth a Beijing businessman throwing $20,000 or $30,000 at a speculative dig complete with JCBs; if he turns up a couple of decent finds he can easily triple his money. The exponential effect is that there is only a short-term future for this kind of mining; come back here in five years and all you will see is a vast, dusty river bed of worthless stones.

Down the river bank is a tented settlement where the miners live for the eight dry months. They return to their families in various corners of China for the few short months when the waters return and digging is impossible again. In the camp everyone has some jade to sell. Mr Chen advises me to be on my guard as this is a market flooded with fakes. I reassure him that I am in his hands and wouldn't dream of buying anything without checking with him first.

We move through a crowd of miners in the middle of the camp who are selling their finds. The men hold stones on their palms, out flat in front for all to see. Everyone seems to be both buyer and seller, and they move around each other picking up and scrutinizing each other's stones. Mr Chen looks at stone after stone; he can clearly tell what is good and what is bad. He passes me a stone and asks what I think of it. I am wrong, missing that it is a fake. Thank God he's here.

Mr Chen finds a man with a stone that he likes the look of. He turns it over and over several times. The stone is a white jade pebble that is typical of Hotan. This river throws out all kinds of jade but the most prized is its white jade, often called 'mutton fat' because of its milky texture. The bigger the piece, generally the more valuable it is, but there are other qualities to look out for: a bit of reddish brown discolouration on part of the stone is particularly treasured, and the really big money comes if the white part of the stone is unblemished. A fist-sized pure white lump with no blemishes and perhaps a corner of red 'skin' could easily fetch upwards of $50,000. Mr Chen buys this thumb-sized pebble for around $100. This one is not for me; there is nothing for me here.

Halfway back to town is a roadside jade market. Mr Chen and I park the car and cross the road into another throng of men peddling their stones. There are even more fakes here than there were on the riverside. We pass under a sign that crosses the entrance to the market. The sign is in Chinese, Uighur and, for the first time since I arrived in China, English. It reads: 'Foster the correct competitive spirid and oppose trickay to promote the jademarket (sic).' I'm glad I have Mr Chen to help me with any residual 'trickay'.

The market is laid out in three rows of Uighur men sitting behind metal basins that resemble kitchen sinks filled with water and jade stones. The stones look a little like ornamental fish beneath the water. The idea is to add lustre to them and make them look a little bigger than they are. Mr Chen will not be so easily fooled. There are hundreds and hundreds of stones for us to look at and we pass from basin to basin, Mr Chen picking out several interesting looking stones, sometimes asking a price, sometimes not, but every time discarding the stone back into the water. On the one hand it's incredibly frustrating that we aren't finding anything good enough to buy but on the other it's terribly reassuring that Mr Chen is going to such lengths to find the right stone. We find nothing by the time the market traders are beginning to pack up for the day around 5 p.m. Beijing time. What a neat trick: start at 9 a.m. Xinjiang time and finish at 5 p.m. Beijing time. That's what I call making the most of the two time zones.

Mr Chen has seen enough today and wants me to make a decision as to how much I want to spend. I have been deliberately vague until now, always saying that I am flexible depending on the stone, but I can see from the range of stones that we've seen today I need to help him focus the search a little. I'm budgeting no more than $5,000, I tell him. In that case, he tells me, I have a choice to make.

Do I want a small pebble that has no flaws and a good skin, the kind of stone that should never be carved? This kind of stone will be worth more in the east, no doubt, but the margin will be small: 10 to 15 per cent. Or, do I want a larger stone that will certainly have some flaws but could be carved by a master cutter, at some extra cost, in one of the ancient carving towns such as Suzhou, near Shanghai?

If I go for the bigger stone then its true value won't be known until after it has been carved. Some people have made five or six times their investment this way while others have found that the stone is heavily flawed on the inside, or the cutter has done a bad job, and lost money. Well, you can guess which option I like the sound of. Tomorrow we'll look for a big rock.

The next day, I take advantage of the extra couple of hours in bed and I meet Mr Chen at around 11 a.m. for tea at his friend's jade shop, which is almost identical to the one I'd met John at in Kashgar. The road is one long line of shops, all selling much the same thing. Any significant finds on the river tend to be whisked away to here immediately. We're waiting in the hope of intercepting one of these deliveries before they reach the shop owners. We don't have to wait long.

A large Uighur man whom Mr Chen recognizes as a dealer pulls up in an old Datsun Cherry. I'm not surprised he recognizes him as the man has a bald head and a two-foot-long beard that looks as though he bought it from a joke shop. We go straight over to him and, after a few quick words from Mr Chen, the man opens his boot to reveal two metal basins full of freshly mined jade. The familiar process of scrutinizing the stones begins, except this time Mr Chen finds two particular stones genuinely interesting. He suggests we take them inside for a proper examination.

The first stone is huge: eight kilos, the size of a loaf of bread. Mr Chen strongly recommends that I break my budget and buy it. However, it's going to cost at least $30,000 and so I'll have to pass. I'm in an unfamiliar market and that kind of investment could seriously derail me if it turned sour. I'm certainly on the lookout for a final double or nothing trade but I'm not sure this is it. When I'm ready to head for home, I want to put everything I've made into one last deal, but it'll have to be something so convincing that I simply can't say no to it. And this expensive lump of rock isn't it.

The other stone is more to my budget and, at 3.5 kilos, it still looks pretty hefty. Mr Chen says it's a good bet. There are some flecks on the surface that could be an indication that the stone is not pure white underneath but Mr Chen uses his torch to pass a strong white light through it. The stone has a good translucency to it and Mr Chen believes that the flecks are only superficial. The initial asking price is as large and as ridiculous as the man's beard: nearly $10,000.

What would usually follow here is a long protracted negotiation: I say $3,000, he says $8,000, and so on until I pay slightly over the odds, only to find out further down the road that I was ripped off. At least, after the experience with the horses, that is how I'm beginning to feel.

However, Mr Chen is most definitely on my side and he and the bearded man exchange some harsh words for a couple of minutes. Mandarin always sounds harsh to me. Mr Chen turns to me. The asking price is now nearer to $5,000. Good work, Mr Chen. I'm now ready to weigh in with a fresh round of negotiations and make my offer of $4,000. The poor man doesn't know what's hit him. He's being tag-teamed. No sooner has he been beaten down to a third of his asking price than this cheeky foreigner is asking for more off. Another volley of cross words follows between him and Mr Chen. In my head they're both talking in the voices that Kung Fu masters use in the old John Woo films. I imagine it goes something like this:

CHEN: 'He says he'll only pay $4,000.'

BEARD: '$4,000! We just had an agreement for $5,000.'

CHEN: 'Yes, but it's not me buying it. It's his money.'

BEARD: 'You've swindled me, Chen!'

CHEN: 'What are you going to do about it? $4,000, yes or no?'

BEARD: 'Damn you, Chen, whose side are you on anyway?'

CHEN: 'His.'

BEARD: 'You have betrayed me, Chen, where's your loyalty?'

CHEN: 'He's paying me.'

BEARD: 'Oh, OK then. Fair enough. But $4,000 is still too little anyway.'

CHEN: 'OK, well how about you split the difference, $4,500?'

We agree. $4,500 for a 3.5-kilo lump of Hotan white jade. I have no idea what I've just done and I have no idea how this is going to turn out. Mr Chen's advice is to go to Suzhou, find the best carver that I can afford and get it carved. All being well, he thinks it could reach $20,000 if I find a collector in the east. As I hand over his $100, I pray to God he's right. What I do know is that, unlike a herd of horses, if I don't find a buyer immediately, it's small enough to put back in my bag to try somewhere else. At least I've learnt something.

Thirteen
YES, MASTER

INVESTMENTS:
— **Wine:** $15,218
— **Jade:** $4,643
IN THE BANK: $32,084

I elected to take the train to Shanghai. It would have taken two days less to fly but something about the idea of a fifty-six-hour train journey sounded too romantic to pass up (and it was only $30). The trains are all equipped with sleepers and everyone gets a bed. I thought this was a great opportunity to see the Chinese countryside and catch up on some sleep before I arrived in Shanghai. When I found my sleeper, the bottom of three bunks in a six-bunk compartment, I was just about ready to sleep for the whole fifty-six hours. The strain of the last six weeks, during which I had covered twelve thousand miles, was beginning to take its toll. I unpacked and straight away got my head down. As I fell asleep I wondered what the metal tray beside my bed was for.

At around 6 a.m., people on the train began to stir. So did their lungs. One by one everyone in the carriage began their early morning clean out, coughing and hacking up whatever had grown, collected or congealed in their airways during the night. I soon worked out what the trays were for as every hack was immediately followed by the pinging sound of the reclaimed mucus as it was forcibly expunged into the metal receptacle. There were well over a hundred people in my carriage and I lay in my bunk listening to every one of them. So much for romance.

I did, however, manage a good few hearty kips, and was impressed at the sheer size of China as two and a half days passed by the window. Deserts, mountains, plains, rice paddies and more rice paddies; China has them all. It needs them to feed 1.3 billion people every day. China's one-child policy, introduced in the 1980s, has been remarkably effective in maintaining its population at a sustainable level. What was considered cruel in the Western media was in fact a calculated act of survival on their part. Every possible inch of land I saw from that train was being employed to produce food. It simply couldn't handle another billion mouths to feed.

With around five hours to go, the landscape began to change as we passed through fewer and fewer areas of agricultural use and the conurbation of eastern China became apparent. The buildings got higher and higher and closer and closer together until we were arriving in the outskirts of the fourth-largest city in the world and the economic success story of the new millennium: Shanghai. I could hardly contain my excitement to be here. This was a new China and I had travelled a long way to see it. Now I was here, I wanted to get straight into it. But the wine was still on the sea, and I had a piece of jade to cut; Shanghai would have to wait while I finished the job in hand.

*

Suzhou is a city of 5 million and yet not many people in the West have even heard of it. I hadn't until I went there and, had I not had a 3.5-kilo piece of jade to get cut, I probably never would have either. I arrived on the bullet train from Shanghai which covers the 100 miles between the two cities in a little over half an hour. Western China had been hot, but dry and dusty, so the 80 per cent humidity in Suzhou was instantly tiring. Five minutes outside was enough to leave your shirt wringing wet.

Mr O, owner of a local jade shop in Suzhou was, I figured, a fairly objective person to seek an opinion from. I'd come to ask him who I might talk to about cutting my expensive lump of stone. A funny-looking, short, fat man with a spiky head of black hair, he had his own jade shop, at the back of which he also ran a cultural centre where two actresses and a band of players were rehearsing songs for an upcoming production.

Mr O showed me his jade and I showed him mine. He said he liked my piece but he couldn't be sure of its value until it was cut. This was consistent with what Mr Chen had said in Hotan so I decided he knew what he was talking about, at least. He had a few ideas about who might be interested in cutting it. There were over one hundred cutters in Suzhou and it was vital to find a good one, so I put the jade back in my bag and we jumped on a tuk-tuk to visit his contact.

A quiet, run-down building, down a quiet, run-down turning, off a quiet, run-down street wasn't where I had expected to find a master cutter. The downstairs had no door and the two flights of stairs we climbed smelt strongly of urine. Down a grey corridor that had never seen a coat of paint was a door. I could hear the sound of drills buzzing noisily from behind it. Inside, rows of workers were bent over drills mounted like sewing machines, cutting out stone in the shapes of Buddhas, frogs, dragons and other traditional Chinese iconography. A couple of them looked up for the briefest of moments.

In the office next door was the cutter and his son. Mr O introduced me and I showed the cutter the piece I had brought from Hotan. He passed it immediately to his son. He explained that this was more his son's sort of thing. I hoped this wasn't a slight on its quality. The son turned it over in his hand, passing his long little fingernail over it. It is the vogue in China for men to grow the nail on the little finger to emphasize that their job is not a manual one. He reached inside his pocket for the key to the safe, from which he produced a piece of jade of similar size to mine. It was carved ornately into an image of a Buddha. I was impressed with the skill of the work but I was keen to avoid getting my own piece carved in a religious theme. I thought that this might limit me too greatly when it came to selling, as I was still not sure where my final market for this would be.

Unmoved by my request for another design, the young master explained to me that he was an artist and his artistic opinion was that the piece would be best suited to a carving similar to the one he was showing me. If I liked it and wanted to pursue it, he would charge me 60,000 renminbi (¥), or $10,000, for the work. I knew immediately that even if I had liked it, I couldn't afford it, but I wanted to see how much I could knock him down. I suggested half of that, around $5,000. No way. To complete this work would take many hours in his workshop, and owing to the large size of the piece there were only a couple of his workers who could do it. His best price was around $8,000 and I could take it or leave it. I suppose he had a lot of expensive nail varnish to buy. I doubted very much that any more than $500 of my $8,000 would make it to the sweatshop workers in the room next door. I decided to pass.

When we left, Mr O was rather animated, considerably more animated than I'd seen him before, at any rate. He was very keen for me to go back and take the man up on the offer. I was keen to try somewhere else. Mr O, though, was adamant that I wouldn't be able to find anywhere else. Hang on a minute. This was the same Mr O who had said that there were one hundred cutters in town only an hour ago; something was going on. A little interrogation of Mr O revealed that he had negotiated himself a tidy 20 per cent commission with the cutter. Now he was happy to reduce that to 10 per cent if I went ahead and said yes, which would reduce my price to $7,200. Nice try, Mr O.

This was a warning to keep my eyes open for hidden charges. Even in the West, where we speak the language, we get caught out by hidden costs in the small print. You only have to speak to someone who's taken a budget flight recently and they'll tell you about excess baggage charges, or 'wheelchair fees' even. These charges are everywhere, and that includes the Chinese jade-cutting market. If you're not careful these can eat away at your profits, and right now I simply couldn't afford to be paying anyone unnecessary commissions.

I told Mr O I'd get back to him and in the meantime I'd sleep on it. In reality I packed him off in a taxi and went it alone. A bit of internet searching later and I had the phone numbers for half a dozen top jade cutters in Suzhou, and half a dozen calls later I had half a dozen meetings with half a dozen jade cutters.

I could describe the half a dozen meetings in detail but, believe me, you'd be as bored as I was, and I don't want to inflict that on you. The highlights were that the stone was liked by a few, and actually scorned by a few, more than one cutter saying they wouldn't even waste their time cutting it. The highest price was $17,000, which seemed remarkable considering the stone only cost $4,250. No offer I received was less than $10,000. With one shop left to visit, I was very disheartened, and was even considering taking the uncut rock to one of the jade markets in Shanghai. At this point I'd have settled for making my money back.

Mr Zhao's jade workshop and shop were in a fashionable district of Suzhou and as soon as I arrived I could see with my untrained eye that his work was remarkable. I'd been in several jade shops by now and I hadn't seen anything to rival the quality of stone and workmanship on show here. I waited for him to come down from the workshop upstairs, feeling a little silly to be even considering asking him to cut my stone, which by now I was beginning to doubt a little.

He lit up a cigarette and pushed his rather arty fringe out of his eyes while he turned the stone over. I told him about my route, how I was heading east from here to Taiwan and then Japan. He said that he knew there were many collectors of this kind of jade in Taiwan, he didn't know about Japan. I explained that I wanted to have it cut by the best cutter I could afford so as to maximize my chances of a sale. What could he do with it? On a budget?

He pulled out a stone from his safe about a third of the size. It was carved with immaculate precision to depict a lonely traveller riding a donkey in the snow through a mountainous landscape. The work was of the highest quality; if my stone could look half as good as that, I'd be ecstatic. I suddenly realized how much trust I was putting in the cutter of my stone. If I didn't pick carefully I could return to find that my investment had been downgraded through bad workmanship.

Mr Zhao spoke like a man who had at least mastered the art of circular breathing. And most of what he said, I'd already heard that day. The stone had imperfections that would have to be dealt with. There was no guarantee that inside the stone would be very good. He would need to work around the clock to have it ready in time for my schedule. Despite all this, he could do it for $4,500. This was not a commercial price, he explained, but he wanted to help me because I was a foreigner. He wanted people outside of China to see how jade was a precious gemstone to rival any other, and he wanted people to see how good his designs and the workmanship of his cutters were. He would do it for me and he wouldn't be making anything from the deal. I couldn't believe what I was hearing; at $2,500 less than the next best offer and considering the quality of his work, I didn't even haggle. I left the jade with him and promised to return to collect it in a few weeks.

Jade represents a strange contradiction in modern China. You have only to look at the styles of the carvings that are still the fashion today to see that not much has changed in the last couple of thousand years. Just take Suzhou; it has been the jade-cutting centre for all that time. This is true in much Chinese art; the techniques have modernized but the themes are still the same as they were back during the Ming dynasty. No matter how developed China becomes, people here will still appreciate the same characters and stories as their forefathers. However, China has developed considerably and I'm betting that there's also room for a few new ideas. In fact, I've staked 3,000 bottles of South African red wine on it.

Fourteen
YOUR WISH IS
MY COMMAND

INVESTMENTS:
— **Wine: $15,218**
— **Jade (including carving): $9,214**
IN THE BANK: $27,513

David Lu can make anything. At five foot two, he's the smallest
trader I've come across so far and no amount of spiking his hair
with gel is going to fool me otherwise. He speaks English at a
hundred miles an hour at a pitch that suggests he may have a secret
helium habit. Here in his factory, on a pouring wet day in a grey
industrial estate in Yongkang, he's explaining to me how he came to
make inflatable boogie boards.

A few years ago, David was in the textile business making the
kind of cheap T-shirts that you can buy on the high street for $4 a
pop. One day, in walked an American businessman with a brand
new design. He wanted David to make a boogie board that could
be inflated for surfing and then deflated again for travel. David has
never surfed, in fact David has never even been to the beach, but he
and the American agreed a price and David simply changed his line
of production; no more T-shirts, he was now in surfboards.

I wanted to find something else to buy in China before I left for
the Americas. This should have been a relatively easy purchase.
China is now by far the largest manufacturing exporter in the world

and a good percentage of that finds its way across the Pacific. I considered many things, from toys to toilet bowls, but I thought it a safer bet to look for something seasonal. I would be arriving in Mexico in the height of summer when millions of Europeans, Americans and Mexicans would be hitting the beach, so it made sense to find something in China that could fit into that market. And if that meant I'd have to spend some time at the beach myself to sell it, then that was a cross I'd have to bear.

I had made a tidy profit on coffee and chilli sauce but factoring in the $1,000 loss on the horses, I was only up a little under $2,000 – still a long way short of my target of $100,000. I was putting a lot of faith in red wine – $15,000 worth of faith to be exact – and I'd now committed $9,000 to a lump of jade. I was getting a little twitchy because I was spending more than I was earning but I reassured myself that these were my golden eggs; the key investments that would determine how much money I made overall. And I still had enough money in the kitty to take on one more.

I'd found David through a website called alibaba.com. There are a few websites like this springing up to help buyers from around the world find Chinese manufacturers like David. There are thousands of small factory owners who advertise and if the price is right they can make you anything you want. It puts businesses in contact with each other. I was scanning it to see if I could find somewhere in China that was making inflatable boogie boards because I'd seen them on beaches in the UK the previous summer and I thought they were a great idea. Up popped David's website.

If there's one thing that you can be sure about in China, it's that if someone elsewhere in the world is making something then someone in China is copying it. The country is flooded with copies of everything. Even Coca-Cola isn't safe from rip-offs; there's a product that comes in red cans which looks and tastes like Coke,

The third Kashgar.

Rush hour in Kashgar.

Did you watch the game last night?

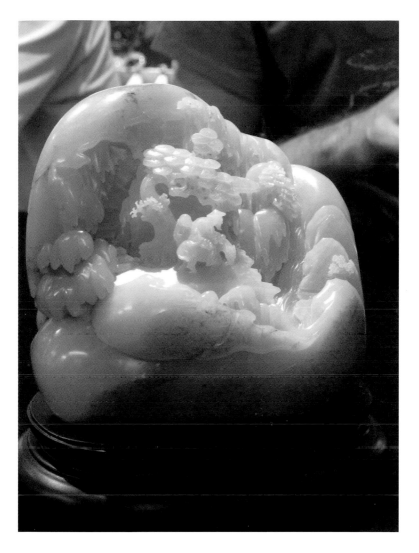

Searching for plum blossom in the snow.

*One of us has just got
a real bargain.*

My future father-in-law?

Bloody sushi.

Now, what to buy in Mexico?

How to make…

… and drink a Margarita.

See how you get on with that one, son.

Who says money doesn't grow on trees?

All photos taken by Kirsty Mitchell, Zoe Page and Clare Gibs

but isn't Coke, yet no one seems to think that's a problem. If you put yourself in the Chinese government's position it makes perfect sense. This guy in some part of China has a factory making rip-off Poka Cola and along comes a big American conglomerate who cry foul and try to enforce copyright law. Guess whose side the Chinese Communist Party are on? Yes, well it makes perfect sense; protect the little man who has started up a factory and you get to be good communists and promote free enterprise at the same time.

It might be interesting for us in the West to look at the Chinese capitalist model. I returned to the UK to find the credit crunch ravaging our economy as we run short of both money and the faith to lend it to each other. The implications for our way of life are yet to fully play out, but one country in the world has stockpiled enough foreign currency to ensure it does not suffer a crunch of liquidity: China. A strong command economy that ensures a solid bedrock for capitalist entrepreneurship may ironically prove to be a new model for how we organize ourselves in the future. Time will tell.

I liked David the minute I met him. Something about this spiky-haired, squeaky-voiced man encapsulated the new Chinese attitude to global economics. Who in the UK would be able to so easily switch from running a textiles factory, sewing garments, to making inflatable surfboards, just like that?

The boards I had so carefully sought out were not the kind of flimsy lilos that you get in most beach-side stalls. These were heavy duty. Rigid when fully inflated and covered in the thick neoprene that you usually find wet suits made from. The idea is that you can replace your usual styrofoam board with them. The problem for most tourists who like to boogie board on their holidays is how to transport the cumbersome thing back home with you at the end of your holiday. No problem for the inflatable; just let the air out and it rolls up to the size of a towel. They were just the kind of thing that I bet would sell well in Mexico, where the waves on the east coast are perfect for surfing.

David didn't have any customers in Mexico. No customers in Europe either. My idea was that he would give me a good deal on the surfboards and I would take them to sell in Mexico. All being well, I would find new customers whom I could then put him directly in touch with for future orders. It was the same tactic that I'd used so effectively on the coffee trade, and he seemed to go for it. He usually sold the boards to his American client for $15 per board. Or so he said. I got him down to $13.50. It was hard work to even get that $1.50 out of him. I had to basically take the whole board apart piece by piece and price each one separately and then add it all back together. I worked out that they only cost him around $9 to make so he was still making his cut. Perhaps I wouldn't be so forthcoming with any new customer details. Anyone who wants to become an inflatable boogie board salesman between China and Mexico, read on, and you'll have all the information you need before David does.

David needed a couple of weeks to get the order of 750 boards filled. I agreed to transfer a 20 per cent deposit to his account right away and the rest of the total cost of $10,182 would follow once the surfboards had been delivered to Shanghai port. I was a little wary of paying any more upfront because, although I liked him, I'd been warned never to put down such a big deposit that it's worth the factory owner just upping sticks and setting up a new factory elsewhere with your juicy deposit in his back pocket. Given the ease with which David had switched industries, switching premises would be a cinch.

I arranged for the shippers to take delivery from Shanghai and I was set. I had around five weeks before my surfboards would be ready to collect from Manzanilla port in Mexico. These windows of time were crucial to my plan; I now had leeway to get back to

Shanghai to collect and sell the wine. After that, I'd find out how the jade carving had gone in Suzhou and, all being well, it and I would be on a flight to Taipei next week.

*

There have always been boom towns. All over the world and throughout history, many of the world's major cities have had their day: London and Paris, after that New York, more recently Tokyo, Hong Kong and Singapore and now, it seems, is the turn of Shanghai, the flagship of China's newly emerging open economy. This new economy had produced a new middle class, and I wanted their money.

I had always suspected that reaching Shanghai would feel like a significant milestone on my trip, and I wasn't wrong. My logic had been that if I'd made it as far as Shanghai then things must have been going at least partly right. When I'd left the UK three months ago, I'd had a clear idea of the route that I would take, but no firm plans of what I'd end up trading. I did, however, always feel that Shanghai was one of the places where I could make some serious money and take a big step towards reaching my target of $100,000. I hadn't ever been to Shanghai before, so this belief was only based on what I'd read and what everyone was saying about the place.

Shanghai's location at the mouth of the Yangtze River meant that it became a significant port when China first opened itself up to foreign trade in the middle of the nineteenth century. By the early twentieth century it was one of the world's foremost hubs for marine trade. It was always more open than the rest of China. Traders from all over the world came to Shanghai to establish their businesses. French, British, Americans and Russians established their own quarters, or concessions, where they lived, and they traded everything from opium to silk. From the window of my hotel in the French concession, I had a bird's eye view of the bustling, tree-lined streets, cafés and boutiques; I had to remind myself that I was in China, not Paris. But I only had to step out of the hotel, turn and look the other way to see exactly where I was.

Just to the east of the river in the centre of Shanghai is Pudong. Some of the bars and restaurants in the older parts of town today have framed photographs of Pudong twenty years ago. Colour photographs taken as recently as 1990 show it as an area of undeveloped paddy fields. Look at Pudong now and you'll see how, in only eighteen years, the Chinese have developed a paddy field into a major global financial centre. The area is covered in skyscrapers, including several of the world's tallest. Looking at it gave me an uneasy feeling; as if somehow time worked differently here. It's as though they just built Manhattan overnight.

This was the kind of spending power that I'd come hoping to tap into. I was no different to all the traders who had come to Shanghai all those years ago to make their fortune. Shanghai was having its day all over again and all around me was evidence of this new middle class of Shanghainese with bags of cash to spend. This was why I'd thought of Shanghai when I'd been in South Africa two months ago. I felt confident that it was the right place to send 3,000 bottles of red wine. Wherever you are, as people get wealthier they start to crave imported products and luxury goods, and my wine ticked both of those boxes.

I had learnt from my experience in Delhi that the way to go was not to waste time targeting bars and restaurants; I simply had too many bottles for that. Instead I decided to take the direct route and go to the distributors. There are around a dozen serious players in the wine distribution sector in Shanghai and I'd contacted a friend called Geoff De Freitas, whose magazine, the *Shanghai Business Review*, has good links with the industry. Geoff had given me email addresses for most of them. My plan was to organize an evening of wine tasting and invite all the distributors to come along. I'd found the perfect place at a swanky wine club in the wealthiest part of Shanghai where all-gated mansion houses are, called Vino Venue.

Vino Venue has a unique approach to marketing wine. The proprietor, Carol Lee, has imported some shiny new chrome-and-glass dispensing machines from Italy. You put your credit card into the slot and choose the size of glass you want and then the machine dispenses the wine. The Venue chooses a selection of wines to showcase every week and its members can come down and sample them by the glass. If they like a wine then the hope is they'll buy a bottle or, better still, a case. I needed to find someone who would buy fifty cases.

The turnout was a little disappointing. Around forty people had made the effort but they were mostly club members who'd only come out of curiosity. There were also two representatives from the distributors and a couple of buyers for restaurant chains, which was encouraging. I did a short introduction to the assembled crowd about my trip so far and the wines that I'd brought from South Africa, and then answered questions while everyone had a taste. I took a lot of questions about the trip and a few about the wine.

For quite a few years I have done a bit of training for bankers and accountants from some of the bigger firms in the City, so I was well used to standing in front of this many people and answering questions. What was strange was to be answering questions about myself. It's one thing explaining again how the dividend valuation model works; quite another to explain why I'd chosen to quit my well-paid job and trade my way around the world.

I survived the cross-examination from the floor, although the Chinese punters who had fronted up gave me a mixed reception. There is a wine snobbery that has sprung up here and some of the comments I heard were a little surprising. 'South Africa doesn't have the culture to make wine. Only France makes good wine,' was my particular favourite; a quote that could have come straight from *Revue du Vin de France* itself. Bearing in mind that the two wines were fairly simple, accessible reds – in fact the Arniston Bay was fruity to the point of tasting a bit like a soft drink – I was amazed to hear people describe them as 'smoky', 'spicy' and even 'oaky'. One thing was clear: the Chinese people who had come to my wine evening liked to sound as though they knew a lot about wine, but most of them didn't. I wasn't too surprised, considering how new wine is to China – you don't have to think back very far to remember when people in the UK were drinking Blue Nun and Liebfraumilch.

It's interesting being in a market that seems to be following a pattern you have seen before. Of course, it's common for economists to look at past experiences to try to predict future trends, so what lessons can be learnt from how the UK wine industry developed that can be applied to the Chinese experience? German wines that used to be popular in the UK were very easy to drink and drew in a lot of new wine drinkers. Gradually people became more ambitious and their tastes expanded to include more sophisticated wines; this opened the floodgates and wine sales have increased year on year for the last twenty-five years.

The Chinese wine industry is now working hard to build a solid base of wine drinkers using the same tactics: establish wine as a cultural norm rather than something for the rich by importing easy, unpretentious wines. There are only 60 million people in the UK and there are 1.3 billion in China; if the Chinese market takes off in the same way then some people are going to get very rich indeed.

Despite the mixed reviews, I did manage to set up a couple of meetings with some of the people I had been targeting. The most promising were Jon Benn, a former star of the old Bruce Lee movies who was now a buyer for a chain of restaurants called Malone's, and an Australian distributor called Michael Lee who was looking at expanding his list to include South African wine. There was also a long shot, a junior buyer for one of the big firms, Aurélie Mazella, who liked the Rozier Bay but would need to show it to her boss before we could take it any further. I agreed to meet with Michael again tomorrow and Jon told me to visit his bar manager to discuss how much wine he needed right now. Aurélie said she'd call me in the afternoon.

I couldn't help but notice that all these 'players' in the market were not Chinese. This is still a market dominated by people from wine-producing countries. Australians, French and Americans are leading the sale of imported wines in China right now, cashing in on their invaluable know-how and their contacts from back home.

All in all, it hadn't been a bad evening's work. The next day I still hadn't heard back from Aurélie but Michael had arranged for us to meet over lunch; I brought the wine. Michael had come to Shanghai from Australia and had previously worked for the biggest distributor in town, ASJ wines. Now he was at a smaller distributor and they were looking to expand their list. He really liked the Rozier Bay and wanted to know how much I was selling it for. Remember, I'd promised Adam in South Africa that I wouldn't sell it as a cheap wine, so I felt honour bound to ask for as high a price as I dared: ¥85 (around $12.50) per bottle. This was a true crunch moment. Michael was the first person I'd floated a price to and he really knew the market. His opinion of the wine and the price counted for a lot. It was a massive relief that he liked it. He had another big gulp and nodded: 'That's a really good price for this wine.' He even smiled as he said it. So? Was he going to buy it?

As Michael started the sentence with the words: 'The problem with being a small distributor . . .' I started to tune out. There was an end to the sentence and I'm sure it was coherent and reasonable but as I looked at him all I could hear was, 'No. No. No.' And I didn't want to hear any more. I was already wondering whether

Aurélie had left me a voicemail or whether my meeting with the bar manager at Malone's would be more successful than this had been. We wrapped up pretty soon after that and Michael seemed genuinely sorry not to be able to help. His advice was to target his old boss; ASJ wines had the buying power to take it all from me.

That night I went to Malone's with a bottle each of Rozier and Arniston Bay under my arm. I felt like a drinks rep, and I suppose that's exactly what I was. The bar is the kind of typical all-American sports bar that I usually avoid. The big screens at either end were showing events from the Beijing Olympics and the bar was lined with both Chinese and Western drinkers; my first thought was that everyone was drinking beer.

I knew what was coming as soon as I met the bar manager, Sean, an Irish-American who was doing very nicely out of Shanghai's new economic miracle selling beers to its sports fans both here and at another bar he'd opened on the other side of town. Beer, not wine. Sean liked the wine, everybody liked the wine, but as he said, 'When you look at my clientele during a soccer game [by which I think he meant 'football match', but anyway] they aren't all sipping on a glass of wine, they're knocking back beers and tequila shots.' It sounded like great fun, and I made a mental note to come back someday and taste the full Malone's experience when I was next in town, but right then I just wanted to get the hell out of there. I felt like a complete fool for trying to sell wine in a beer house and a little pissed off at Kung Fu Jon for sending me off on a wild goose chase. His words, 'Well, we get through a lot of wine', were still stinging my ears.

I was up against it again. This time I really had to hustle. I was in a foreign town with a great product but a shortage of leads. Over the next couple of days I contacted every half lead I had, every contact in my book. The big distributor that Michael suggested had an exclusivity contract with a large South African supplier already, so there was no deal there. Two other distributors weren't ready to put South African wine on their list yet. One Chinese distributor I waited an hour for didn't show up. A large discount wine supermarket was interested but the head buyer was in Australia for a fortnight. I even tried the Marriott hotel chain; they liked the wine (everybody liked the wine) but said they could only take a dozen bottles on a trial basis. If I'd had six months in Shanghai then fine, but in my current timeframe, no deal. Then Aurélie called; she'd tried to persuade her boss but she was sorry, this wasn't for them. I was beginning to get really panicky.

I had come to Shanghai with a good product (I think I may have mentioned already that everyone liked the wine) and I was offering it at a good price. Every meeting had gone much the same way: there was no problem with either quality or price but there always seemed to be something getting in the way of a deal. I was a little surprised because I could see people all around me in Shanghai making money. There seemed to be a real get-up-and-go, entrepreneurial spirit about the place and I had felt sure that would throw up someone who would see this as a great opportunity. I was leaving lots of margin for a distributor to make their profit but no one seemed interested.

The other thing I had going for me was that it is very difficult to get new wines into China these days. Even the experienced distributors here were saying that there is too much paperwork involved and Chinese customs have started to be a bit tricky. I'd done all that paperwork while the wine was en route from Cape Town with the help of a local freight forwarding agent, and it had all gone very smoothly, so my wines were now registered in China. Anyone who bought these wines would be able to import more quite easily. Everyone thought that I'd been lucky – but not lucky enough, it seemed, for anyone to take the next step.

I had only one more day in Shanghai and I was beginning to make arrangements for what I was going to do if I couldn't sell the wine. The agent I had used could store it for me but I would have to continue to find leads by email and phone. I might even have to come back to Shanghai later in the year. It was far from ideal and it meant a lot of money tied up that I wouldn't be able to use for other trades, so I wasn't happy. Then I had a call back from a tiny distributor that I'd cold-called the day before; they wanted me to come in to see them. Excited? I put the phone down and had to put a hand to my chest; my heart was racing. This was my very last chance.

The Merchant is a very small outfit in a grubby, industrial-looking building in Shanghai. The outside is grey concrete and the corridors inside are raw breeze block. It wasn't somewhere I expected to find a wine merchant, but once inside the building I was surprised that the first unit along the corridor was the office of a model agency and the next an advertising agency. It was the kind of industrial chic that you see in the trendy areas of London, such as Shoreditch. The Merchant actually occupied a swanky office space further along the corridor and I waited in reception for the director, Jonathon Lim. While I was waiting I spotted a copy of Geoff's *Shanghai Business Review* on the coffee table; I always take this sort of coincidence as a good omen.

Jonathon was five foot two and looked like he went to the same barber as David Lu. He didn't appear much older than the average boy band member so I was glad that he'd brought his director of wine, Kelvin, along too. Despite their assumed English names, Jonathon and Kelvin were actually Chinese Malaysians.

We sat in their boardroom, either side of a long, mahogany table surrounded by shelves of 'award-winning' wines in presentation cases. Why is wine always 'award-winning'?

The wine tasting started the usual way. Big glasses, lots of swirling, followed by sniffing and slurping and sucking of wine through teeth. All the things that you do if you're tasting the wine and never do if you're actually drinking it. I was just praying to God that nobody shouted, 'Marzipan!'

Kelvin was the taste man and he said he liked it. In fact he liked them both. Time for Jonathon, the money man, to get involved. How much? I was firm on the Rozier at ¥85 (around $12.50) and I suggested ¥65 for the Arniston (around $9.50). The two boys gave each other a sideways glance, giving away how good a deal they knew they were getting. The Rozier at that price was a bargain and they didn't even try to negotiate. The Arniston was a little different. Jonathon thought it a little expensive and so I let him knock me down a little to ¥50 (around $7.50) on the condition that he take it all. At these prices I'd still be making a huge 80 per cent on my investment. They would put 50 per cent more on that to calculate their wholesale price. The retailer would then double it, so by the time these wines were sold in a supermarket or a restaurant they would cost around $30 each.

It's so frustrating when people say they want to 'sleep on it'. I say it all the time so I know what a good negotiation technique it is. Jonathon wanted to go through the numbers with his finance director, and in any case he doubted they'd take it all, but they'd let me know tomorrow. I knew that in China it's always better to do business face to face so I said I'd be back same time tomorrow.

I hardly slept. If the deal went ahead then I was out of jail, so by the same logic, if it didn't, then I was in it. Or at least my capital would be locked up until I could find someone to take the wine. If it had been hard trying to sell it while I was in Shanghai then it would be a whole lot harder once I'd left.

Jonathon wasn't there when I returned to the swanky office. Kelvin was in his office behind his desk. He had both bottles in front of him. 'You said ¥85 for this one, right?' He tapped the top of the Rozier bottle, 'And ¥45 for this one?' Trying to pull a fast one.

'It was 50 for that one,' I corrected him. I did appreciate the effort. I was surprised that he was actually interested in both; I'd felt that he would either want one or the other.

'If we are going to build South Africa into our portfolio then it would be better to have two wines to offer our customers. We couldn't pay for it all now.'

I was like a dog with sight of the rabbit. 'How much can you pay now? 50 per cent?'

'Yes, those are our standard terms, 50 per cent now and 50 per cent in 30 days.' That sounded like a deal to me. I would have $15,000 to bank now and I'd still get the rest before I had to head home. Given the circumstances, this wasn't so much a get-out-of-jail as a last-minute reprieve from the governor.

There's a great drama to doing last-minute deals. I suppose every deal is last-minute, but this was too last-minute. I'd gone right to the wire. One second my whole trip seemed in jeopardy, the next I was back on track with my first really significant profit. Sure, I'd made money on chilli and coffee, but nothing like this. A cool $14,344 profit to put alongside my earlier profits. Even with the losses on the horses, I was up over $16,500. My target of $100,000 looked possible for the first time. If I could maintain this momentum I'd make it, and maybe even make more. I had money in the bank now to buy something in China and I had a date with a certain carver in Suzhou.

*

I had been worrying a bit about cash flow. With all the money I had tied up in jade and wine, I was also waiting for the second instalment from Puneet Gupta for the chilli sauces, and I was going to have to pay the jade carver on collection. Now that I'd offloaded the wine I was feeling much more buoyant. I boarded the bullet train to Suzhou in high spirits. If the cutter had done a good job on the jade then best estimates were that I could make three or four times as much when I came to sell it. The recommended market in this part of the world that everyone was directing me towards was in Taiwan.

Fortunately for me, I had a good cutter on board. I returned to the shop to find him exactly where I'd left him: sitting in his shop, having a fag. I'd emailed to say I was coming, so he wasn't surprised to see me and if anything he seemed excited to show me upstairs to the workshop. His workers were hard at it, fifteen of them all busily drilling away on other pieces; with the jade running out, every workshop is now working at full capacity to make sure they cut as much of it as they can while it lasts. A small gold box on the corner of the master's desk immediately caught my eye. He ushered me over towards it. The moment of truth had arrived.

Master cutter is a big title to fill. I had high expectations of him and he hadn't let me down. I opened the box to reveal a totally transformed stone. He had cut right into it to carve out the shape of a mountain with a frozen river running through it. There were stalactites dripping from caves and the mountainside was covered with pine trees that in turn looked as though they were covered in snow. The imperfections in the stone were fairly marked but where possible he had used them to create the impression of freshly fallen snow.

In the centre of the stone was a lonely, pitiful-looking man riding on a tired donkey, accompanied by his manservant. They were in such a cruel environment it made me wonder, what are they doing?

'They are looking for plum blossom in the snow.' He traced the flecks in the stone with his cultured, long little fingernail. 'These flecks are plum blossom. He has become lost so is now looking for refuge. And up on the mountain here,' my eye followed his finger to a small house almost hidden behind a snow-laden branch, 'is his refuge. It is a story about how a traveller must persevere in his search for what he seeks and fate will keep him safe.' I didn't realize it but I'd actually started to cry.

I don't know if it was the beauty of the piece, the poignancy of the story to my own quest or just plain relief that he hadn't made a complete pig's ear of it, but either way I was an extremely happy man. Chinese society isn't particularly tactile but he got a great big bloody hug anyway. I was so proud of him, he'd done me proud; I had a beautiful piece of genuine Chinese art and I wasn't going to have any trouble selling it. I handed over the ¥32,000 ($4,500) and promised to let him know how I got on selling it in Taipei.

Fifteen

A BIRD IN THE HAND

LAST TRADE:
— Wine: $14,344 profit
INVESTMENTS:
— Surfboards (including tax and shipping): $12,156
— Jade: $9,214
IN THE BANK: $44,919

There's a new trend of late for countries to advertise themselves as places for us to visit. Tourist boards have come up with slogans that are supposed to capture the very essence of their countries, to let us know exactly what we will get from going there, like a holiday mission statement for us. So, the Irish tourist board invites you to 'Discover your very own Ireland'; Taiwan's tourist board promises 'A surprise round every corner'. Over the course of my time in Taiwan, this is exactly what I found to be true. Unfortunately, nearly all of those surprises were unpleasant.

I'd come to Taiwan with my tail up. After the success I'd had in China with the wine I felt like I was finally on a roll. I'd put the failure of the horses behind me and learnt from my mistake of putting all my eggs in one basket. However, if China was the perfect platform from which to launch myself towards my target of $50,000 profit, then Taiwan proved to be the arsonist below the platform loosening all the screws, lighting a big fire and running away. I was going to learn a whole new set of lessons and experience a whole lot of surprises.

Surprise number one came as soon as I arrived. Chatting with taxi drivers on the way in from the airport often gives me an idea of the lie of the land. Contrary to what I had been reading in the press over the last few years, Taiwan was not abuzz with economic confidence but was actually, well, quiet. Granted, I had just come from the mania of Shanghai, but I felt the city of Taipei must be suffering a collective hangover so nauseating that it had decided to stay in bed all day and watch videos.

Taiwan is an ethnic Han Chinese island off the east coast of mainland China and south-west of Japan. The Japanese have had various periods of influence on the island and actually ruled it for the first half of the twentieth century, until the end of the Second World War. As such, there is a definite Japanese influence that makes it very different to mainland China, despite the island having a distinctly Chinese feel. Driving in from the airport, you only have to look at how many karaoke bars there are in Taipei to see how much they still embrace Japanese culture. This, I thought, was an opportunity; I had already decided that Japan would be my next stop.

There's also a fair amount of American influence in Taiwan. They're obsessed with baseball, for one thing. This probably all stems from the massive amounts of aid thrown Taiwan's way in the 1950s, which helped the Taiwanese to begin the move from being a largely agricultural economy to an industrialized one. They invested wisely in education for all and quickly set the foundations for Taiwan to grow into one of the 'Asian Tiger' economies of the 1990s. Over the years it has become a massive exporter of electronics and textiles to the big markets in the US and Japan, but here I was listening to a taxi driver telling me how things have started to slow considerably.

The Taiwanese economy was facing a massive problem. Chinese

and Vietnamese labour had become so much cheaper that two things had started to happen in the last couple of years. First, Taiwanese firms were relocating manufacture away from Taiwan; second, Taiwanese investors were moving their money overseas. Private Taiwanese investors alone now have over $100 billion invested in China. Taiwan was starting to feel a bit like somewhere that had had its day and was now a little overshadowed by the success of its big brother. Not necessarily the place to find yourself with three-and-a-half kilos' worth of 'luxury goods' in your pocket.

Often the buyer will 'fall in love' with a product, and this is especially true with a piece of art. If I could find the person who felt that they simply had to have this jade, then it was a licence to charge whatever I liked for it. On the other hand, dealing in luxury goods comes with a downside: they are the first things that people cut back on when the purse strings are tightened. News from back home suggested that the dark clouds of economic recession were gathering there, too. I didn't know it then, but there was a real storm coming that could have a profound effect on future trades.

I had arrived in Taiwan in time for the weekly jade market. Every Saturday, the space below one of the city's concrete flyovers is transformed into an underground market where hundreds of traders from across the island come to sell jade of various colours, cuts and sizes. At this time of year Taipei was a seasonal 38° and humidity was running at 98 per cent. This meant that the driest you would be all day was when you were still in the shower; after that, you'd be really wet.

I strolled into the market with my jade under my arm early in the morning to meet the president of the Jade Association. I'd sent him a couple of emails earlier in the week from China to ask for his help with organizing a stall. The market was already buzzing with traders; no evidence of any economic slump here. Well, not on the face of things, anyway.

In an attempt to relieve the extreme temperature and humidity in the jade market, the traders have clubbed together to introduce an air-conditioning system. Unfortunately for me, I'd arrived a month too early to reap the no doubt considerable benefits. Instead, the market was still using an old, improvised system of releasing water vapour from pipes that ran along the ceiling. The result was a little like an overhead dry-ice machine. As this impacted on my ability to see anything above shoulder height quite considerably, I decided to go back outside and wait for the president on the street. He eventually emerged from the mist and introduced himself.

A cheery, small man with a tendency to nod a little too much at everything, the Jade Association president looked a bit like the dog on that annoying insurance advert back home. He had received my emails asking for a stall and was expecting me. Of course, a stall at the market was no trouble. The Taiwanese have a very refreshing attitude to foreigners: they actually practise the now almost universally forgotten art of universal hospitality. It will only take a few more years before enough of them have explored the wider world and worked out that the rest of us are all xenophobic bastards and they give up and become just like us. But for now, this was a slice of luck.

The jade market contained approximately five hundred stalls arranged in long aisles that disappeared into the distance below the flyover. I had been given a very good pitch in one of the centre aisles, around 50 yards from the entrance. This was the spot where most of the people arriving stopped chatting and started shopping. I also noticed that I was the only stall to be displaying just one piece of jade. I hoped this would make me eye-catching.

The stall next to me was run by a charming Taiwanese girl called Jenny, around twenty-five, with big, round glasses that quite deliberately made her look both more learned and more mature than she really was. Her stall was displaying thirty or so smaller ornamental pieces of what looked to me like green nephrite jade, although she corrected me; they were actually made from chrysocolla, another green gemstone. The jade market was not entirely restricted to jade.

Jenny's uncle actually owned the stall but spent most of the day playing draughts with his mates while Jenny looked after the customers. When he did come over to check on things he showed a little interest in my piece. He turned it over a few times, curled his bottom lip and gave me a nod as if to say, 'I'm impressed.' Then he asked me how much I wanted to sell it for. A very good question.

The truth was, I had no idea what to expect to sell this piece of jade for. When I had been in Suzhou and Hotan, I had asked people what to expect and the answers that I received had been very ambiguous. There is no set price for jade, no per carat value like there is for, say, diamonds. So I had to pick a number. I decided to chance my arm and go for an optimistic valuation: $40,000. That was obviously negotiable, but my logic was that I could allow someone to knock me down to half of that and I'd still be doubling my money. Remember, I'd paid around $9,500. I was preparing myself for the Taiwanese to haggle as much as on the mainland. Jenny's uncle didn't haggle; he just put it back down.

The president returned with a friend who he thought could help me out, a young Taiwanese chap called Rolf, who'd grown up in Los Angeles and had returned to Taiwan to sell chrysocolla and other quartzes back to the US via his online business. He didn't know the first thing about jade but he could translate from English to Taiwanese for me. Rolf had left his wife in charge of his own stall and seemed more than happy with the idea of hanging out at my stall. One thing I had begun to realize on this trip is that trading in markets can get a bit humdrum, and when a crazy foreigner turns up trying to sell something that he clearly knows nothing about, it's good entertainment for everyone else. There's a healthy balance between wanting to help him out and wanting him to fall flat on his face.

I was quickly the centre of attention and there were no shortage of people prepared to offer their opinions on the jade. Good piece, bad piece, it's from Hotan, it's a fake, very big, not big enough, good cut, bad cut, not white enough, if it were whiter it would be worth more; on and on. The Taiwanese jade-buying fraternity were out in full to give me their assessments of my piece. No serious buyers, though, until finally the president introduced me to a friend of his who had come over to have a look: Mr Chen.

Mr Chen had one of the adjacent stalls and sold a fair amount of similar pieces to mine. He and the president sat down to give the buying of my piece some serious consideration. I was sticking to my $40,000 price tag and they were having a very animated conversation about it, in Taiwanese. Fortunately for me, Rolf was listening and translating their conversation. It seemed that the president was interested in buying the piece himself, only he wanted Mr Chen to go in halves with him. Mr Chen was mulling it over. They were agreed on two things: this size of piece was becoming increasingly rare in Taiwan as the Hotan jade mines were beginning to dry up, and the price of white jade in particular was on the rise. The argument was over how much each was prepared to put in and how long they would have to hold on to it to make a profit.

I couldn't believe it. If I managed to sell it that easily for four times what I had paid for it then my entire trip would be in jeopardy because I would have to give serious consideration to packing the whole thing in and becoming a full-time jade dealer. I would be on the next plane back to Hotan, make no mistake.

The deliberation between the two men continued for an hour.

Many cups of tea were drunk. The president began to persuade Mr Chen. Then he began to get cold feet, and Mr Chen started to do the persuading. Eventually the president got quite cross that Mr Chen was putting too much pressure on him to make a decision, and the two men actually started to have a row. I had to ask them to leave. They were becoming bad for business and there were other buyers beginning to queue up.

I was confident, really confident. I was in the Taipei jade market along with lots of other jade traders and mine was getting lots of interest. OK, not everybody liked it, but I was getting offers. OK, those offers weren't a lot more than I had paid for it – $10,000, $12,000 – but they were offers. I even haggled with one man to get his offer up to a whopping $13,000, but I wasn't going to take it. It was still not even lunchtime. Why should I settle for a paltry $3,500 profit now?

One thing that was dawning on me, however, was that the offers were probably telling me to revise my $40,000 asking price to something a little more realistic. I felt that could still be $20,000, or even $25,000 if I found the right person. The sort of person who gets up on a Saturday morning and thinks, 'I know. Instead of buying a new car today, I'll go down the market and spend the money on a pretty rock.'

Rolf agreed that my new asking price of $25,000 seemed more realistic but as the day went on there were fewer and fewer people even asking what my price was. Eventually the market started to empty out, and it became clear that when I'd first arrived I'd had the best offer I was going to receive all day. Now that the afternoon had come and gone there simply weren't any more takers. As the market started to draw to a close I began to wish I'd grabbed the offer of $13,000 when it was there.

Taiwan had lived up to its promise and surprised me by teaching me a lesson I thought I already knew: a bird in the hand is worth two in the bush. I'd been greedy and I was being punished for it. I'd also been guilty of trying to play a market I knew little about. Unfortunately, I didn't let that sink in before I rushed off to make the same mistake again.

Sixteen

OUT OF THE FRYING PAN

INVESTMENTS:
— **Surfboards: $12,156**
— **Jade: $9,214**
IN THE BANK: $44,919

I decided to put the jade back in my bag for the time being and look into what I was going to buy while I was here in Taiwan. If the state of the economy made selling luxury goods hard, the flip side should be that they would be easy to buy. It wasn't an ideal situation as I had $9,000 tied up in the jade and another $10,000 in the surfboards. I was also still waiting for the second instalment of $4,000 from India for the chilli sauces. All in all, with $23,000 tied up, I was really looking for a small deal to keep me busy. If I could put a few more grand in the kitty before it was time to leave for Japan then I'd be delighted.

The thing that I was particularly interested in was a product that I knew sold for big money back in London: oolong tea. A friend in London who sells fine teas to Harrods and Selfridges had suggested getting in touch with a French tea trader based in Taiwan, so I set up a meeting with him to try to pick his brains. His address was a mansion block in the suburbs of Taipei, where a peak-capped doorman eyed me suspiciously as he let me through a gate into a traditional Chinese courtyard. Inside, a middle-aged French man was sitting at a low table, watching his children playing on a slide that stood rather incongruously in the corner.

Stefan was looking after his children while his Taiwanese wife was working; a very Western role reversal that he explained to me was still rather unusual in Taiwan. As a way of staying sane (as well as making a little cash on the side), Stefan had put his well-informed French palate to good use. He used to be rather a connoisseur of French red wine, he told me, but now he had developed a good understanding of Taiwanese oolong tea.

There is a delicate art to making a good cup of oolong (I always want to insert another o when I write it, like Typh-ooo). The pot has to be warmed, the cups have to be warmed, then the hot water is added to the tea in the pot, which then also has hot water poured over it and then, finally, after a few moments to soak, the first cup is ready.

You can repeat this ceremony several times and each cup will taste a little different. There are many different oolongs and they display different taste profiles in much the same way as wines. Some get better with age. The best teas generally are the ones that grow at the highest altitudes. This is also the hardest place to grow tea and so, like nearly everything else in the world, the best is also the rarest – and the most expensive.

Stefan had two suggestions for me: either I could seek out a tea expert in Taipei to sell me a top-notch vintage tea that would be worth big bucks to a collector overseas; or I could try to find a little-known estate that he had heard about recently from another Western enthusiast, a Russian, who had told him about a farm that could only be reached by crossing a deep ravine and which lay at the top of one of Taiwan's most beautiful mountains. Well, I had been feeling like it was time for a trip to the countryside.

*

Leaving Taipei, all I had was a sketchy idea of where Stefan thought his Russian friend had found the secret plantation. It was nothing more than a cross on a map showing where I would find an '85 kilometres' sign by the side of the road; I had no idea what it was 85 kilometres to, or from. Stefan thought there was a ravine that needed to be crossed at this point, but I would have to ask when I got there. The nearest village, Lishan, was a couple of miles down the road.

It was a relief to be getting out of Taipei. I had spent far too much of the last few weeks in urban environments and I was really hankering for some country air again. It didn't take long before Taipei was left far behind and I was driving south along the motorway that traces the west coast of the island. I took the turning for Lishan and found myself on a smaller winding road that snaked up into the luscious green mountains. Small farms clung precariously to them; evidence that I was in tea-growing country.

The road to Lishan continued to climb up and up and the ravine to the side became deeper and deeper. Steep green mountains reached into picture-perfect cotton-wool clouds. The cross on the map indicated that the plantation I was looking for was nearly 7,000 feet above sea level and Lishan was the nearest village at 6,000 feet. I drove through Lishan and started looking out for road signs showing '85 kilometres' on them. Amazingly, spot on where Stefan had said it would be, there was the sign and, opposite, a tea processing plant. I pulled over and went in to ask for more specific directions

An oolong tea processing plant looks much like any other industrial factory from the outside, and inside it's pretty similar too. The biggest difference is in the types of machines and other paraphernalia that you get on the factory floor. One giveaway was the large, circular drying racks that still had the odd stray tea leaf left on them. Another was the two long, cylindrical drums into which the leaves are thrown once they have dried, to be tumbled into small, pea-sized balls. This is how you find the tea when it eventually gets packaged. But the plant wasn't doing much processing right then, and the whole place was pretty quiet except for two middle-aged men having a cuppa in the office.

The men seemed happy to have a visitor and welcomed me in to join them. The first man, in his fifties, wearing glasses and a smart striped shirt, was Mr Him, who owned the plant. His friend was Mr Ho who owned the plantation across the ravine. It was Mr Ho's tea that we were about to drink and Mr Him was quick to tell me just how good it was; the finest in the Lishan area. Amazingly, I had just stumbled across the very man I was looking for, and here he was inviting me in for a cup of his own tea.

After our cup of tea, Mr Ho invited me to come back to his farm to see for myself where it had come from. We wandered down the road from the plant while he talked ten to the dozen about his farm on the far side of the ravine. It looked like at least a day's walk. The ravine dropped down more than 3,000 feet to a wide river, then rose up on the other side through a band of woodland, and from there went steeply up to where I could see his tea fields, almost directly opposite where we stood. I was concerned as to how we were going to make it there before dark and, as Mr Ho was at least sixty, I was even more concerned as to how he was going to make it at all. He didn't seem concerned.

Further down the road we stopped at what looked and sounded like a noisy mechanic's workshop on the edge of the ravine, where a few men were smoking cigarettes while they repaired an old engine. The engine seemed to turn a wheel, which turned a metal cable that stretched across the half-mile span of the ravine. Two other men were replacing a length of the cable at the same time, holding their cigarettes in their pursed lips while they bolted the new piece on to the old. Attached to the cable they were repairing was a large basket. I'm as averse as the next guy to the annoying 'health and safety' culture that we have allowed to take over all our lives, but this looked like a situation that could really have benefited from, at the very least, somebody with a clipboard being present.

Concern is a funny emotion in that it can be classified in degrees. I am mildly concerned that I may have accidentally put a dark sock in with my white wash; I am deeply concerned that my employer will have to make redundancies and I will lose my job. Well, I was mildly concerned that we had a long walk to reach the tea farm on the other side of the deep ravine with a fast-flowing river at the bottom of it; I was deeply concerned when Mr Ho proposed we cross it in the basket attached to the cable that was being repaired.

When the banging and bolting eventually stopped, Mr Ho indicated that we were ready to climb into the basket suspended from the cable. Stunned, and blindly following the small mountain farmer because I didn't want to look like a big baby, I climbed into the basket with him. From up there I could see that all across the valley there were similar cables criss-crossing the huge ravine. Small baskets hanging from miles of cable were transporting people from the road to the tea fields and back. I could see how important this somewhat unusual means of transport was to this community, but I was still scared stiff to be having a go myself.

The ancient engine belched out a dark cloud of diesel fumes and the rusty wheel turned itself over. As the cable moved, the basket started coming away from the edge of the ravine, and through the holes in its floor I could see all the way down to the river, more than 3,000 feet below. The pace of the basket picked up, and soon Mr Ho and I were zipping across from one mountain to the other in little more than a washing basket dangling from a wire. At times like this I find it helps to make loud screaming noises. Mr Ho tried to reassure me that no one had ever died making this journey, and even though I believed him, I continued with the screaming until we reached the other side.

The day was drawing to an end and the sun went down quickly behind the mountain. Mr Ho suggested that we have some dinner and then look around the farm in the morning. The house was on two storeys and Mr Ho lived with his family upstairs. He made a bed for me where his workers sleep at busy harvest times, in a kind of man-sized rabbit hutch downstairs. I climbed into my hutch and made my bed for the night. It had been a remarkable achievement to find this place and now that I had made it here I was determined that tomorrow I would buy some of Mr Ho's tea for a discount price.

As with most farms, the day here began early. Just before dawn. While Mrs Ho was preparing our breakfast, I went on a bit of a wander. Outside, the mountains were shrouded in mist and the sun was starting to rise behind them. Shafts of yellow light reached up into the sky and the mist began to break up. Stray patches drifted past me, momentarily enveloping me in a grey gloom. I felt cold for the first time in as long as I could remember. Pretty soon all the mist would be burnt off by the sun and the resulting humidity would be felt by everyone down in Taipei but for now, up here, the air was crisp and fresh and the silence was broken only by the occasional coo from Mr Ho's racing pigeons.

Mr Ho was a racing pigeon fanatic. Like many Taiwanese, he regularly enters his birds into competitions where, I was amazed to discover, the prizes can reach hundreds of thousands of dollars. Mr Ho's number one bird cost him $40,000 the previous year and he was hoping to enter it into Taiwan's million-dollar race the following year. The pigeons in the race are taken far out to sea on a ship and launched at the same time. The first bird back to its coop on the island wins the million. It attracts TV and radio coverage and Mr Ho and his bird were in training for it. I asked him what he would do with the money. 'Build a better coup,' was his reply, which spoke volumes for how content Mr Ho was with his lot in life.

Doing a deal with Mr Ho was fairly straightforward. He took me down to the fields to show me around and as he did so he explained that I'd come at a good time. His spring tea had just been picked and was being processed right now. The spring harvest is when the best of the oolong tea is picked. He still had some left to sell but most of his supply had been sold to a distributor for export to Europe and the US. Mr Ho seemed a little deflated by the price at which he'd had to sell to the distributor but, brilliantly for me, he was very open about what that price was.

I could have stood there negotiating with Mr Ho all day and would never get below the price that a big distributor had paid. He'd already told me what price he'd sold to the distributor for, so I wasn't going to pay more than that and, in any case, he seemed reconciled to that being the actual price that he'd sell to anyone for. All I had to do was piggyback on the distributor's negotiation. When I asked him if I could take his last 600g (equivalent to forty bags) he said he was happy to sell to me for the same price as he had to the distributor. He could have pushed me to pay more as I wasn't really a bulk buyer, but he didn't. We shook right away on a price of $1,000 in total, or $25 per bag. I'd had all the benefit of the distributor's negotiation without having to do any of the hard work myself. Instead, I was free to enjoy the scenery and prepare myself mentally for the basket ride back.

*

On the way back to Taipei I received a call from Stefan. If I was interested then he had an opportunity for me to source some of the very rare oolong tea he had told me about previously. He would set up a meeting with a tea master who went by the name of Mr Teaparker at his address in downtown Taipei. The plan definitely wasn't to buy two types of tea, but I'm always interested to meet anyone who claims to be a master of anything; at the very least I might learn something more about the product I'd chosen to invest in already. I let my curiosity get the better of me and told Stefan to go ahead and arrange the meeting.

I got off the underground train in the centre of downtown Taipei, a far cry from the serene mountainside of Lishan. Even though it was nearly 9 p.m., the streets were still light from all the neon signs advertising the latest in electronic gadgetry and the new Batman film. Young people hung out in groups dressed in fashions inspired by what Japanese youth are wearing. There is a sense in Taipei that people are strongly influenced by what is going on elsewhere and they have become very good at copying anything that they find interesting.

It didn't come as much of a surprise, then, to find that Mr Teaparker's address was a swanky pad decorated *à la mode* of a west London flat. What was a surprise was that what I'd expected to be a casual meeting turned out to be anything but. Mr Teaparker was a short, middle-aged man with round, dark glasses that made him look a bit like a nerdish schoolboy. He had put on quite a spread.

We sat down either side of a long, pine table along which Mr Teaparker had prepared some samples of collectable teas, some of which were nearly thirty years old. We were not alone; six attending waitresses brought kettles of hot water for Mr Teaparker to prepare cups of the various brews so as to educate me in the qualities of oolong that made it so collectable. He also had a PowerPoint presentation with highlights from his nineteen books on the subjects of oolong tea, tea sets, tea cups and tea ceremonies. He didn't just look like a nerd.

The oolong leaves are a very dark green and come rolled up in little balls which could easily be mistaken for drugs. To my unsophisticated palate the tea tastes a bit like green tea, and even by the time I'd left Taiwan and tried several of them, I still couldn't quite put my finger on why one was so much better than another. It's a little less bitter, perhaps, and the good stuff has a bit of a sweet aftertaste, but it's so subtle that it could take years to develop the taste buds to tell.

I tried to impress on Mr Teaparker that I couldn't possibly learn all that had to be learnt in order to make an informed decision about which tea to buy. If I went with one of these teas then I would only be trading on his reputation. If he said it was good then it must be good and a potential buyer would trust that that was enough endorsement to make an investment. I needed to do a bit of research and Mr Teaparker needed to find out which, if any, of these rare teas he would be able to get hold of. We agreed to sleep on it.

The next day, Mr Teaparker had found an interesting tea that he wanted to show me, so I went to meet him again, this time at a markedly less salubrious address. As I arrived I had begun to think about why I was interested in buying another tea from Taiwan. After all, I already had $1,000 invested in oolong and if I could double my money on it then I had a great trade to get me to Japan, from where I could connect to Mexico in time to meet the surfboards. Did I really want to get into another tea deal? I must admit that my curiosity got the better of me.

Mr Teaparker had 100g of 1980 vintage oolong to show me. It was presented beautifully in a pewter canister held in an ornamental mahogany box. The tea had sold at auction a few years ago for around $1,000 and its value was rising fast. I could tell that Mr Teaparker was excited to have found it for me and he handled it as though it was the Holy Grail. He said there were three collectors that he knew personally in Japan who would be 'very excited' by this tea. The price, he thought, would be three to four times the price in Taiwan. 'Whoa!' I thought. Why isn't Mr Teaparker taking it to Japan to sell it himself?

Mr Teaparker's story went like this: Mr Teaparker has written nineteen books about all aspects of tea and its importance to

Taiwanese culture; he has become an ambassador for Taiwanese oolong tea all over the world; he cannot be seen to be involved in the 'business' of tea any more as this would compromise his reputation, and even if that weren't the case, his reputation was worth a lot more than the $1,500 that this tea would cost me.

This had come down to exactly that. I needed to trust his reputation if I was going to make a profit on this tea. I was intrigued as to who would pay three or four times as much for it in Japan. Collectors fascinate me and this was a rare opportunity to glimpse this often hidden world and find out what drove it. It was also potentially a chance for a quick $4,000 profit. I decided to take a punt and trust Mr Teaparker to deliver the goods; at worst, I'd have a very expensive pot of tea to take home and drink with my Chinese takeaway. I had two types of oolong to sell and $2,500 invested, again in something that I knew very little about.

I took a short flight from Taipei and threw myself straight into the middle of another of the world's great cities. The climate in Tokyo was no less oppressive than it had been in Taipei; 90 per cent humidity meant that the last thing I wanted to drink was a cup of hot tea, but I hoped that I could find enough people among Tokyo's 30 million inhabitants to persuade otherwise. So as long as I could find a route to market, I felt that this shouldn't be too hard a sell.

Seventeen

TEA BREAK, ANYONE?

INVESTMENTS:
— **Surfboards: $12,156**
— **Jade: $9,214**
— **Tea: $2,500**
IN THE BANK: $42,419

My plan in Japan was to focus on selling the forty bags of Mr Ho's tea first, while Mr Teaparker set up meetings with collectors for the vintage stuff. My idea was to approach speciality tea shops, so I emailed the biggest three in Tokyo, but not one of them would even agree to see me, no explanation offered. I decided instead to explore the idea of a street market. Friends who have lived in Japan had described to me how the Japanese like to get involved in anything 'a bit kooky' and so I thought that if I could get something interactive and fun going with a kettle and a stall then I could draw some people in. Unfortunately, the Japanese had other ideas. I tried and tried to get permission from several Tokyo market authorities to rent a stall for the day, and was turned down every time. Phone calls, emails and personal visits bearing gifts all drew blank after blank. I was being denied access to my potential market.

In an act of desperation I struck on the idea of doing some direct selling via another route, and with the aid of a normal tray, a poster and a roll of twine, I set myself up with an usherette-style tray from which to sell my tea. I decided on the busiest street in Tokyo, in the

Roppongi district; right in the middle of town. My plan was simply to stop people and try to convince them to buy some great Taiwanese oolong tea. It was a long day. After six hours and hundreds of approaches I had managed to sell a total of five bags of oolong for a total of $175. At that rate, I would be in Tokyo for three weeks before I had gotten rid of it all. That night I went to bed a little disheartened and running short of ideas.

On my evening run through the financial district, the one quiet place in the whole of Tokyo after everyone has gone home, I struck on an idea. There must be somewhere in Japan where people drink lots of oolong tea. I was having little success selling my tea to the Japanese, so I decided to have a go at trying the Chinese ex-pat population in Chinatown, in nearby Yokohama.

One Chinatown looks much like any other. There's a 'look' that all Chinatowns have, as though they were all designed by the same person. The format involves a big Chinese-style gate at one end, then a few streets of Chinese restaurants and supermarkets, and then a big gate at the other end. Yokohama is no different. Along one of those streets I found a small Chinese tea shop run by a man who I estimated was at least 120.

At first I was keen to keep my cards close to my chest and I did a quick scan of the teas that he had on sale. There were some older teas but mostly they were oolongs of a comparable quality to mine. They were packaged similarly, anyway. I decided to try my luck and ask the world's oldest man if he was interested in buying teas and, to my surprise (I could have been in Taiwan), he said that he was. I showed him some of my tea and he took a sample, smelt it, fingered it, smelt it some more and finally asked if I minded him tasting a bit. That's the idea.

We sat and had a nice cup of tea. He said he liked the taste and the Lishan area was a good part of Taiwan for me to have gone for tea. I said thank you, and would he be interested in buying thirty-five bags (remember I sold five in Roppongi yesterday) for, say, 3,000 yen (¥) per bag. He laughed.

The advantage to selling oolong tea in Chinatown is that they know their oolong tea in Chinatown. The disadvantage to selling oolong tea in Chinatown is that they know the price of oolong tea in Chinatown. Not only that, they already buy a load of it directly from their cousin's mate's cousin's farm in Taiwan for a knock-down mate's rate.

The bottom line was that ¥3,000 ($30) was not going to fly with this guy. He was a buyer but only at a knock-down price of ¥750 ($7.50) per bag. Much less than the ¥2,500 ($25) that I'd bought it for. What could I do? I realized that I was on a hiding to nothing with this trade but I had to do my utmost to reduce my loss as far as possible. I tried to push the old fellow up a little: even ¥1,500? He wasn't budging. Not even a little. He would leave the offer on the table and if I changed my mind I was free to come back, but the offer stood at ¥750 per bag. I decided to press on and see if I could do any better elsewhere; I didn't have to go far.

Next door was another tea shop. Literally next door. I had to check that they weren't the same place. The owner was a man from mainland China with a fascination for Taiwanese tea, so I thought things were going pretty well when he said that he liked mine. Unfortunately, he had a good thing going with his distributor already and he didn't want to upset the apple cart. He kindly offered to buy a few bags for his own personal stash (another $100 in my pocket) and offered some free advice into the bargain: 'Save yourself a big problem,' he said, 'foreigners can't bring products to Japan to sell them without all the necessary import and taxation documents. Most Japanese will simply refuse to trade with you. If the old man next door says he'll take it off your hands then do yourself a favour and accept. A distributor wouldn't be able to sell it for more than around ¥1,000 [$10] anyway.'

After my experience with getting permission to trade at the Japanese street markets, I could believe what he was saying. Japanese bureaucracy was pushing me into a corner. Not to mention the slow realization that I hadn't got as good a price from Mr Ho as I'd thought. Time to face facts; I had nowhere else to go.

The old-timer was happy to see me back. If his colleague next door was right then he was saving himself around ¥250 ($2.50) per bag on what he'd normally pay a distributor for this kind of tea. If his neighbour was just spinning me a line, too, then he was saving himself a whole lot more. Either way, I was out of my depth. I wasn't qualified to argue with anyone about the quality of this tea, and I knew it. I had dabbled in a market that I knew absolutely nothing about and, like the jade, I was finding it hard to sell as a result.

I offloaded the remaining 35 bags of oolong for a paltry ¥750 per bag, making a grand sales total of $525, which translated into a $475 loss. I made a note never to dabble in the unknown again and took heart from the fact that at least my vintage tea came with the seal of someone who knew what they were talking about. I left Chinatown chastened but determined to make up the losses when I met Mr Teaparker's tea collector contacts the following day.

*

After a great sushi supper and a good night's sleep, I started the day refreshed and with a new spring in my step. Mr Teaparker had emailed me the details of a collector in Tokyo and I was on my way to meet him. I had 100g of a 1980 high mountain oolong under my arm for which I had paid $1,500 (around ¥150,000). The Taiwanese tea master had assured me that I could ask for between three and four times what I'd paid, and I was intrigued to find out if he was right. More than that, I was intrigued to see what such a person looked like – someone who would pay nearly ¥1 million ($10,000) for a pot of tea.

The address that Mr Teaparker had sent me to was a vintage book and art shop in a smart suburb of Tokyo. Mr Yoshi ran the shop with his wife. As I climbed the stairs to his office, the walls were covered in stunning Hiroshige landscape prints; Mr and Mrs Yoshi clearly had very discerning taste.

Mr Yoshi was a lot younger than I had imagined, in his early thirties. He was wearing a khaki shirt, trendy glasses and he spoke fluent English. A very modern Japanese man with a taste for very old Japanese culture and, I hoped, old Taiwanese tea.

I presented him with the mahogany box and his face lit up when he lifted the lid and saw the impressive pewter pot inside: 'Oh my God!' I took this to be a good first reaction. I gave him the go-ahead to open it and he poured out a few of the leaves into its upturned lid so that he could give them a good once-over. He was extremely impressed. 'The shape is good, the size is even, it's very nice,' he cooed. Then he gave it a sniff. 'Wow, it's just so great.' I could tell he was serious about the tea, but at what price?

I explained to him that Mr Teaparker's assessment of the tea was that it could be worth as much as ¥1 million. Did Yoshi think that was a fair price for it? He laughed nervously. 'That's too much money.'

'What is your assessment of its value?' I asked.

'Obviously, I can't pay ¥1 million for tea. I can pay ¥100,000.'

That was less than I had paid for it.

'That's less than I paid for it,' I told him. 'I think you need to offer more like three times that, ¥300,000.' I'd worked out that that would cover my losses on the other tea, and still leave me with a respectable profit overall. I also felt that the tea belonged with someone who would appreciate it, and it was so clear that Yoshi was falling in love with it.

Unfortunately, not enough to lose leave of his reason. He had to stand firm and he wasn't able to sanction a ¥300,000 ($3,000) payment. I left him my number in case he changed his mind and said goodbye. Mr Teaparker had told me there were two more collectors I could approach here in Tokyo. It was time to call on the next one.

Mr Teaparker had sent me to another shop, this time selling the owner's own work. Mr Lim made exquisite teapots and sold them in his gallery shop. He was expecting me. We went through the now familiar tea-smelling ritual and Mr Lim wanted to know how much I wanted for it. I explained to him that Mr Teaparker's assessment was very high and, as I wanted a quick sale, I was offering it at the knockdown price of ¥400,000 ($4,000). I wanted to leave a bit of room for negotiation, in fact I would have happily taken ¥250,000 ($2,500).

Mr Lim liked to drink oolong tea and sometimes he would pay ¥5,000 or even ¥6,000 for one he liked, but nothing like the price I was talking about. He wasn't a collector, just a keen amateur enthusiast. I liked him but this was a dead end.

So far, Mr Teaparker had found me just one collector and one amateur enthusiast. In Taiwan he had promised to find me three collectors. I was in Tokyo where I didn't know anyone and I was trying to sell a product that, let's face it, I knew next to nothing about. I was utterly reliant on Mr Teaparker to deliver more leads. I got him on the phone and explained all this to him. I didn't expect him to do any more than provide me with telephone numbers but he wasn't able to help me any further. He promised to call me straight back with another number but that was the last time we spoke. I'd come undone again, and I could only hope that I wouldn't be stuck with the tea for too long.

Taiwan had been a disaster for me. I had failed to sell the jade even though I'd had a perfectly reasonable offer for it, because I was too greedy, and so had missed my opportunity. Even though I should have learnt from that not to deal in products that were foreign to me, I made the same mistake almost immediately when I decided to buy not just one but two types of oolong tea. I then compounded my own stupidity by entering into a trade that was completely reliant on the efforts of a man I didn't know. Was it any wonder that I'd lost $2,000?

I was feeling pretty sorry for myself. All the momentum that I'd built up in China seemed to have been derailed in Taiwan. I had to get back on track; if the horse throws you off, you have to get back on. I had to find something in Japan that I could make some money from and reverse my bad run of luck. I had to find something that would sell one way or another, something that had a definite market, a trade that couldn't end up with a 'no sale'. There seemed to be one obvious choice. It won't be a surprise.

Eighteen
GONE FISHING

LAST TRADE:
— **Mountain oolong tea: $475 loss**
— **Vintage oolong tea: $1,500 loss**
INVESTMENTS:
— **Surfboards: $12,156**
— **Jade: $9,214**
IN THE BANK: $42,944

We all know that prices change with circumstances. Take, for instance, the price of oil, which was peaking at nearly $150 per barrel when I arrived in Japan. A combination of massive demand for oil coming largely from China's rapidly expanding economy and a shortage of supply because of, amongst other things, trouble in the Middle East, was pushing up prices for everyone around the world. From motorists back home to fishermen here in Japan, the effects of being in a truly globalized world were being felt and they were hurting.

They say that wherever you are in London, you're never more than ten feet from a rat. Wherever you go in Japan, it's a good bet that the same holds true for fish. Sushi and sashimi are a national obsession. Tuna, salmon, mackerel, octopus; if the Japanese could get their hands on the fabled giant squid you could count on it ending up in a Shibuya sushi bar. Of course, before it arrived there it would have to be sold through Tokyo's fish market in Tsukiji.

Tsukiji is simply the world's largest fish market. It's vast. It's seventeen acres or twenty-eight football pitches or the size of Monaco, or something equally arbitrary. The market is in the south of Tokyo and lies right on the Sumida River. From the front it resembles a typical wholesale market: a vast car park, unloading bays for trucks on the outside and rows and rows of stalls selling fish on the inside. As it is a fish market it also has a dock, which allows boats to come straight from the sea and up the river to unload.

Millions of fish pass through it every day in the most carefully ordered and systematic way imaginable. In many ways it's a feudal system. Only seven families are allowed to land fish from the boats that pull into its dockside. Tuna is the big money fish here, and after it is landed, it is auctioned. There are approximately 250 licensed wholesalers in the market who are authorized to bid at the auction, which happens behind closed doors and is over before 4 a.m. Then the fun really starts.

I arrived at Tsukiji around 5.30 a.m. to research how the Japanese fish market operated and I was immediately almost knocked down by a kind of battery-powered, high-speed mini-lorry. It was transporting boxes of fish from one side of Tsukiji to the other and it was not alone; there were hundreds and hundreds of them scooting around the market, transporting fish from one place to the next.

The tuna auction had just finished, and the mini-lorries were whizzing the hefty tuna carcasses out from the auction room to the wholesalers' stalls at around 400 miles an hour. The wholesalers team up in groups of four to lift the whole bulk of the fish off the mini-lorry up and onto a chainsaw, the kind that you would ordinarily see in a timber yard. There were dozens of these dotted around the market.

The tuna get carved into half a dozen pieces and then they're sold via the wholesale market on to retailers: sushi bars, restaurants and supermarkets who come every morning for fresh fish to feed their customers. By 5 a.m. the wholesale market is teeming with retail owners and buyers competing for the best cuts of fish. Each large tuna will eventually fetch anything from $4,000 to $30,000, and this amount will have nearly doubled by the time the slicing and dicing at the retail end is done. Big business. Before dawn, $25 million worth of fish will have been sold twice and be heading its way to a Japanese belly somewhere in the city of Tokyo. What's really frightening is that this occurs all over Japan, in every city, from Choshi to Nagasaki, and from Kyoto to Osaka.

Even in my days in the City I'd never seen this much activity at such an early hour. The wholesalers were chainsawing tuna the size of cattle, the stalls were set up and already the restaurateurs were aggressively piling in to pick the best-looking fish for their diners. The energy of the place was infectious and fresh and seething, and people were clearly enjoying being at the heart of something so vital. I was hooked, so impressed with the scale of opportunity here that somehow I wanted to find a way to tackle this market and take a slice of the profit that was coursing through it. There were two options I could see: either go for a wholesale pitch, whereby I would buy from the auction and sell on to the retailers, or go back a step, land the fish myself and sell at the auction.

This next bit could be very boring for you. It's the bit where I describe the enormously bureaucratic nature of Japanese business and the reluctance of Japanese authorities to let foreigners do anything out of the ordinary. I was bored by it and no doubt it would be even more boring for you to read about second-hand. Just trust me when I say it is impossible to go out, catch some fish and rock up at Tsukiji market to sell them to a wholesaler; if you are not connected to the fish mafia, it is impossible to get a wholesaler's licence unless someone you know happens to have one already, and they die, leaving it to you. I was beginning to think that the whole Japanese fishing industry was a closed shop, when suddenly I had a breakthrough: the fishing union of Fukuoka consented to give me permission to negotiate with its fishermen. If – and only if – I could come to an agreeable arrangement with one of its members, I would be given dispensation to sell fish in the market at Fukuoka.

Fukuoka is on the southernmost of Japan's three main islands. As you move further from Tokyo, everything starts to feel a little more relaxed. By the time you reach the fishing village of Kanasaki, outside of Fukuoka, it actually starts to feel like a tropical paradise. Forget the gaudy neon and crowded streets of Tokyo; this is a sleepy community of fishermen, average age 128. As it was now July, the beaches were packed with holidaymakers, the hillsides were verdant and the rice paddies were full. When I pulled into the dockside, a smallish dock of around thirty medium-sized fishing boats, the place was deserted but for a lonely figure waiting by his boat to meet me; he was Kirisaki-san.

Kirisaki-san was pushing fifty but he didn't look a day over fourteen, a testament to the benefits of living his days in the fresh air and eating a diet of fish and boiled rice. Even though he had three teenage daughters, he still looked as though he had never experienced a moment's stress in his life. His face has remained as wrinkle-free as any of theirs. He welcomed me with a cheery 'Konichi-wa', and invited me to walk over the gangway to his boat.

It was what fishermen call a day boat, around 30 feet long, designed for catching mackerel with two large holding tanks built into the middle of the deck. The Japanese taste for raw fish means that fishermen keep the fish alive until the last minute. This means that once they are hooked, they are instantly transferred to the tanks and kept alive all the way back to shore. Kirisaki-san explained to me that this last week there had been a national fishermen's strike and the boat had been sitting unused in the dock for two days as a result. Just like truck drivers back in the UK, the fishermen of Japan were protesting that the high global price of oil and government taxes on it were prohibiting them from making a profit, and something had to give.

This might have been a worrying sign for me, considering as I was investing in the business of fish, but I saw it differently. I could see that events in China and the Middle East were creating an opportunity for me here in a tiny fishing port in the far south-west of Japan.

No fishing for two days meant that the market had been starved. Just like the price of oil, when the supply of fish is constrained, its price rises, as long as demand stays steady – and, as we've already established, when it comes to fish the Japanese are very demanding. What clinched it for me as an opportunity was the weather forecast. There was a typhoon on the way from Taiwan. Tomorrow was looking like it might be the only viable fishing day this week. Kirisaki-san seemed agreeable to the idea of chartering his boat; he even presented me with various options.

Kirisaki-san's first suggestion was that I charter the boat from him for ¥60,000 ($600) and then we split the value of the fish we caught after we'd sold it at market. A little probing revealed that a good day could yield $1,200, a bad day only $500 or less. This didn't seem like a very good option to me. His alternative was that I charter the boat for a flat $800 and keep all the fish to myself. Again, this seemed to involve him passing all the risk to me and then taking all the juicy guaranteed return for himself. I tried to explain to him the adage of the bird in the hand and the two in the bush. He seemed to find this particularly amusing. I think something must have got lost in translation, as I still don't think it's that funny an adage.

I thought I may have had a fairer option. What if I covered his risk and guaranteed him $600 whatever the catch? That way, he knew he was going to have at least an average day. He liked this. In return for my covering his risk, I would keep the first $600 of the catch, so if we only caught $600 of fish then I'd be no worse off and he would still have the $600. He agreed that only seemed reasonable. Any fish we caught in excess of $600 we split; I needed his skills as a fisherman to make this work for me, so it was important that he had a stake in our success. The last thing I wanted him to feel was that he was on a jolly for the day and it didn't matter how many fish he caught.

He mulled over my offer for a moment and then he surprised me. He agreed, and he also offered to cap his return at $800. If we had a $1,200 day then he would only take $800 and the profit of $400 was all mine. I took this as a sign of good faith and we shook on it. Deal. Now all we had to do was catch the fish.

We shook hands on the boat as the sun fell on the harbour. The schedule for the next thirty-six hours was explained to me. We would reconvene here at 4 a.m. and head out to sea. The fishing would be shared between us. Once we had caught our load we would return to harbour and get some sleep. We would then come back to the boat at midnight to kill the fish, box them and take them to market. We needed to arrive in Fukuoka before 3 a.m. to be in time for the auction, which would start at around 4.30 a.m. and be over before 5 a.m. It sounded like a day and a half to me! I was raring to go. All I needed to know was, what did I have to bring? Kirisaki-san said that was easy: just some wellies and a hat.

It was still pitch black in my hotel room at 3.30 a.m. as I peeled the price tag off my new wellies and put them on. I had gone with some shorts so as not to stain my trousers with the inevitable stench of fish. With my wide-brimmed fisherman's hat, I thought I looked like I was dressed more for Glastonbury than a Japanese fishing boat. I was pretty sure the fish wouldn't mind; in any case, by the time they had seen what I was wearing it would be too late for them anyway.

I stopped off at the Seven Eleven – which was actually more like a Seven Seven as it was open at 3.45 a.m. – and bought an apple for breakfast, a bento box for lunch and a five-litre bottle of water for everything in between. With any luck it would be calm enough at sea that I could stomach at least some of it.

I have to say I was a little put out to arrive before Kirisaki-san, considering the hour, but eventually he arrived, full of beans. His little truck was loaded up with half a dozen foul-smelling trays of bait in the form of defrosting miniature prawns, so the beans were probably a direct result of simply not having to be in the truck with them any longer. We carried them over the gangway and onto the boat with a cooler and our lunches, and soon we were ready to cast off and head out to sea. It was only minutes before the first crown of dawn peeked above the horizon.

There are few things that I have enjoyed more than the sight of the sun rising over the sea. To be on the water at dawn, to feel the warmth of the sun on your face and to see its rays slowly light up the sea below is a pleasure beyond any other. I know that it is easy to become desensitized to experiences, but surely fishermen the world over still delight in this every time they set off on an early-morning expedition. Certainly Kirisaki-san's happy mood, despite the hour, suggested a fulfilment with his lot in life.

It took us less than an hour to reach the spot from where we would fish for the day. There were another six or seven boats within view. Kanasaki is one of several ports that lie along a channel where the current from the south meets the current from the north. This makes the water particularly rich in food for the fish that we're after: the horse mackerel.

Anyone who's been on holiday in Cornwall and fished for mackerel will know the drill. The line is fairly thick, like a washing line with four or five hooks attached. Just above the hooks is a small wire mesh pot, packed with the smelly mini-prawns that Kirisaki-san had brought along. You throw the whole lot overboard, let the line out until it reaches the bottom and then slowly draw it back in, a few feet at a time, pausing at the end of each pull to check that you haven't snagged a fish. You'll know if you have by the discernible tug on the line. It sounds simple. It wasn't.

Over the next two hours or so I filled and refilled the bait holder, throwing it over the side and pulling it back in once I felt the tug on the line. Often there was nothing there at all. Sometimes, rather annoyingly, there was a fish (or two) on the line, but when I went to pull them over the side they swished and turned and freed themselves, escaping back into the depths, safe from my net.

Kirisaki-san, on the other hand, operated smoothly and deftly, landing a fish (or two, or three) every time. He also happily chattered away about life and everything in it. Every time I let a fish off the hook, he erupted in fits of laughter, never tiring of finding my mishaps profoundly amusing. Every fish I managed to land earned a comment. Nine times out of ten this was either 'big size' or 'small size', depending on the size. So we proceeded with the day.

By around 8 a.m. I was starting to get the knack. I began to feel how the tug of a fish is different to the underlying tug of the ocean and I started pulling up fish with something like the same regularity as Kirisaki-san. I even got a complimentary 'professional' from him. I have never been more proud.

We started to hit a rhythm and the tanks in the heart of the boat began to look more respectable. I was curious as to how we were faring, and was encouraged to hear that if we kept up this pace we should be on for a good profit. No pressure then, just keep catching fish. I started to think what it would be like to make a profit. After the recent disasters I'd had in Taiwan and Tokyo, I was desperate to start making money again. Somehow, the physical labour of this pursuit made me feel better. I was trying, and I could actually feel that.

To break up the monotony and to up both our games I suggested a little competition: first to ten. I'd like to say I'm not a betting man, but I am. However, I wasn't convinced by Kirisaki-san's wager: if he reached ten first then I had to marry his daughter. No matter how he dressed it up – I would inherit the boat, I would get Japanese citizenship, she's a very good cook – I was reluctant to accept, but he carried on regardless. He pulled out his first catch before I'd finished the 'o' of 'Go!' and proclaimed: 'One–nil'.

The easiest way out of this, I decided, was simply to win, so right on cue I struck back: 'One–one'. And so the game continued until 'two–two', after which he started pulling two or three up at a time in quick succession and won ten–two. Coolly, he turned to me and told me that from now on I should call him 'Dad'.

The other fishermen and Kirisaki-san kept each other constantly amused with their on-board CB radios. In theory, they all compete for fish, but in reality they are a community. Survival in bad weather necessitates that they look out for each other, and they share jokes and observations on the day's fishing to keep each other company and, probably, sane. When one of the neighbouring boats turned and took off for the shore, the radio chatter picked up. It wasn't even 11.30 a.m. and I was a little surprised to see someone leaving early. Why was he leaving? Was the typhoon early? Was our day going to come to a premature end, too? I was worried that this was going to scupper my chance to make a profit. 'No,' Kirisaki-san explained, 'he's run out of cigarettes, so he's going home.' It's good to know that the pursuit of profit is not always so desperate that there isn't room for a little self-indulgence.

By lunchtime we seemed to be doing well and the tanks were carrying at least eighty fish. Kirisaki-san revealed that 'big size' can fetch up to $8 each and 'small size' more like $4. We had about half of each, so after a quick mental calculation I thought we had around $400 worth of fish. We had enough time to reach the $600 mark but Kirisaki-san pointed out that we were starting to run out of bait. All those wasted casts in the first couple of hours were starting to look like the 'profit that got away'. It was now crucial that every cast brought home a fish.

We continued after lunch but a couple of blanks convinced me that I should slow down to allow Kirisaki-san to make more of the bait. I dropped to around one cast for every three of his and, as he continued to pull out at least one fish with every cast like a well-oiled machine, this looked like a very prudent course of action. Right to the last mesh full of prawns, he brought home the goods, and when the final fish dropped into the tank we did a quick head count. I reckoned we had around one hundred fish of varying sizes. Our chances of breaking even? Kirisaki-san thought it was possible but, as always, it would depend on the market. We needed to head back, store the fish and get some rest before that.

Back at the harbour, the boat was tied up and the bait trays unloaded over the gangway. Thankfully, Kirisaki-san's daughter hadn't made it down as promised, so I could relax and help him. We scooped all the fish out of the tanks and into a huge holding net that we threw over the side of the boat. The fish would remain there for the next seven hours while we went to get some rest. Once the boat and the tanks had been hosed down, we were ready to go. I'm usually not very good at sleeping during the day, but after twelve hours hauling line off the boat I was utterly exhausted. I headed back to the hotel, my arms burning, wondering if we had caught enough fish to make my money back at market.

Nineteen

PLACE YOUR BETS: RED OR BLACK

INVESTMENTS:
— **Surfboards: $12,156**
— **Jade: $9,214**
— **Fish: $600**
IN THE BANK: $42,344

Midnight is a rude time to be woken. It's not even tomorrow. It's still today. At least it still feels like the day that I woke up in earlier. My head is heavy and dark and I don't want to get up. Then I remember where I am, sigh and get out of bed. If this is a fisherman's life then you can keep it. I'd rather go back to getting up at the crack of dawn and heading off to my desk job in London. Well, almost.

Thankfully, Kirisaki-san is already waiting for me when I arrive back at the boat. If he'd been late again then we'd have fallen out. I've discovered that it's quite hard to get a cup of coffee in a small fishing village in the south-west corner of Japan at 12.30 a.m. What you do get here, and in fact all over Japan, are vending machines. Climb to the top of Mount Fuji and there's a vending machine; find yourself on a remote beach and there's a vending machine; go looking for a vending machine in the middle of the night in a small fishing village and you won't be disappointed. So, a couple of cans of Coke later, I'm ready to put on my big, yellow, rubber fisherman's pants and start killing fish.

Kirisaki-san and I remove all the fish from the holding net and throw them roughly into a box on deck. Kirisaki-san has filled two other large buckets with iced water. He points to the left one and tells me: 'Big size,' the right one: 'Small size.' He then lifts a fish out of the bucket, slips his middle and index fingers under its chin and into its gills and then, with a backward tug, he breaks its neck and drops it into the left-hand bucket. Just to check that I was paying attention, he reiterates: 'Big size.'

I've caught mackerel before. Many times. I've always enjoyed the catching bit but, I must admit, when it has come to the killing bit in the past, I've never been quite sure what the most humane way is. I have tried beheading with a sharp knife, bludgeoning with a heavy object and even suffocating in a plastic bag. Now, having been educated in how easy and simple and painless the correct way to do it is, I am experiencing years of residual guilt. If only I had known what I know now.

As a way of overcoming this delayed emotional burden, I throw myself into the humane slaughter of as many fish as I can. Each humane killing reduces the percentage of fish I've killed inhumanely. Kirisaki-san may have won the fishing contest, but I am the executioner. In a couple of minutes we have made light work of the whole catch. Fingers in, break the neck, pick the size, choose the bucket; next. Simple. I haven't even time to notice that each dead fish has sprayed a little bit of fishy blood onto me until after the last fish is deposited into the bucket and I realize that my face and arms are covered in specks of blood. I look like a crazed psycho killer from a fishing-based slasher movie – *Nightmare on Helm Street*.

On a little bit of a bloodlust comedown, I start analysing our catch. Kirisaki-san thinks we've done alright, but no better. Am I on for a profit? He doesn't know. It'll be close and, crucially, it will depend on market conditions. The best thing we can do now is to package them well and get them to market on time. We've done everything so far to preserve the freshness and thereby maintain the price. Now Kirisaki-san shows a real artistic flare when it comes to packing them up.

I fetch a dozen polystyrene boxes from inside the hold and we begin to lay out the fish according to size. One by one the boxes fill, and we get around fifteen small or eight big fish to a box. I start to picture each fish that got away through the day and imagine how many extra boxes we could have had if I'd only been quicker with the net or more careful pulling on the line. It is these small things that a fisherman lives or dies by. We have sixteen boxes in total, which we load up onto the back of Kirisaki-san's mini-van. After giving the buckets and the boat a quick scrub down, we're ready to head into the night, towards the market at Fukuoka. In a few hours' time I will know whether I'm Jonah or Ahab.

Kirisaki-san and I whiz through the streets of Fukuoka, as every reasonable soul in the city of 6 million is still fast asleep. When the morning comes they'll all be heading off to work and at lunchtime they will be expecting fresh sushi. To furnish this nationwide obsession the market has to start early. We arrive by 2.45 a.m. and it's already teeming with traders and fishermen. As at Tsukiji, ankle-length white wellies are the shoe of choice here, and everyone who isn't walking around in them is probably scooting around in them on a high-speed mini-lorry. I'm a little disappointed when our fine catch is deemed too small to warrant having a mini-lorry assigned to us and we're merely waved through by the official at the gate.

We back Kirisaki-san's little van up to a conveyor belt in a large warehouse next to the dockside. Some of the bigger boats are actually landing their catch straight into the market. Kirisaki-san explains that this is how the large fresh tuna are usually brought to the market; their value is so high that every second counts. Our boxes of mackerel are literally small fry in comparison.

Each of our boxes has a label inside bearing Kirisaki-san's logo so that the market official can keep track of them. He is a small, old man with a long, grey beard. I think he looks very wise. Maybe he isn't, but somewhere along the line I've been programmed to believe that all Japanese men with long, grey beards look wise. The boxes are offloaded at the other end by a team of market labourers and placed in rows according to size along with other mackerel brought by other fishermen. In all, there are around 200 boxes of mackerel in this patch of the warehouse. The warehouse is a vast area, around the size of four tennis courts, covered in fish of every variety you care to name. On one side of us is the squid and on the other side is the shellfish, and then there are the whitefish, crabs, scallops and eels. It goes on and on and then back up the other side until the shark and swordfish, which are opposite us, and then at the very end, the big money: the tuna.

The auction starts with the tuna. The auctioneers all wear white hats. The only people allowed to bid are the traders, who wear red hats. As it starts, the auctioneer stands at one end of a row of ten huge tuna carcasses. The twenty-five buyers gather round him so that from above it must look like a messy game of snooker. He lets out a massive cry from his belly and begins gabbling. Five seconds later, he lets out another cry, with a downward stab of his hand toward the tuna, and then moves on to the next fish. It takes no more than two minutes for him to scream his way down the line of fish, then he lets out a final cry and he's off. He has auctioned off ten fish for between $3,000 and $7,000 a pop. So that's $50,000 dollars in two minutes. And even though I followed it myself, and saw with my own eyes all the mysterious hand gestures that the buyers were making, I was none the wiser as to who had bought what.

The hierarchy of fish determines the order in which the auctions occur. Mackerel comes fairly far down the line and, by the time the auctioneer makes his way to my boxes, the mini-lorries have scooted in and emptied over half the warehouse. It's still not even 4 a.m.

Our auctioneer is a tall, well-built man in his late twenties. He takes a minute or two at the end of the first line of mackerel to establish that all the mackerel buyers know he is about to start, then he lets out a loud scream and starts the auction. He walks at pace down the line, never really stopping at any one box and never really stopping for breath. The noise is constant: jabbering prices in a monotone and then intermittently letting out a louder cry, which I assume means 'Sold!' He works his way down the first line and up the next. Each time he cries 'Sold!' the relevant buyer tosses a slip bearing their logo onto one of the boxes of fish and the auctioneer's assistant walking behind him makes a note on his clipboard. In no more than five minutes, every box has a wholesaler's slip inside it and he has sold the lot.

How did it go? Kirisaki-san says prices were better today than last week. As I'd expected, a combination of this week's strike and the predicted typhoon meant that prices were pushed higher. Had I made a profit? It was still too early to say. The auctioneer's assistant would now take his clipboard back to the market office and the accounts department would make sense of who had bought what from whom and for how much. In an hour or so, they would work out the money, and only then would the fishermen know what their catch sold for. Until then we could only wait.

The wait for an answer from the market office takes a little longer than expected, and I'm still waiting at 6 a.m. Three herons have flown in from the dockside and are tentatively creeping into the market hall on the hunt for discarded scraps of fish. A market worker washing down the floor turns his hose on them when they fall within range and they open their huge wings and fly back out to safety. The sun comes up over the harbour and the lights on the suspension bridge are turned off.

Eventually, Kirisaki-san reappears, holding a brown envelope that I know must contain our takings from the auction. I am physically and mentally exhausted. I could have gone back to my hotel and waited for an answer over the phone, but this is too important to me; I desperately want to have made a profit on this endeavour. I've agreed to pay Kirisaki-san $600, or ¥60,000, so anything less than that in the envelope will have to come directly out of my pocket.

Kirisaki-san hands me the envelope and at first all I can see is indecipherable Japanese script. Then I can see the bottom line; that's the same in any language. It says ¥60,150. It takes me a second or two to process. I have to pay Kirisaki-san the first ¥60,000, so that means I've made ¥150, or $1.50. I am overjoyed, ecstatic, a little over-tired and a little emotional. I should be devastated; I've been up for forty-two of the last forty-eight hours, I'm sun-damaged and aching all over from what has been the hardest two days of physical exertion of my trip so far, but I'm not. I almost crush Kirisaki-san with the biggest hug I can muster. We are both laughing hard and I'm even more delighted that he gets it, he understands that the important thing for me is that this is not a loss.

Kirisaki-san takes the envelope from me and takes out his share of the spoils, the ¥60,000, and then he offers me the two coins that are left over: 'Cashback!' He laughs. Call it cashback, call it what you like. I'm looking at two small, silver coins in my hand and to me they represent the importance of persevering. I pray they also represent a turning point in my adventure.

For Kirisaki-san this has been an average day. Well, maybe not usual, but you know what I mean. Today he had the luxury of knowing that he would make his $600, but I can't forget that he has to work this hard every day to make that. Some days he makes a lot more, but others less. The rising price of oil is narrowing the fishermen's margins all the time and they are typical of many businessmen the world over who are feeling this cost acutely. As long as the world depends on oil as its primary power source, then from British lorry drivers to Japanese fishermen, everyone's way of life will hang on an economic precipice. If they can't afford to do their jobs we will have to pay more for our fish.

But for me, I now have the feeling that things have turned in my favour. I've put all the bad luck I had in Taiwan behind me and I'm back in the black. My pecker is up again. Now it's time to move on from Japan and make some serious money in the Americas, 5,000 miles across the Pacific Ocean, where I should have a delivery of surfboards arriving any day.

Twenty

GOING LOGO DOWN IN ACAPULCO

LAST TRADE:
— **Fish:** $1.50 profit
INVESTMENTS:
— **Surfboards:** $12,156
— **Jade:** $9,214
IN THE BANK: $42,345

What's in a brand? It's more than just a name that tells you who the manufacturer is; it's also about fashion, design, quality and other, looser associations that convey to a customer the very essence of what a product represents. Without a brand, a product seems cheap. The brand is a way for the seller to reassure buyers that they can trust the product. A successful brand takes time to build, but once established it becomes a reliable route to making some serious cash and a means to expand and diversify into new markets. Everyone in the market is trying to establish new brands, and once they have a successful brand they'll fight tooth and nail to hold on to it.

China, India, Brazil, Mexico and South Africa are now part of the G8+5. Rapid economic growth has meant that they have far outpaced most of their developing counterparts and they are now key markets for international companies. According to the IMF, Mexico is now the eleventh-wealthiest economy in the world in terms of purchasing power, which is the best indicator of what the average person on the street has to spend. Mexico has built much of its success on exporting to the rest of the world, but as people get richer they start wanting imported goods too. One thing that is clear when you arrive in Mexico is that they are importing goods with strong brands; from clothes to cars, household brand labels are in evidence everywhere.

I had crossed the Pacific from Japan and crossed the date line in the process. It's a very strange feeling because you wake up in the morning, go to the airport, spend all day flying and then arrive at the same time on the same day as you just left. I felt as though fate had somehow given me a bonus day, a day that shouldn't be wasted, so I hit the beach.

I had decided to try to make some profit from bringing inflatable surfboards (boogie boards) to Mexico. Along with oil and manufacturing, the big industry in Mexico is tourism. Most lower- and middle-income families take their holidays on Mexican beaches every year, along with over 20 million foreigners. I was arriving in Mexico at the height of summer and I'd banked on being able to sell a brand new product that I'd bought in China: 750 inflatable boogie boards, for which I'd paid $12,000 including shipping and taxes. Each board had cost a total of $16 and had been carefully branded with the 'Hola' logo.

The manufacturer in China had taken the order for the boards unbranded; 375 blue and 375 black. It was up to me what I put on them. As a way of conferring a sense of quality to them, I'd asked Peter, a friend in London who's got an artistic flair for these things, to draw up a design for the boards. I had come up with the idea of calling them 'Hola', where the H was shaped like a wave. *Hola* is Spanish for 'hello', and *ola* means 'wave'. Well, I thought it was clever, and Peter came up with a cracking image. I'd had it printed on every board and it took them into a different league.

I have surfed for many years. I'm not terribly good at it; I can stand up well enough and I can turn left. I never quite got the hang of turning right. I don't like the wave to be much bigger than I am, or I get scared. Surfing looks serene when it is done well; it can result in distress and even drowning if done badly. Surfers often look down on boogie boarders as lesser beings, but drowning is drowning in my book, whatever position you choose to do it in.

The first thing I had to do was get my board and therefore my brand endorsed. It was all very well turning up with a branded product and claiming it was the next new thing, but who was I, with my unidirectional turning skills, to be selling surfboards? I needed to find someone with the credentials to say whether the Hola boogie board was any good. If I could find someone with credibility the market would have to listen. I thought the best place to look for such a person was on the beach that's known throughout the world as being home to one of the world's largest surfing waves, the Mexican Pipeline.

Puerto Escondido was once a deserted beach resort on the hippy trail but now it's a world-class surf resort. The reason is this huge wave that runs the length of the beach. Along the shorefront are a dozen beach bars selling *cervezas*, tortillas and sushi. Every morning and evening, the sea fills up with surfers who risk it all to take on the colossal wave. At dusk, those not brave enough to surf sit in the bars, sipping on a beer watching the small, dark figures out at sea paddle, squat and ride. Some of the tricks and stunts they perform are simply breathtaking.

If you sit for long enough, you're sure to see one figure stand out among the crowd. Literally. Angel Salinas has been riding this wave for nearly twenty years, originally as a surfer but now as a power-boarder. Powerboarding involves standing on the board the whole time (with the aid of a paddle), so you can see him a mile off. He paddles in and out of all the other prostrate surfers waiting for the perfect wave. You will also recognize him because he nearly always wears a Mexican wrestling mask.

I'd contacted Angel because of his reputation in Mexico. Not only has he been a professional surfer on the international stage for twenty years, he is liked and respected throughout the surfing community. I'd found countless articles about him on the internet and in surfing magazines over the years, all complimentary. He also owns a surf shop.

Central Surf is right on the Zicatella beach in Puerto and I found Angel behind the desk, a strong, powerful-looking man approaching forty with a warm, infectious smile; instantly likeable. I introduced myself as the one who had been emailing him about the inflatable boogie boards and he seemed intrigued to see one. I was equally keen to show him, but first I wanted his word that he would come out on the Pipeline with me tomorrow at dawn to try them out. I explained that I wanted a professional opinion, and his was the best in town. All surfers like to hear this kind of thing.

Angel agreed, so I inflated one of the boards. It was the first time I'd seen an inflated board with the Hola logo on it so I was a bit nervous as to how they'd turned out. I wasn't disappointed. The board inflated well, actually going quite rigid. The logo looked magnificent on it and Angel seemed quite impressed. We compared it to the conventional styrofoam boards that he was selling in his shop. They were selling for upwards of 1,000 pesos ($100), and when I told Angel that I was selling the Hola board for 300 pesos ($30) with a recommended retail price of 500–600 pesos ($50–60), he liked it even more.

I thought I had done my homework properly on this trade. If you recall, the logic for the board being inflatable was that tourists, mostly kids and novice surfers, would like it as a board that they could take home with them when the holiday was over, unlike the conventional board. For this to work the price had to be attractive to that market, so I'd set it deliberately at around half the cost of the conventional board. Angel agreed that this was a good strategy. If it worked tomorrow, he'd even buy twenty for his own shop. No pressure then.

*

The next morning we met at first light on the Zicatella beach. There were already a dozen surfers in the water and the waves were pounding in on the shore. The Pipeline was at least twelve feet high at its peak. I was trying to look confident in front of Angel but I'd never surfed anything like this big a wave before.

Angel and I pumped up our boards and discussed tactics. There was a very strong rip tide that pulled you along the shore so we were better entering the water a little further up. After that, we needed to paddle out to where the waves were breaking. Angel warned me that this would be 'very fierce' and I would need to duck dive to get through. Duck diving is a way of pushing the nose of the board under the incoming wave so that you go under the wave rather than getting smashed by it. Angel was a little concerned that, because the boards were inflatable, this would be more difficult than with a conventional board. I reassured him that I knew how to duck dive but I was a little scared about his point.

We wished each other luck and headed out, skipping over the first few waves and then throwing ourselves onto the boards and over the incoming surf. We paddled hard against the rip tide for five shoulder-aching minutes, getting closer and closer to where the waves were breaking. Up close, twelve feet of water looks a lot bigger and I knew I was going to have to give it everything to paddle my way under and through it. Safety lay on the other side.

Angel, being heavier than me, had drifted further on the rip so he was well out of shouting distance. I was on my own and I was right up to where the humongous waves were breaking. I paddled towards a wall of water twelve feet high that was coming at me with an awesome power. I gave one last paddle just as I met it head-on. I pushed the nose of my board down and kicked as hard as I could. The front of the wave raced over my head and I could feel that I was moving through the middle of it, hanging onto the board for all I was worth. Then the tow of the wave came dragging behind, grabbing hold of the board, and me attached to it, with overpowering strength. It dragged us down and then down again. It was like being inside a washing machine on the full spin cycle. I couldn't tell which way was up or down, my feet were spinning right over my head and my arms were being pulled from their sockets. I was really, really scared. I concentrated on holding my breath. Hang on, Conor. I was urging myself to hold on to the last of my breath. Wait for it to end; it will end.

It did end. I felt a calmness return to the water and righted myself by putting my feet on the ground. Incredibly, I was on the sandy bottom. I pushed up and kicked for the surface, taking a massive gulp of air as soon as I broke through. I was alive. What the hell was I doing here? I wasn't experienced enough to be here and I'd nearly drowned as if to prove it. I still had hold of the board, which was one thing. I would have liked to have time to think about what I was going to do to get out of this, but I didn't have time. There was another wave coming.

Again and again I went into the wash cycle. Each time I took a battering. Up and down inside the water, gasping, gulping and clinging on to life. Each wave mercifully pushed me a little further until, finally, I was beyond the break and back in the manageable shallow surf. I could feel the sand beneath my feet so I was able to lift the board out of the water and stumble back to the safety of the shore. I had a cramp in one leg and I was chronically short of breath. I got back on dry land and vomited.

When I had finally composed myself enough to look again, I could see that Angel had made it through the break and was taking his place in the line-up next to the other surfers, waiting his turn for a wave. When it was just right, he paddled with his huge, strong arms and got ahead of one of the waves that had almost done for me. The wave reared up, revealing a smooth face of water. Angel and the Hola board were on the top edge of it and seemed to hang for just a moment before he pushed the nose of the board over and down the face. He expertly tilted his body so that the board ran along it, always staying a few feet ahead of the breaking edge. He seemed to ride it for miles, and as he got closer to the shore I could see his beaming, infectious smile. He was having fun.

He came back to shore and we walked along the beach towards each other. He was concerned about me and wanted to make sure I was OK. I was fine now, and only wanted to know what he thought about the board.

'Everybody out there said to me, "Angel, what is that?"' he started to tell me. 'They said, "Angel, you can't catch a wave on that," but I did. I caught a good one.' What a hero. There's something primeval about surfing and a simple, ancient heroism that accompanies anyone who can do it well. I was full of admiration for this giant of a man.

'But what about the board?'

'It's good, my friend.' He beamed at me. I noticed for the first time that his board looked in bad shape. One of the handles was torn and the safety leash had been ripped right off. 'This is a great board for kids and for beginners. In the white water near the shore it is perfect. But maybe not too good for the Mexican Pipeline. It was very difficult to get out past the breaking water.'

'You're telling me, Angel, you're telling me!' I gave him a pat on the back because he'd said all the right things and because he will forever be one of my heroes.

Angel bought twenty boards for his own shop. I gave him a knock-down price of 250 pesos ($25) as a thank-you for his endorsement. Now I had that, I could look anyone in Mexico right in the eye and say, not only did Angel Salinas ride the Mexican Pipeline on the Hola board, he bought twenty for his own shop. Who was going to argue with that?

*

The endorsement had given me enough confidence to go for a one-off deal with one of the really big players in the Mexican sports goods sector. If I could get rid of all remaining 730 boards in one hit, it would free me up to spend some time looking for a quality Mexican product to buy while I was here. It would also be a first: selling something the easy way. So far, things were going well, so I was reasonably confident.

I contacted the enormously helpful Chris Wall at UK Trade & Investment (UKTI) in London for any contacts that he had in Mexico. The UKTI is a fully funded body that aims to help British companies find new opportunities overseas. Chris had lived and worked in Mexico for years and he was a great source of contacts and support, as was Hugo Martin, the owner of a UK-based venture company, who set up a meeting with the buying executive from Mexico's number one sports retailer, Marti Group, at their store in Acapulco.

The Marti store was a general sports superstore. It was on an out-of-town shopping development. It was glass-fronted with automatic sliding doors. It had a jet ski in one window and a display of tennis equipment in the other. It was a sports shop and had no pretensions to be anything but. Alejandro Gamez had flown all the way down from Mexico City to meet me, which he assured me was perfectly normal behaviour for him if there was a big deal to be done. He was a tall, Spanish-looking Mexican dressed in a smart striped shirt and suit trousers. He spoke in polished English.

It took me about five minutes to explain to him the origin of the boards and why I had gone with the Hola brand. I was a bit worried that it might not translate in Mexico. I don't actually speak Spanish, so it was entirely feasible that I'd missed the double meaning of *hola* somehow. Maybe it meant hello but also meant drown; I didn't know. It was alright; Alejandro said it was good. He liked it. He did a sort of half nod, half shrug, as he played around with it. 'Hola. Hola. Yeah, I like it. How is the board? Does it work?' Bingo. I relayed my Angel Salinas story. Every time I referred to the board it was 'Hola Board' this, 'Hola Board' that. I pumped it up as I spoke, but Alejandro started to look impatient; he kept looking at his watch.

'How much is it?' he asked.

'Well, for a small order, 300 pesos ($30). But if you were interested in the lot I could knock that down to 280 pesos. I think that leaves you lots of margin to retail them around the 500 peso mark.'

The moment of truth. 'Well, it's no problem to take them all, we have one hundred stores nationwide. I'd rather pay around 250 pesos [$25] for them though.'

'A little low for me; how about we split the difference?' This was becoming my catchphrase. I could have pressed harder but I'd learnt from the jade market experience: close a deal while it's there.

'So, 265 pesos per board? OK you have a deal.'

We shook hands and he said something that I'll never forget:

'See? It's easy doing business in Mexico.' And with that, he was off. He had a flight to catch back to Mexico City. He fired off some instructions to me about emailing him all the details, and his purchasing manager would send a purchase order and arrange delivery next week. He had done his bit. He'd made the decision that I wanted him to make – needed him to make – and next month the Hola Board would be the new brand on the shelves.

Finally, I had managed to effect a deal that had gone smoothly. From its start on a rainy day in China to its end in an air-conditioned sports shop on a baking hot day in Acapulco, it had gone to plan. OK, I had nearly died along the way, but apart from that, ten out of ten for planning and execution. I gave myself a pat on the back and went out to spend some of the $8,000 profit on getting thoroughly pissed.

I was back in the money-making groove. Behind me was the misery of Taiwan and ahead of me the way home. I was beginning to think again of what that all-important last trade was going to be, but I didn't feel that I had quite enough money made yet. I was up around $21,000, which wasn't enough to go for a double or nothing to make the $50,000. I needed to squeeze in one more trade first.

Twenty-one
IT MAKES ME HAPPY

LAST TRADE:
— **Surfboards: $7,719 profit**
INVESTMENTS:
— **Jade: $9,214**
IN THE BANK: $62,220

The *jimadores* arrive in the agave field half an hour before dawn. The men climb out of the bus that has brought them here from the town, each carrying a kind of axe called a *coa* in hand. They are all dressed in cowboy hat, boots, denim shirt and jeans, with their left leg covered in a protective leather pad. After a few minutes spent sharpening their *coas*, they are gathered together by the foreman. Last year the Herradura distillery, one of Mexico's oldest, was taken over by a large American company. The American parent's corporate health and safety policy means that now the men must engage in a group warm-up exercise. The *coas* are put to one side while they form a circle and begin a routine of hip-wiggling and shoulder-stretching. They look a little nonplussed; some have never been injured in forty years, even without a warm-up.

Once the men are ready to begin work they spread out in the field amongst the agaves. These are blue agave, so called because they have a very faint blue hue to their enormous spikes. An inadvertent brush against one of these will cut deep enough to draw blood. The *jimador* places his left foot carefully onto the agave to hold it still and then, with several deft chops, goes about removing the spiky crown to shape the plant into what looks like a giant pineapple, called the *pina*. The men work incredibly fast; a team of twenty *jimadores* can clear a whole two-acre field in four hours, the length of a normal working day. They are paid by weight for the *pinas*, which are collected up in the back of a high-sided truck and driven away to the distillery. A *jimador* can expect to earn an average of $500 per week; not bad for a four-hour day, five-day week. Little wonder, then, that to become one, your father had to have been one.

José is a *jimador*, like his father and grandfather before him. He's meeting me today in his huge, white Stetson hat to show me around. His job is to persuade me to buy something from the Herradura range for my next trade. I want something that is typically Mexican and I want a strongly branded product. The two best deals that I've done so far on this trip have been red wine and boogie boards so I want to combine what I've learnt and take tequila to Rio de Janeiro, where I think there should be a good market for it. Brazilians traditionally drink cachaça but are famously open-minded about new products; I reckon the bars and clubs of Rio might be ready for a little of Mexico's most famous export. It's worth a shot (sorry).

I've always thought that tequila was a drink best drunk drunk. It's hard for me to envisage a situation where I am sober and I order tequila. It's OK in a margarita or a tequila sunrise, but otherwise it's a 'last orders' moment of madness for which you always pay the price the next day. José is keen to show me why they see it a little differently here.

In Mexico they have over one hundred brands of tequila and the vast majority of them hail from this small part of the country north of Guadalajara, after which the drink is named: Tequila. I've taken a ride up here to find out a little more. I was interested in the idea of exporting tequila to Brazil and I was intrigued by the idea that it could have so many brands. In my mind all tequila was equally foul and so I wanted to know more about what made one brand more expensive or better than another. That's where José comes in.

Back at the distillery, José is showing me the long and complicated process by which the agave is twice distilled to produce white tequila. Contrary to my previous misconception, this is how all tequila is made. The gold tequila that I thought was supposed to be 'better' is actually the same tequila, only it's spent some time in an oak barrel before bottling. This gives it a slightly different flavour. José has a few of them lined up to show me.

On a small bench inside the hacienda, José and I sit to sample the white, gold and aged (or *añejo*) varieties of the Herradura brand. The way to drink tequila, he tells me, is not to knock it back, but rather to sip it into one's mouth, leave it on the tongue for five seconds and then slowly swallow it back. One by one, we repeat this process with some of the finest tequilas available on the market. José swirls each glass with flamboyance to show me the variety in body and colour, pushes his nose into the glass to marvel at the hints of chocolate and lemon in the aroma, and I copy. I have a strong sense of déjà vu about it all. Remember Cape Town?

The proof, as they say, is in the pudding, and unfortunately José is with the wrong guy, because each glass of tequila tastes just as bad as the last to my palate. I try not to wince and contort my face, I wrestle with my gag reflex so as not to paint the hacienda a new shade of sick and I even manage to discern a flavour or two beyond the simple 'disgusting', but it's no use. I don't get it. The Mexicans know how to appreciate this drink and I have no doubt when José tells me that, in time, I too could learn, I could educate my palate to develop the same degree of appreciation that he has for this 'Mexican champagne'. But I haven't time and neither, I suspect, does the rest of the world. The vast majority of us will forever be ordering tequila as an ill-thought-through, desperate late effort to get a little more drunk before we go home to pass out in front of the telly, and I was reasonably confident that this would be the case in Rio, too.

To his credit, José persisted long enough to change my mind, although it did take a vintage tequila that retails for nearly $200 per bottle to do it: a twenty-year-old aged tequila that, he assures me, is Herradura's finest ever concoction. I take a sip and let it swirl in my mouth, preparing myself for the inevitable retch, but it doesn't come. He's done it. José has found a tequila that actually tastes great; all kinds of warm flavours of cocoa and a real sweetness on the tongue make this the one and only tequila that I would actually consider sipping. But it is way too expensive for what I'm trying to find. I want a reasonably priced tequila that I can sell in the bars and clubs of Rio. The kind of tequila I want is one that people can drink the uneducated way – shots and margaritas – and nobody wants to pay $200 for that.

That's not to say that the Herradura brand wasn't a good asset. We may all regard tequila as disgusting, but there is another preconception that successful brands have played to their advantage in the tequila market: the idea that a good tequila gives you a better hangover. Better hangover. There, I've said it. The idea that hangovers come in different flavours is another ridiculous claim, as far as I'm concerned. I've heard many an unremorseful drinker blame the quality of the booze from the night before for their suffering, when the reality is that too much alcohol gives you a hangover. But what I think doesn't matter. José is confident that the rigorous way in which Herradura is distilled makes it the only tequila in Mexico that comes with a 'no hangover' guarantee. Now that, I can sell.

José is unable to negotiate a price for the Herradura tequilas with me and so I have to say goodbye and wait for a call from the boss, who is actually in the United States. Once the American colleague has had a report from José on which tequilas I'm interested in, he'll contact me with the prices.

The next day the call comes and their man lays out his best prices for me. I'm not interested in the expensive stuff. I've made my mind up to go with the cheapest two tequilas in his range but he needs to give me a cheap enough price for me to be able to sell it in Rio at a little below what they might already be paying there. I'm going to flood the market with a new brand and I want some room to manoeuvre on price, but he isn't playing ball.

Herradura is a very successful brand of tequila in Mexico, and around the world. Their man seems to be very interested in the idea that I could find new customers for them in the Brazilian market, which they seem to feel they haven't yet fully explored, but he is concerned about my strategy. If I want to sell Herradura in Rio then he wants me to respect the brand and that means respect its price. I'm offering to find him new customers in Rio but I need to be able to compete with other brands there, and they sell for near the $35 mark. At the price that is his best offer I don't think I'll be able to compete.

Unfortunately, he won't budge. Selling their product at such discounts is not part of the brand they are trying to build. If I were to go into Rio selling Herradura cheap, people would get the wrong impression about the brand and that's not what they want. He is convinced that I can sell Herradura on quality in Rio and still make a 25 per cent mark-up. I don't agree. I think that, like me, most people in Rio don't really appreciate good tequila and the 'no hangover' guarantee is a nice gimmick, but it's not enough to make the difference. I'm really sorry, Herradura, but the answer has to be: 'No.'

The Herradura experience has cemented my thoughts and now I know what I want: a good brand of tequila but at a price low enough that I can afford to sell it in Rio for $30 or even $25 per bottle. Fortunately, there are plenty of options, and after a little ringing around I find an interesting lead at a well-known Mexican brand that actually bottles in Guadalajara: Sombrero Negro. I call their sales director to explain what I'm doing and he tells me that Brazil is a new market for them right now. They have recently begun exporting there but so far have concentrated solely on São Paulo, not Rio. He invites me in for a chat.

Inside a walled hacienda in Guadalajara, the Del Señor distillery that makes Sombrero Negro is not as picturesque as Herradura but the economics of using a plant in town makes their costs lower. The company is family owned and run, and has a good history going back nearly one hundred years. Like Herradura, they produce a fine twenty-year-old expensive tequila but, unlike Herradura, they also produce a cheap, bottom-of-the-range tequila specially made for drinking in shots or mixing in cocktails. Its price tag is a mere 15 reales (R$), or $10, cleared in Brazil. And each bottle even comes with a small sombrero hat; black, of course.

*

I now had four days in Rio and 400 bottles of Del Señor Sombrero Negro tequila to sell. I arrived in Lapa, in the heart of the old town, to do a little research. Lapa is the party district where the cool young people of Rio head at the weekend. The cobbled streets are lit by lamps strung overhead and the crowd is thick with people moving in time to the beat of the samba rhythms pumped out by invisible sound systems inside graffiti-adorned houses. The crowd breaks open sometimes, clearing way for a couple who have broken into an impromptu dance, and stalls sell barbecued meat and chilled beer. Weaving their way through the crowds are young men carrying trays of lime, salt and, you've guessed it, tequila.

In the space of ten minutes after arriving in Lapa, I had been accosted five times by the tequila salesmen. For around $1 they offered me a small shot in a plastic cup with a pinch of salt and a slice of lime. At first glance this should have been an encouraging sign; Rio is clearly embracing the idea of drinking tequila. I had thought my main adversary in this would be the indigenous cachaça, but I was wrong. On closer inspection it was clear what I was up against. Every tequila pusher on this street was selling the same brand: José Cuervo.

'See how you get on with this one, son.' I took a bottle of Cuervo from one of the street sellers and offered him a bottle of Sombrero Negro in exchange. He looked a little confused at first. Then he realized what was going on: I was offering him a full bottle of Sombrero Negro for his half-bottle of Cuervo. Would he take the swap? No way. He took his bottle back and went back to working the crowd.

I had a similar experience at the first bar I tried to sell to later in the evening. I met up with Marcelo, who ran a Parisian style café-bar not far from my hotel. He was a jowly man, and camper than a row of tents. He sat with me at a small, round table next to the road and I showed him my sample bottles of each of the tequilas.

'Sombrero Negro.' He read the label and turned the bottle over in his hand. I think he liked the little black hats. 'But I have a deal with Cuervo. I only buy tequila from them.'

I had suspected this kind of reaction; but everyone has their price. This was a good chance to test the price at which I could undercut Cuervo.

'How about if I offered it to you for R$30 [around $20] per bottle?'

'No. I only buy Cuervo.'

'How about if I offered it to you for a special price of R$25?'

'No.'

'Well, what price would you not be able to say no to?'

'Even if you paid me, I will still say, "No". I only can buy from Cuervo. I have a contract. You will find most bars in Rio are the same.'

Well, that certainly set the bar high. If Marcelo was right then I had 400 bottles of unsaleable tequila. I had to hope that he was wrong.

Hooray; Marcelo was way wide of the mark. The very next bar that I went to bit my hand off for 48 bottles of tequila at R$30 ($20) per bottle. The bar was listed on the worldsbestbars.com website as one of the world's best bars, so I was a little apprehensive when I turned up to meet the Italian boss, a colossus of a man called Washington, who bore a passing resemblance to Marlon Brando circa *Apocalypse Now*. Washington's bar, Scenarium, was a labyrinth of rooms filled with antiques and curios. The walls and ceilings were draped with odd collectables, mannequins, clocks, even a full-size rickshaw. Washington was rightly proud to be the owner of the bar that is credited with kick-starting the Lapa club scene.

I showed Washington the Sombrero Negro. I was waiting for the excuse about Cuervo and an exclusive contract, and I wasn't disappointed. Well, I was and I wasn't. Scenarium sold Cuervo, but Washington was his own boss. Nobody told him what he could and couldn't sell; given the size of him, I could well believe it. He did tell me however that I'd have to make it worth his while to try something new. I suggested R$30. He said fine. Simple? It was. I dropped off 48 bottles and he handed over R$1,440 ($960). I was on my way and I'd made a 100 per cent mark-up. At this rate, if I could get rid of all my tequila then I stood to make a tidy $4,000.

Deal after deal over the next three days. Every bar I hit wanted to get in on the cheap tequila deal. My undercutting strategy was working. Sure, I had to drop to R$28, R$27 and even R$25 a couple of times, but I could afford to. I was still making R$10 per bottle at that price. I met João (Mexican restaurant), Padraig (Irish bar), Angelo (Tex Mex bar), Leo (nightclub), John (Irish bar), Anna (Mexican restaurant), Michelle (backpacker hostel) and, last but not least, Mila, who owned a chain of bars and restaurants and took the last 120 bottles. All in all, I'd sold 400 bottles of Sombrero Negro to Rio for $7,800 in total. Allowing for transport and costs that left me with a tidy $3,200 profit.

I'd love to look at the success of the tequila deal and find a message about the power of the brand, but the simple reality was that it all boiled down to money. Bars and restaurants work on tight margins and I'd been able to come in under the radar of the big brands with a cheaper option. The real test of the Sombrero Negro brand now is this: when those 400 bottles have been slammed, will the customers come back for more? And if they do, what will they pay next time? I had opened the door; now it was up to Del Señor to keep the momentum going.

I had a momentum of my own, too. I had as much cash in the bank as I needed to turn for home. I had been five long months on the road and I was ready to get back to London. But I had one more trade in me. If I was going to make it to my target of $50,000 then I still had to make nearly $25,000. I would have to risk every penny I'd made so far. And the last trade would need to be something I could buy here in Brazil that would sell back in Blighty for a big margin. I had enough profit put aside now to go for that last double or nothing bet – as long as I could find the right product.

Twenty-two
YOU WOOD SAY THAT

LAST TRADE:
— Tequila: $3,143 profit
INVESTMENTS:
— Jade: $9,214
IN THE BANK: $65,363

How do you get someone to pay more for something than it cost? This is the question that every entrepreneur must find answers to. After travelling over fifty thousand miles in five months, I was starting to feel as though I had discovered a few answers of my own. If I was going to hit my target then the time was coming when I'd have to put some of them into action in one final 'all or nothing' deal.

Entrepreneurs must convince their customers that they are buying something that will enhance their life. They're on to a winner if they have a product that can make the customer feel younger, stronger, sexier, happier. It's often enough just to imply as much, through the strength of a brand such as Ferrari or, dare I say, Hola surfboards. I wanted to find a product that could do 'all of the above', that could claim be the newest, most exciting product in the newest and most exciting market of recent times. And what might that market be? It's a market that has grown rapidly by successfully convincing its consumers that they can make the world a better place.

226

The trick lies in the premiss that the clearest representation of our moral choices is in how we spend our money. You say that you are concerned about global warming and deforestation of the rainforests. I say to you – well, that's easy for you to say. What if I can convince you that the only way to truly express this concern is to put your money where your mouth is? That if you really care about the planet's future then you have to buy sustainable products and be prepared to pay more for them? Unless you actually buy that sustainable pine kitchen table rather than the mahogany one (and pay twice as much for it), then it's all just hot air, isn't it? You should put up or shut up.

The trend over the last five years in the West is for more and more of us to do exactly that – put up and dig a little deeper in our pockets to support 'ethical consumerism'. This catch-all term simultaneously means boycotting products which have a negative impact on society (such as mahogany or blood diamonds), and actively choosing products with a positive impact on society (such as energy-efficient light bulbs or organic vegetables).

The failed Elephant Pepper deal had been troubling me since I'd been in Africa all those months ago. I really liked the idea of finding a product that fits into this green market. At the time I'd felt that chilli sauce eaters would pay extra if they thought a few elephants were benefiting. Now I wanted to blaze a trail doing something similar, but with a new product, just as I'd done with Craig's coffee in Cape Town. And this time I wanted to bring it back to the UK to get my 'green premium'.

The best thing about the green premium is that it's often disproportionate to the extra costs involved in producing the goods, so there are even greater bumper profits to be made for manufacturers and retailers. From energy companies to chilli sauce manufacturers, firms can charge more simply because consumers have been convinced that the product has green credentials. What do they really get for this premium? How valuable is the feeling that they're making the world a better place? I don't know, you had me at the 'premium' bit.

*

Flying in a light aircraft doesn't quite create a barrier between you and your surroundings like a jumbo does. You are more aware of what is around and below you in much the same way as you might be in a car. I've read lots about how the rainforests of Brazil have been chopped down and reduced by 50 or 60 per cent. Even since the millennium we've chopped down an area the size of Greece. But none of these figures can prepare you for seeing it with your own eyes.

In Mato Grosso, in the far west of Brazil, there are huge patches in the forest: missing trees that have been cleared for farming. What would once have been 100 per cent forest is now a land pocked and scarred by deforestation. OK, people need to live and that means that food needs to be planted, animals need to graze and so it follows that trees need to be cut down. But even knowing that, was it any less shocking to see it? Not a jot.

The plane circled over the vast Río Paraguay, which flows through the heart of the Pantanal, a vast tropical wetland. A flock of bright pink birds skimmed over the water and trees along a bank teeming with nesting storks. Deforestation has a profound indirect effect on us all; there would be nothing indirect about its effect round here.

I had flown here to meet Sylvio Coutinho and his son Sylvinho: two men who had started to make money out of ethical consumerism. Only these guys had come up with a twist. Their scheme involved chopping down trees – in Brazil. It sounds so wrong. I just had to check it out.

Sylvio senior had begun planting a teak forest on reclaimed swamp land in the Mato Grosso region fifteen years ago. The plantation had grown to over 150,000 acres when Sylvinho joined the business. Their company, Floresteca, had taken Burmese teak plants and used cloning techniques in a laboratory to produce a fast-growing variety that could reach maturity in twenty years rather than the hundred years it usually takes in the Burmese rainforest. The conditions in Brazil are perfect for teak even though the tree is not indigenous. It actually grows better here, ten thousand miles away from where it's meant to grow.

The massive cloning programme already has over 6 million saplings ready to go into the ground. The idea is simple: cut one down, plant a new one.

As we drove out from the airstrip, I wondered whether Sylvio derived a sense of satisfaction from doing his bit for the rainforest. I assumed he probably had a personal connection to it, perhaps raised by wild animals after surviving a plane crash in the heart of the forest as a child? 'You mean, why we're doing all this?' The minivan bounced along the muddy track. 'It's not because we're nice guys; it's because we saw a market for this way back in '93.'

*

Brazil has two seasons: wet and dry. It was coming to the end of the dry season and hundreds and hundreds of acres of tall, slender trees had shed their enormous leaves, laying a golden blanket for us to walk on. The plantation had grown in waves as new investment funded each new phase of expansion. Sylvinho and I were crunching our way over the leaf fall in one of the first areas planted fifteen years ago; the trees on either side of the track were already forty feet high.

Once again, I found myself in a beautiful place, talking about business. Sylvinho, at thirty-five already a widely travelled and extremely cultured man, was passionate about what he and his father were aiming to achieve here. I was full of respect for the pair of them – to have had the foresight to plant all these trees fifteen years ago, before the true importance of the green dollar was known, they had taken a huge gamble, and they have since waited patiently to cash in the coupon.

Sylvinho was talking quickly because he had to fly back to São Paulo for a polo game in the morning (as you do). So we got down to brass tacks. The thing that interested me most here was the opportunity to tap into the UK ethical timber market, but that meant going up against anyone who was already supplying sustainable hardwoods. This area was growing fast but as yet there was no teak available from sustainable Brazilian forestry. And Floresteca hadn't even started looking at the UK as a market yet.

My question was: how could I prove to a UK customer that the teak was genuinely sustainable? I knew that there were tons and tons of 'dirty teak' making their way into the UK every year. This is teak from Burma that has been banned in the EU but comes via third parties such as Thailand and Malaysia. I didn't want to be left with a load of wood that I couldn't prove the provenance of. Sylvinho was prepared for this question. The wood was all certified by the Forestry Stewardship Council (FSC). They certify every log and it comes stamped with an FSC code. All the wood that arrived in the UK would have a clear paper trail, all the way from the bill of loading back to the plantation. This could be the all-important brand I'd been looking for.

So I needed to know what Sylvinho wanted from the deal. Was this a one-off, or did he want to develop a long-term relationship with a UK customer? A one-off didn't strike me as being particularly helpful to either of us. If I could find a returning customer for him then he could offer me a better price now and I could guarantee him more return in the long term.

Sylvinho wanted to give me a good price which would allow me to act competitively when I arrived in the UK. For the first time on this trip, I was actually considering a deal as a long-term opportunity for me. Why not? Here was a great product with an admirable goal. I'd be happy to be involved in it in the future – but how that would happen was for the future. Let's stick to now. I needed this wood at a really low price. But of course, I would say that, wouldn't I?

My tequila deal had been a roaring success because I'd been able to undercut all the big players in the market. I got a great price because Del Señor had been so desperate to get into a new market that they were prepared to sell to me at just a little above cost. My overheads were almost nothing and so I could offer the cheapest tequila in town. Here was a similar situation. With no UK market penetration, I was taking on the risk for Floresteca and they'd have to reward me with a bargain basement offer. There'd be lots of legwork to do in the UK as there had been in Rio but, as I found out there, a good price opens doors.

At times during the last five months I'd just been scrambling, hustling and blagging to either haggle for a better purchase or convince someone to take my remaining stock so I could dash off to catch the next bus, train or plane; but I'd been learning. Horse trading had taught me not to get myself backed into a corner and I said I'd never do that again. But there's no fear of wood going off. I didn't have to sell it all in one day. I could wait, bide my time, until I found the right person for it.

I felt I was being offered a deal that combined the strengths of my successes and avoided making the same mistakes as I'd made in my failures. I'd found my double or nothing final trade. I was ready to go all in.

*

I have made $24,000 on this trip on top of the $50,000 I started with. That's still $26,000 short of the $100,000 target. I'm in the market for a whole container load of sustainable teak, and a Brazilian forester whom I've only just met is throwing some prices at me. I have two choices: kiln-dried planks that are ideal for furniture and flooring, or air-dried blocks that are bigger and therefore more versatile. The air-dried blocks may need to be kiln-dried at a later stage depending on what they're used for, and are therefore a little cheaper.

Sylvinho is opening the negotiation at what he claims is little over cost. He wants to charge me $1,400 per cubic metre for the planks and $1,000 per cubic metre for the blocks, plus he reckons that I'll need to allow another $1,000 for shipping. I know that there'll be another couple of thousand at the UK end for duty and fees. So, leaving aside $5,000 for total costs, I'd say I have $20,000 to spend on wood.

The usual haggle over prices is mercifully short. I go for a 20 per cent discount on the grounds that I'm taking a big risk here, but I can tell from his reaction that this would work out at less than his cost. He's happy to give me around 10 per cent off, and eventually we settle at $1,300 for the planks and $800 for the blocks, and he'll even pay the shipping. My $20,000 will afford me a total of 24 cubic metres – the dimensions of the container that I've just convinced Sylvio to pay for. With no shipping cost, that means I've knocked nearly $5,000 off his original price.

I'm heading home to the market that I know best. And I have a product I believe in at a price I can make a great margin on. Assuming no outbreaks of woodworm en route, I'll meet my container of teak back in London in five weeks. I should be able to line up some potential buyers in the meantime. That is, if the world I find there bears any relation to the world I left behind.

Twenty-three
DONE AND DUSTED

INVESTMENTS:
— **Wood (including fees and UK transport): $22,146**
— **Jade: $9,214**
IN THE BANK: $43,217

It's easy to see yourself as an individual operating in your own world. When you have your head down, charging at a problem, you can focus so hard on it that you simply forget that what you do is affecting and affected by everything else around you. This is especially true when you arrive back in the UK with $25,000 worth of top-of-the-range timber and find that you're in the middle of an economic holocaust.

While my teak from Brazil has been merrily meandering its way across the Atlantic Ocean, the wheels of the Western world have totally fallen off. Recession has taken hold, the property market has slumped and even banks are going bust. The mood is gloomy to say the least, and therefore not ideal for finding a buyer for a shedload of teak. Add to that the fall in the value of the pound relative to the dollar, and the wood is suddenly 20 per cent more expensive than it was in Brazil. All in all, you could say the world has moved on even more than I have in the last five months.

This is a problem that all importers face. When the pound is worth $2 it's a lot easier to buy goods from the Americas than when it's worth $1.60, as it is now. If I was importing a car from the US that cost $20,000, a few months ago that was the equivalent of £10,000. Now it's more like £12,500. To make a profit it is necessary to push the increase in price on to customers and when you are in the grip of a recession this is not what your customers want to hear.

This may prove to be an even greater problem for producers of ethical goods. It's all very well asking people to spend a little bit more to save the planet while everyone is rolling in it and times are good, but once things turn sour and people start tightening their belts then things may be a little different. Ethical consumerism is about to face its biggest challenge yet.

So the good news is that I've made 20 per cent on the wood already just because I paid for it in dollars two months ago. The even better news is that I have a lead.

Sean Sutcliffe runs a furniture-making business that operates at the high end of the market. They work with some of the UK's top designers, including Sir Terence Conran, and their branding is very 'green'. When I spoke to Sean on the phone he explained to me that he has a self-imposed ban on all tropical hardwoods, including teak, because he prefers to make furniture only from sustainable materials. Even his plywood comes from an FSC certified source. He sounds a little sceptical, but is nonetheless curious to hear that I have some sustainable teak, complete with the all-important FSC branding.

The great thing about Sean is that, come rain or shine, he's only in the market for ethical timber. No matter how bad the economic climate gets, his branding is so dependent on sustainability that he can't replace materials for less ethical ones. This should mean he's the perfect person to bring the teak to. When it arrives.

*

Remember that millstone of jade I carried all the way back from China? Well, guess what: all is not lost.

I tracked down a jade dealer in London. His gallery was at one of Mayfair's swankiest addresses. Roger Keverne is a tall, handsome, well-appointed man who makes his living dealing in Asian antiquities. He certainly looks the part. And he's agreed to take a look at my jade.

We're sitting in his gallery, surrounded by glass cabinets displaying ancient jade, some of which is thousands of years old. This is Roger's bread and butter, but as one of the leading authorities on jade in the UK he also has a pretty valuable opinion on what (if anything) my piece could sell for here. After the slating I (and it) got all over Taiwan, my expectations are low, to say the least.

Roger opens the box and carefully lifts the stone onto a felt-covered tray on the table between us. There follows a well-rehearsed routine of scrutiny as he lifts and turns it over, giving it a careful examination.

'It's a bloody good piece,' he confidently asserts, returning it to the tray. 'Where did you get it?'

I explain to Roger how I came to be in the possession of £4,500 worth of Hotan jade and the journey it and I have been on together. As the words come out of my mouth it sounds preposterous, like an adventure that happened to someone else. I tell him all about the offer in Taiwan that I let slip through my fingers and I tell him about the subsequent experiences in Taipei where everyone told me it wasn't white enough or big enough.

'Ha!' Roger lets out a loud snort. 'Take no notice. These jade dealers are all bloody bastards when it comes to negotiation. They'll say anything to get your price down. Pay no attention to that. It's a good piece.' Relieved? I could have cried!

The stone, it seems, is the real star; a fine example of white Hotan jade. The carving is good but could have been better. Possibly the carver was a little rushed and would have benefited from having more time, but nevertheless he's sure it's worth a lot more than I paid for it. However, it would be a challenge to find a buyer for it in the present economic climate and I may have to listen to offers.

If I can wait, the best idea would be to put it in an auction some time next year. And the asking price? 'Between £10,000 and £15,000.' Well, well, well. It cost me around £4,500. I'll have to wait, but perhaps there may yet be a profit to be made from this rock. 'In the meantime,' Roger sagely suggests, while he turns it over again in his hand, 'why don't you just put it on top of your television and enjoy it?'

*

I turned up at the appointed time to meet Sean with a full container-load of teak on a cold, crisp November morning in Berkshire. It couldn't have been more different from the searing 44° heat of the Pantanal two months earlier. The truck pulled into the courtyard of a converted dairy farm where instead of cows Sean now has saws and wood stores. There was a reception committee to meet me, a factory full of curious faces gathered to see their first glimpse of sustainable teak.

Sean was there too, and was keen to get samples off the back of the truck and onto a planer. First the wood had to meet their basic requirements. We started by checking its moisture content, which involved putting an electronic device of some sort onto a few samples of the kiln-dried planks. The digital reading needed to come in at below 15 per cent, and it did – 10, 11 and 12 per cent on successive tests. Sean was happy that the kilning had been done well. Next, the paperwork from Brazil had to be verified. The FSC are very fastidious when they come for their frequent audits, and the paper trail needs to be airtight. After a few minutes in the office with Sean's accountant we were given the green light. It was kosher FSC certification.

The final test involved planing a sample to see how it would 'come up'. This is where it got really exciting because Sean and his partner Steve had never had teak in the workshop before. For a real timber enthusiast like Sean this was the equivalent of a new toy. Up to then, he'd been using a teak replacement, Tatachuba, and he made no bones about how little regard he had for it as a wood. 'Teak is the king of woods,' he proudly asserted to me. As if I didn't know.

The teak came through the last test proudly. The planing machine removed the top layer to reveal a spectrum of earthy green and golden hues. This was wood with character. Sean explained that as it aged a lot of the greens developed into silver shades, which was very desirable. All in all, I could tell he was very excited. This teak could open up a whole new avenue for him.

So with no problems over quality it was time to settle down to discussing prices. I wanted £1,400 per cubic metre for the kiln-dried planks and £1,000 per cubic metre for the blocks, totalling around £27,000. I was relieved that I'd bought the teak in dollars back in August when the ratio was 2:1. That meant that my wood had cost me 20 per cent less than if I were buying it now. Making that profit before I'd begun was pure luck, nearly as lucky as having sold my flat to fund the trip when the market was at its peak. I'd probably made more money out of that one transaction than all the others put together.

It made sense to work in pounds sterling from now on. The target was clear: I'd set out to double my £25,000 investment and I'd put all my profit into this timber so I needed to sell it for £25,000. Easy. By asking for £27,000 I felt I was leaving a little room to offer a discount and still hit my target. Unfortunately, Sean had other ideas.

Sean was playing hardball from the off. My heart sank when I started to hear the pre-negotiation patter: recession, hard times, uncertain future, different climate; get used to hearing this sort of thing, because it's a sign of the hard times to come. Sean may have loved the idea of the wood but he wasn't going to offer me anything like what it was worth. Straight off the bat he said my £27,000 was too high, so I floated the idea of a discount. I could come down to £25,000 if he took the lot. He offered me £15,000.

Now let's look at this situation. Here's a man who has just told me that he buys Tatachuba and he doesn't like it. He's told me he would rather use teak any day of the week. He buys Tatachuba for nearly £800 per cubic metre. And yet, bold as brass, he's telling me that he won't pay more than that for my teak. Clearly, in the time I'd been away, Britain had become a buyers' market.

Our body language said it all; we were both sitting back in our chairs, arms crossed, faces fixed.

We were at a stalemate. Sean was just as resolute as I was and we were too far apart in our valuations of what the teak was worth to agree a deal. It was time to leave. I felt a profound disappointment that I hadn't felt since Cape Town, but if I'd learnt anything from that experience, it was that when things don't go according to Plan A, you have to come up with Plan B.

*

The setback with Sean meant that I was on familiar ground in more ways than one. I was hustling to find a buyer and I was back on home soil. I started by putting a few calls in to some of the UK's boat builders, traditionally the biggest importers of teak. These guys are experiencing great difficulties at the moment because the EU has banned all imports of Burmese teak since March 2008. After talking to a couple of them I found out that the price of rainforest teak in the UK is normally between £4,000 and £6,000 per cubic metre.

My teak was clearly not from the rainforest, but from a plantation. It differed in several ways that relate to the speed at which it grows and its sap content, but this basically boils down to two things. First, it was worth less by at least 50 per cent. Second, it was no good for boat builders but ideal for garden furniture.

I was surprised to find from a simple internet search how many teak furniture makers there still are in the UK, but unfortunately once I started calling them I realized that many of them have their furniture made in factories in Vietnam and simply import the components for assembly here. They can still advertise as 'Made in the UK' that way.

Eventually, I found a genuine British furniture maker in Nottinghamshire. John Green runs a company called Wood Newton who were in the middle of a job refitting a house in north London. He thought that there might be an opportunity to use my teak on it. He could only use the kiln-dried teak planks (around half of what I had in total) but if it proved to be what I said it was then he could offer me £11,000 for it. I said I'd come to see him. He said he'd need to see the whole lot before he could agree a final price. I had a Plan B.

I organized for the planks to be picked up from Sean's yard and delivered to Nottingham, and I would then go up to meet John when they arrived. I was pretty confident from Sean's analysis that the quality of the planks was good, and this was much closer to the price that I was looking for. In the meantime, I had to pick up one of the logs myself to deliver it to Plan C, a small workshop outside Portsmouth.

New Dawn Furniture is owned by Dennis Wingham. He hasn't had teak in his workshop since 2002 because of the Burmese political situation. Like Sean, he was concerned about the FSC paper trail (because 'they're worse than the bloody VAT man'); he has seen the market for sustainable materials in the garden furniture business and can't take any chances losing his FSC certification.

Dennis is a sixty-year-old man who looks like he enjoys a pint. He can also talk the hind legs off a donkey. He works on his own every day in a workshop that he built himself next to the house that he built himself. Not much of a commuter, Dennis. When I arrived he was in the middle of crafting a bench for next year's Chelsea Flower Show.

I helped him lift the block up and onto his machine saw. He trimmed off an inch-thick plank, which he then moved over to plane on another machine. His eyes lit up as soon as he saw the green colours in the wood. This was what he'd been missing for the last six years. Bingo. I could smell a sale. But how much of it could he take? After all, he was a one-man band and I had a lot of timber; 13.5 cubic metres, to be precise. Dennis didn't bat an eyelid. If the price was right then he could take the lot. It would keep him busy all winter. I stuck to the price I'd asked Sean for: £1,000 per cubic metre, still a fraction of the cost of 'dirty' Burmese teak and, as far as I was concerned, a fair price. 'That's a really good price.' Dennis's face lit up.

'So we have a deal, Dennis?'

'We certainly do.' His hand shot out to shake mine so readily, I think I could have asked for more.

'Done and dusted.' He beams.

I have to admit to having a soft spot for artisans like Dennis. The British craftsman is a dying breed and there is precious little business left in the countryside these days. Dennis may retire soon, but for now his workshop is still turning out garden furniture for the discerning customer. Most teak furniture is now made in Vietnam where labour is cheap, but here in a leafy Hampshire village there's going to be a steady supply of beautifully crafted benches and tables for the foreseeable future. You never know, you might even see Alan Titchmarsh sitting on one at Chelsea Flower Show next year.

As someone who's tried to go it alone for the last five months, it's also heartening to be completing my final trade with a kindred spirit: someone who has eschewed the world of big business and prefers the discipline of being his own boss, dealing face-to-face with suppliers and customers. You might not make as much money and you might not have the security but there's something about standing on your own two feet and doing business like this that makes me thrive. And I think Dennis feels the same.

Dennis told me that the teak would help him make it through the recession. It struck me as odd that Sean had used the recession as a reason not to buy the wood, and yet Dennis was turning that on its head. Who's right? Only time will tell. The crucial factor is how each one perceives risk. Sean's customers tend to be big hotels and bars that want sets of furniture for roof-top bars and terraces, so he would need to convince one of these customers to go for the teak. Until he could do that, he'd be sitting on a lot of stock. Dennis, on the other hand, has lots of smaller customers and so his risk is spread out. He seemed pretty confident that when he offered teak as an option to his ethically minded customers they would go for it. As far as Dennis was concerned, it was a sure-fire winner.

For me, I had one more (I hoped) meeting in Nottinghamshire in three hours' time, so I headed back up the M1 to meet John Green at Wood Newton. All being well, this would be my final trade.

I arrived after dark at a fenced-off industrial estate just outside Nottingham; not exactly the setting I had had in mind for my grand finale. The rain hammered down on the roof of the building and I could barely read the enormous letters on the side, spelling out Wood Newton. There were two lorries parked on the tarmac around the back. One of them contained 9.5 cubic metres of Brazilian teak.

John Green was younger than he sounded on the phone. He was

wrapped up in a trendy body warmer and had a warm smile to match. He seemed to think it all very amusing that I had arrived at his yard with so much timber on spec. We talked over the deafening sound of nail guns assembling the flat-pack houses that Wood Newton were preparing for an eco-town outside Milton Keynes. In a few months they will have built thousands of sustainable, wooden-framed, environmentally friendly homes for a fraction of what they would have cost if they'd been made from bricks and mortar. This may be the future of British house building. These houses are so airtight, John reckons you could keep them warm by simply 'turning the lights on'.

*

The forklift starts to offload the wood and John takes a random sample of planks from the first pallet. It's a common trick for suppliers to 'dress' the wood so that the best pieces are on the top, and he's been burnt before. We take four planks into the workshop to test the moisture content. I'm confident after my experience with Sean that they'll pass the test, and they do. With flying colours. So we're on. I want £14,000. He offers me £10,000. I want £13,000. He says, 'Let's meet in the middle: £11,000' I've been doing this for so long now that I've actually started to enjoy haggling. I do it all the time. Anyone who said that we can't haggle in the UK is talking rubbish, as John has just proved with his deliberately dodgy maths. What an old trick, you'd fall for that?

'OK, let's settle on £11,500.'

'Deal.'

For the last time I shake hands and for the first time I have nothing left to sell, apart from the heaviest, most expensive paperweight in England and a £750 bag of oolong tea. It is over.

So the £13,500 from Dennis plus the £11,500 from Wood Newton makes a profit of £25,000. And I could end up with more once the jade is sold. I'd done what I set out to do and doubled my investment. It felt pretty damn good.

*

I set off five months ago with a goal of £25,000, but the trip was about more than that. If I'd just changed the money to dollars and put it under my bed for the last six months, I would have made nearly £7,000. But I wanted to know if it was still possible for someone to trade the old way, to buy something in one country, travel with it and sell it in the next. I had a hunch it was, and I'd backed myself to prove it. What I found is that the world is not dominated by big business in the way I had thought. Sure, the big multinationals are making the big profits, but the majority of the world's trade is the product of small businesses owned by guys like John and Dennis, like David Lu and Craig Shiel. Of course it's possible to trade the old way, because that's the way the world has always operated. It's easy to sit in an office in the City and think that it's all about the big bucks; the fact is that those big bucks are just the total of all the small bucks swirling round the system, which are generated by people making a living. And that's what it's really all about – living.

I'd found more challenges, more successes and failures, and more life in the way I'd earned my money over the last five months than I had in five years of working in London. I had literally paid the price of backing myself when I was wrong, and I'd felt the sweet buzz of making a profit when I was right. And I'd felt it all the more profoundly because it was my money.

Is this the future? Right now, there are thousands of people being made redundant all over the country. There won't be enough jobs to absorb them all and so they're going to have to find alternative ways of making money. If, as I suspect, necessity is the mother of all invention, then these people will have to reinvent themselves economically. It has often been stated that recessions are a good time for the arts because people are more creative when they are stressed. The last big recession of the seventies gave us punk and we had Britart from the slump of the early nineties. Could the next couple of years of economic gloom inspire a similar renaissance for disenfranchised professionals to become the entrepreneurs of the future? You'd better believe it.

ACKNOWLEDGEMENTS

First and foremost, I'd like to thank Dick Colthurst and all the Tigress team for their first-class ideas and support throughout the production; they were integral to the success of the whole project from start to finish. I'd also like to thank my editor and chief cheerleader, Jon Butler, my agent Gordon Wise and my Mum for all their comments and suggestions that continually refined and improved everything that I wrote; Steve Shearman, Belinda Cherrington and Matt Cole for helping me get this caper going in the first place, Bertie Jenkins for being a great friend through it all and my Dad and Brains for just being great.

There are many, many other people I'd like to thank for giving me invaluable advice over the last year on areas that were far from my expertise. In particular I'd like to say cheers to Dave Azam for all the wine tips, Grant Rattray for explaining the African coffee industry to me in record time, and Paul Wilson and Jonny Bealby for their encyclopaedic knowledge of Central Asia. I owe a debt of gratitude to Tony Wang for all his support in Shanghai, Dunstan Kessler for making those beautiful posters at a minute's notice as well as Peter Ayres for the inspired Hola surfboard design. My appreciation also to Herbert Gleiss and Roger Keverne for all their notes on jade and to Fernando Lomeli Ortega, my man in Mexico. And *muchos gracias* to Chris Wall for letting me borrow his enormous black book of contacts in Latin America. Many thanks also to Paola and Ben at HSBC; without you all I may have lost a lot of time and money.

And of course the biggest thank you of all to Paul, Ed, Nicki, Kirsty, Zoe and Clare for sharing all the laughs and tears with me along the way.